Kauai Underground Guide

Lenore & Mirah Horowitz

Papaloa Press

19th edition

First edition:	1980
Second edition:	1981
Third Edition:	1982
Fourth edition:	1983
Fifth edition:	1984
Sixth edition:	1985
Seventh edition:	1986
Eighth edition:	1987
Ninth edition:	1988
Tenth edition:	1989
Eleventh edition:	1990
Twelfth edition:	1992
Thirteenth edition:	1995
Fourteenth edition:	1996
2nd printing	1997
Fifteenth edition:	1998
Sixteenth edition:	2000
2nd printing	2002
3rd printing	2003
Seventeenth edition	2004
Eighteenth edition	2007
Nineteenth edition	2011

ISBN-13: 978-0-9745956-1-0
ISBN-10: 0-9745956-1-6
ISSN 1045-1358
Library of Congress Catalog card 82-643643

Original Drawings by Lauren, Mirah, Jeremy, & Mike Horowitz, & Devon Davey
Historic Petroglyph Drawings by Likeke R. McBride
Lifeguard Station icon by Winston Welborn, www.kauaiexplorer.com
Photos by Lenore W. Horowitz, Mirah Horowitz, Jeffrey Courson, Lupe & Gaby

Special thanks to Lauren, Larry, Jeremy, Rachel, Mike & Michelle,
for their help with the research, writing, design of this 19th edition
& mahalo nui loa to Keali'i & Fred
Dr. Monty Downs & Robert Trent Jones Jr
& special thanks to Andy, Peter, Marvis, Jeffrey & Hezar, Efren, Lupe, Gaby, David,
Miguel Angel, Michele, John Edmark & his Design Class at Stanford University
and in fond remembrance of John Akana

Printed in Canada
by Kromar Printing Ltd., Winnipeg, Canada

Contents

Exploring Kauai

Welcome!

Kauai is an incredible island – with adventure, natural beauty, exciting things to do and see, countless local treasures. We've been writing this guidebook for thirty years, and are still surprised by new discoveries. When we started this book, a 16-page pamphlet fit the bill coast-to-coast, but as the island has grown, so has our book (and e-book). A little book that emerged from four small kids and two parents now encompasses a growing extended island family – children and grandchildren, husbands and wives, sisters and brothers, neighbors and friends – musicians, photographers, teachers, artists, surfers, doctors, lifeguards, tour guides, boat captains, pilots, fishermen – a Kauai-grown tribe ready to welcome you in! Keali'i Reichel and Robert Trent Jones, Jr. have woven in their own stories as well, and so have many of our thousands of readers, all becoming a part of a network of authors that makes this edition so special.

One thing we have in common is caring about children. Our book profits go to helping needy island kids (read about our *Campaign for Kids*, 238), and we want to help you keep *your* families safe, so be watchful on our island shores (read *Ocean Safety*, 80-83).

It truly takes an island to write a guidebook!

Come be a part of our island, join our island family. We have so many things we can't wait to show you!

Lenore & the Horowitz Ohana

Definitely Don't Miss on Kauai!

* **There's Nothing like North:** If the sun's on your side, hit the North Shore! *Hanalei Bay* has breath-taking beachwalks, gentle summertime tides, and great winter wave-breaks. Kid-friendly *Kalihiwai* has sand perfect for sports: firm and level, ideal for running, football and family fun. Go kayaking in its river, or in the calm summer months, even on the Bay itself. For solitude, try *Secret Beach*, hidden down a cliff trail; or for beach-combing, *Larsen's*, where you can laze in the sun. And for snorkeling there's *Tunnels*, full of tidepools and treasures, and truly great reef fish.

* **The End of the Road:** Go forth, to the North, to the 'end of the road'! Follow Kauai's main road from *Hanalei* to *Ha'ena* and then on to *Ke'e Beach*, as it twists and narrows and winds by the sea. At times you'll cross one-lane bridges, at times you'll hug the cliffs, and at the road's end, you'll discover beautiful Ke'e Beach, a must for summertime swimming and snorkeling. It's also the trail head for the Kalalau trail.

* **Nature's Na Pali: the Coast with the Most**. The spectacular Na Pali Coast is one of the most beautiful places in the world – a wilderness framed by crashing waves and jagged cliffs, dotted wth waterfalls plunging into the swirling sea. See the whole Na Pali coast by *helicopter* or *boat:* one gives you a bird's view; the other takes you up close – right into sea caves.. If possible, try both.

* **Hike the Kalalau Trail**, even if only for the first mile. You experience the Na Pali cliffs from within, along a narrow footpath through the trees, streams and waterfalls that speckle the coast. Seasoned hikers can forge ahead to *Hanakapi'ai Beach, Hanakapi'ai Falls*, or beyond.

* **Snorkel with Kauai's Best Fish**: *Poipu Beach* on the south, *Lydgate Park* on the east, and to the north, *Tunnels* (best in summer or calm winter days) and *Ke'e Beach* (summer only). Or swim deeper and try scuba. Gregg Winston at *Watersports Adventures* will guide even timid first-timers to depth-defying adventure!

* **Find What is Hidden:** Search out the sandy spots that are secret, from *Secret Beach, Larsen's*, or *Kilauea* (north shore); to *Maha'ulepu Beach*

(south shore); to the long beach walk south of *Lydgate Park* (eastside); to *Pakala's* (also called *Infinities*) (westside). Geocaching anyone?

* **Sunrise, Sunset**: Each tropical day has a stunning beginning and end. In the summer, visit the *St Regis Hotel* and watch the sun set into the ocean before dinner in Hanalei. In the winter, try *Beach House Restaurant* in Poipu, or drive father west to the beach at Kekaha. At sunrise in the east, walk the beach south of *Lydgate Park*.

* **Hey, Howzit? Go 'Local'**! Try what Kauai's own have been loving for years: one of 70+-year-old restaurants that keep locals happily well-fed. *Hamura's Saimin, Barbecue Inn,* or *Tip Top* (Lihue); and *Hanama'ulu Café & Tea House* (Hanama'ulu). Here you will find authentic Kauai!

* **Sample traditional (and tasty) Kauai treats**, like *lilikoi chiffon pie, Taro-Ka Chips, shave ice*, and home-made *ice cream*.

* **Fresh from the Farm: Meet and Eat at Farmer's Markets**. Check out Kauai's fab farmer's markets in different parts of the island on different days. Drink milk straight from a coconut, or sample wonderful fruits and vegetables carried in on the back of a pick-up – mangoes, papayas, avocados, tasty bananas and star fruit. Meet local farmers who grow beautiful tropical flowers and make fragrant flower lies. You will be tempted to cook eggplant and stringbeans – even if you're on vacation!

* **Fresh Off the Boat**: Try Kauai's seafood just off the hook! Local fish markets *Ara Sushi Market* (Hanama'ulu), *Fish Express* (Lihue), and *Pono Market* (Kapa'a) cannot be beat, and Pono's *poke* (sashimi grade fish with seasoning and onions) is considered the best on the island. For a terrific lunch or cook-your-own filets, catch your own on a fishing charter, or else go to *Kilauea Fish Market* (north shore) or *Koloa Fish Market* (south shore).

* **Zip it up!** Try the stunning Kipu zipline adventures over Kauai's valleys and streams; fly through the rainforest like a tropical bird!

* **Grand Canyon, Island Style**. Hike the *Waimea Canyon*, Kauai's own mini Grand C. At road's end, hiking trails in *Koke'e* lead into forest unique from the coast and the beach.

* **Voyage to Ni'ihau**: Book a special tour of this private island, off-limits to all but native Hawaiians. Snorkel its reefs with *Holo Holo Charters* and *Blue Dolphin Charters*; scuba with *Seasport Divers* (for certified divers); or explore the island by air with *Ni'ihau Helicopters* (run by the Robinson family), including a beach and picnic stop.

Jeffrey Courson

𝒫lanning your ideal Kauai vacation

Where to Stay: location, location, location

Kauai has a little of everything. Like an America in miniature, it has rolling hills and valleys to the east, sun-warmed beaches to the south, and majestic coastal mountains to the north and west. Such variety is rare, particularly on an island only 32 miles in diameter, but it can complicate deciding where to stay and what to do. Luckily, there is no wrong answer, and planning the perfect vacation is definitely part of the fun.

Almost circular in shape, Kauai has three main tourist areas: Princeville & Hanalei to the north, Poipu to the south, and the 'Coconut Coast' between Lihue and Kapa'a to the east. Families with limited mobility might prefer the gentle surf and primarily pleasant weather of the south shore. Adventurers on the other hand may want to head north to gorgeous cliffside beaches where hiking and camping offer chances to see unparalleled, unspoiled beauty, but where the weather is more variable. Those who locate on the eastside – like our family – can access both: from the eastside you can drive north or south in a little less than an hour, depending (increasingly) on traffic. The towns of Kapa'a and Wailua sit about midway in the road system that goes almost all the way around the island's perimeter, with the Na Pali cliffs of the northwest quadrant off limits to wheeled vehicles.

Before you go: Request a free Kauai Vacation Planner at 800.262.1400 *www.kauaidiscovery.com*. Visit *www.kauai-hawaii.com* for helpful info about attractions, calendars, point to point driving tips, parks, recreation, culture. Check out local news at *The Garden Island* newspaper *www.kauaiworld.com* and *www.kauaiexplorer.com* for beach, hike, and surf tips.

The North Shore

With by far the most spectacular landscape, the north shore combines rugged mountains with beautiful beaches and green vistas – the Kauai of postcards. As the windward shore, the north also gets the most rainfall, particularly in winter months when surf at the beaches is also bigger and more unpredictable. No matter the season, many people love the north shore for its rural tranquility and magnificent beauty, and come here to 'get away from it all,' to wind down to 'island time' in an area made remote by one lane bridges occasionally washed out in winter storms.

The major resort area on the north shore is Princeville, perched high on an ocean bluff overlooking Hanalei Bay. Princeville includes private homes and condos, two championship golf courses, and the newly renovated 5-star *St Regis Hotel*, with elegant rooms and service, gourmet dining, and a stunning cliffside setting. A small beach at the base of the cliff, reached by the hotel's elevator, offers views and, when seas are calm, swimming and snorkeling (from about $400/night) 520 Ka Haku Rd, Princeville; 808.826.9644; 800.826.4400 *www.stregisprinceville.com*.

Spectacular Hanalei Bay in summer, from the terrace, St Regis Resort. In winter, surf can reach twenty feet, and boats take shelter in the south.

St Regis Hotel overlooks Hanalei Bay

Nearby, the *Hanalei Bay Resort* combines the conveniences of a condominium with hotel amenities (from about $200/night/room and $370/night/suite) 5380 Honoiki Rd, Princeville; 808.826.6522; 866.507.1428 *www.hanaleibayresort.com*.

Surrounding Princeville's golf courses are a host of condos and private homes offering gorgeous ocean views, particularly at sunset. Getting to the beach requires a hike down the cliff to one of the small beaches (hotel guests have elevator privileges). For owner-direct listings: *www.vrbo.com*.

Outside Princeville, you can get closer to the ocean, for example in the town of Hanalei, near one of Kauai's finest beaches at Hanalei Bay. You'll also find privacy on or near the beach in the lovely residential areas of Kalihiwai and Anini (east of Hanalei) and Wainiha and Ha'ena (west of Hanalei). The *Hanalei Colony Resort* in Ha'ena offers beachfront condos, a favorite for its rustic simplicity (from about $230/night) 5-7130 Kuhio Hwy, Ha'ena; 808.826.6235; 800.628.3004 *www.hcr.com*.

The South Shore

The south shore, at Poipu, on the island's leeward side, has drier weather and generally calm year-round swimming conditions. It's also flatter, with dryer vegetation than the north shore. For swimming, there is wonderful Poipu Beach, and for sheer beauty, Maha'ulepu.

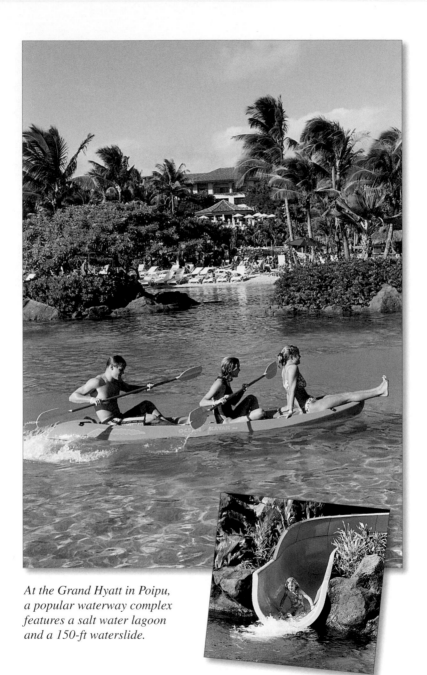

At the Grand Hyatt in Poipu, a popular waterway complex features a salt water lagoon and a 150-ft waterslide.

You have many choices for lodgings, including two resort hotels – the Grand Hyatt Resort and the Sheraton Kauai. *The Grand Hyatt* offers 600 spacious rooms and elegant dining in an architecturally beautiful resort. Because the beach has strong surf and intimidating currents, the Hyatt offers guests an elaborate swimming complex, with river pools, waterfalls, a 150 foot waterslide, as well as a 5 acre meandering saltwater lagoon with islands (from $340/night plus $18/night resort fee) 1571 Poipu Road, Koloa; 808.724.1234; 800.233.1234 *www.kauai-hyatt.com.*

Poipu Beach

Nearby, the *Sheraton Kauai* has 413 rooms located right on beautiful Poipu Beach, great for swimming in all seasons (from $455/night, plus $18/night resort fee) 2440 Hoonani Rd, Poipu; 808.742.1661; 800.782.9488 *www.sheraton-kauai.com.* The most famous south shore hotel, the *Waiohai*, is now a Marriott timeshare, with 238 2BR villas (from $390/night) 2249 Poipu Rd, Poipu; 808.742.4400; 800.845.5279 *www.marriott.com.* Or try the timeshare exchange for last minute bargains *www.redweek.com.*

Newly opened next to Waiohai in the Poipu Beach Hotel location, *Koa Kea Hotel* is intimate and luxurious with spa (from $300/nite) 2251 Poipu Road, Poipu; 808.828.8888; 877.806.2288 *www.koakea.com.*

Beachfront at its best? The best location on Poipu Beach is the *Kiahuna*. Only a few buildings are directly on the beach, however; most are set back, some right next to the road. Competing companies manage the

Kalapaki Beach

property: Outrigger's Kiahuna Plantation (from $175/night) 808.742.6411; 866.956.4262 *www.outrigger.com*. Suite Paradise 808.742.7400; 800.367.8020 *www.suiteparadise.com*. Kiahuna Beachside has the best beachfront units (12 from $365/night) 800.937.6642 *www.kiahuna.com*.

Poipu Kai, set farther back, walking distance from the beach, starts at $175/night, managed by both Aston Hotels: 808.742.7424; 877.997.6667 *www.astonhotels.com* and Suite Paradise: 808.742.7400; 800.367.8020 *www.suiteparadise.com*. At *Poipu Point Resort*, you'll find luxurious suites, but a beach too rough for easy swimming (from $369/night/1BR) 1613 Pe'e Road, Poipu; 808.742.1888; 800.426.3350 *www.diamondresorts.com*.

Choose from condos and B&B's, many close to Poipu Beach Park, with year-round excellent protected swimming (p 67). For more information: *Poipu Beach Resort Association*: 808.742.7444 *www.poipu-beach.org* or check out *www.vrbo.com* for owner-direct rental listings.

The Eastside

The '*Coconut Coast*,' between Lihue (where the airport is located) and Wailua and Kapa'a, has convenient location as its main advantage. It's about midway between Poipu on the south and Hanalei on the north and about a 40 minute drive from each, so you can explore the island with ease in either direction, depending on the weather and your inclinations.

Got pool?
The Kauai
Marriott

You'll find hotels, condos and B & B's, many of which can accurately be described as 'beachfront.' Ask careful questions, however, because eastern shore beaches can have tricky currents, and swimmers must be very cautious. Beachfront at its best? *The Kauai Marriott* in Lihue fronts the magnificent sandy swimming beach at Kalapaki Bay, with a circular pool ringed by five jacuzzis, one of the state's largest. On more than 880 acres of golf courses and waterways, rooms may be smaller than the Hyatt's, but you can't beat its beach (from $370/night) 808.245.5050; 800.220.2925 *www. marriotthotels.com.*

The Coconut Coast near Wailua offers moderately priced hotels, condo resorts, and B & B's. Some excellent beachfront condos include *Lae Nani* 877.523.6264; *Wailua Bay View* 800.882.9007; *Lanikai,* and *Kapa'a Shores* 808.822.3055. The enormous *Waipouli Beach Resort*, a high density complex, features an elaborate swimming pool with waterslide to compensate for a modest beach (from $120) 4-820 Kuhio Hwy, Kapa'a, 808.822.6000; 866.508.9565 *www.waipoulibeachresort.com.*

Moderately priced hotels (about $200/night or less) include a great location for families, the *Aloha Beach Resort Kauai*, only a short walk to Lydgate Park's wonderful rock-rimmed pools and Kamalani playground (from $80/night) 3-5920 Kuhio Hwy: 808.823.6000; 877.823.5111 *www. alohabeachresortkauai.com.* Near Hanama'ulu, the *Kauai Beach Resort* has had a facelift; a sand pool and waterslide make up for a beach with currents too strong for safe swimming ($130/night) 4331 Kauai Beach Dr, Lihue; 888.805.3843; 808-245 *www.hilton.com* or *www.aquaresorts.com.*

Some hotels recently turned timeshares (i.e. suites with mini kitchens) include (for under $200) *Islander on the Beach*: 877.997.6667 *www. astonhotels.com* and *Kauai Coast Resort at the Beachboy*, primarily timeshare but with some rentals: 520 Aleka Loop, Kapa'a; 808.822.3441; 877.977.4355 *www.kauaicoastresort.com*.

The recently renovated *Kauai Beach at Makaiwa* puts a new face on the old Sheraton (from $175/night) 56 Kuhio Highway, Kapa'a; 808.822.3455; 877.997.6667 *www.astonhotels.com*. The remodeled beachfront *Hotel Coral Reef*, once a funky bargain is now being marketed as a "resort" (from $245/ night) 808.822.4481; 800.843.4659 *www.hotelcoralreefresort.com*.

The Westside

Largely undeveloped, the west side is still 'local' Kauai. The weather is sunny, dry, even arid, which you'll appreciate when other parts of the island have rain. Just west of Poipu and Koloa, you'll come to the town of Hana-pepe, with art galleries, a swinging bridge, and an authentic taro chip factory. Salt Pond Beach Park is nearby, a beautiful spot enjoyed primarily by local people. Further west, you'll love the long, sandy beach at Kekaha, great for swimming, surfing, and beachwalking. Beyond that is the awesome expanse of sand and cliffs at Polihale.

Choose from vacation homes, apartments, and B & B's in the towns of Waimea and Kekaha, which has the best swimming beach. *Waimea Plantation Cottages* offers hotel services with old-style charm in vintage plantation cottages with free wireless (from $200/night) 9400 Kaumuali'i Hwy, Waimea; 808.338.1625; 866.774.2924 *www.waimea-plantation.com*. The best swimming beach, however, is at Kekaha.

Finding Home Base: hotels, condos, homes

Beachfront & oceanfront: the truth & the lingo

If you want to be located on or close to a swimming beach, consider these words carefully: 'ocean front' probably means a rocky place, or at least marginal swimming, but even 'beachfront' can be a misleading term. The so-called 'beach' could be rocky or unswimmable due to dangerous currents and strong surf. A property as a whole may be accurately described as 'beachfront,' but actually be shaped like a pie wedge, with the tip on the beach and the wide end (where you may end up being situated) back on the road. Or it may be technically adjacent to a beach, but with a building, a swimming pool (or even a road) in between.

Key questions: What will I see when I open up my sliding glass door? How far do I have to walk (or drive) to get to the nearest sandy swimming beach? If you have children, ask about the closest 'child-friendly' swimming beach. Swimming pools vary in size and location, and yours may end up being a tiny kidney next to the parking lot, so ask how far you have to walk to reach it– a key point if you have toddlers and all their paraphernalia to carry.

Renting condos and homes

New condo developments are going up all over, the result of accumulated building permits issued before Hurricane Iniki in 1992. New luxury complexes with high density and expensive interiors now compete with older, smaller developments in better locations but showing their age. New vs old: that's your first choice. The second is whether to rent from an owner or an agency. Owners give better rates but obviously have less flexibility to deal with changes in your vacation plans, and are less likely than agencies to refund your money if you are unhappy. If you decide to go owner-direct, *Vacation Rentals by Owner* is one of the largest online resources: *www.vrbo. com*. Check reviews *www.tripadvisor.com* and LA Times Travel *www.travel. latimes.com*. For South shore: *Poipu Beach Association*: P.O. Box 730, Koloa, HI 96756; 808.742.7444 *www.poipu-beach.org*.

Expect to pay at least $140/night ($180/night for a condo at or near a swimming beach). If you rent owner-direct, expect a one week minimum stay. Popular months (December– March; August) require advance reservations. Cancellation policies vary from two days to a month. *www.redweek. com* is a clearinghouse for timeshare rentals, often at steep last minute discounts.

For a human voice, try *Kauai Vacation Rentals*, a well-established agency offering personalized advice on rentals island-wide: 800.367.5025 *www.KauaiVacationRentals.com*. Also call *Garden Island Properties*: 800.801.0378 *www.kauaiproperties.com* or *Prosser Realty*: 800.767.4707 *www.prosser-realty.com*. Some agencies specialize:

SOUTH SHORE: Parrish Kauai: 800.325.5701 *www.parrishkauai.com*. R & R Realty: 800.367.8022 *www.R7R.com*. Poipu Connection: 800.742.2260 *www.poipuconnection.com*. Garden Island Rentals: 800.247.5599 *www.kauairentals.com*. Suite Paradise 800.367.8020 *www.suite-paradise.com*.

NORTH SHORE: Na Pali Properties: 800.715.7273 *www.napaliprop.com*. North Shore Properties: 800.488.3336 *www.kauai-vacation-rentals.com*.

Harrington's Paradise Properties: 888.826.9655 *www.oceanfrontkauai.com.*
Hanalei Aloha Management: 800.487.9833 *www.800hawaii.com.* Oceanfront Realty: 800.222.5541 *www.oceanfrontrealty.com.*

Renting bed & breakfasts

B & B's are plentiful on Kauai and come in all varieties and prices,
from a beachfront cottage to the spare room-with-bath in a home with a
gregarious host. Two agencies on Kauai represent many individual owners,
as well as small hotels, inns and condos. *Bed & Breakfast Hawaii* was the
first, with listings on all the islands: 800.733.1632 *www.bandb-hawaii.com.*
Bed & Breakfast Kauai has an exclusive focus on Kauai: 800.822.1176
www.BnBKauai.com. Questions to ask: What's for breakfast (continental,
full meal, or stocked kitchen)? What kind of beds (length, width)? What
degree of interaction with host and other guests (How friendly or private do
you want to be?) What's the cancellation policy? Most require a minimum
stay and are booked 2 to 3 months in advance, so plan ahead.

Renting rustic

If you like hiking and camping (yet amid relative comfort), you can rent
cabins in some of Kauai's loveliest wilderness areas. In the Koke'e forest
region, you can rent a cabin with stove, refrigerator, hot shower, cooking
and eating utensils, linens, bedding, and wood burning stove at bargain
rates, from $65/night (maximum stay of 5 nights during a 30 day period) at
The Lodge at Koke'e, Box 367, Waimea HI 96796; 808.335.6061
www.thelodgeatkokee.net. Also in Koke'e, *YWCA Camp Sloggett* offers
"bunkhouse" accommodations ($25/pp/night), tent camping ($10/pp), lodge
(8-15 people), and cottage (up to 4 people, from $85/night). Contact YWCA
Kauai, 4 Elua St, Lihue HI 96766; 808.245.5959 *www.campingkauai.com.*

NORTH SHORE: *YMCA Camp Naue* in Ha'ena offers beachfront
camping in bunk houses (or your own tent) $15/night: YMCA of Kauai, PO
Box 1786, Lihue HI 96766 808.246.9090 *www.ymcaofkauai.org.* Kapa'a
has an *International Hostel* ($23/night/bunk) internet available: 4534 Lehua
St, Kapa'a. 808.823.6142 *www.kauaihostel.net.*

Getting There: What to pack — how not to lose it

If you travel only with carry-on bags, you avoid the risk of losing
checked luggage on connecting flights, especially when changing carriers.
Some tips (learned the hard way) for checking luggage: We pack a change
of clothes and a bathing suit for each family member, as well as any
prescription drugs, in a carry-on bag just in case someone's suitcase is lost

temporarily. We also distribute every-
body's belongings in every suitcase, so
that no one person is left without clothes
if a suitcase is lost permanently. Because
tags can fall off, we label each bag
clearly inside.

A replacement-cost rider on your
Homeowner's insurance policy may turn
out to be a wise investment, for the
airline's insurance limit is $1,850 per
passenger. Airlines may subtract 10% of the purchase price for each year
you have owned an item, exclude cameras and jewelry, and may take up to
six months to process a claim. If your luggage is missing or damaged, save
all baggage-claim stubs, boarding passes, and tickets, and be sure to fill out
an official claim form at the baggage supervisor's office before you leave
the airport. Most clearly tagged luggage makes its way to the owner within
24 hours (and they deliver). Call daily for an update.

Vacation days are too precious to spend on line in stores. We try to cut
down on clothes (except for swim suits and T-shirts) and use space for other
essentials – beach sandals, walking or hiking shoes, snorkel gear, sunscreen,
hat with brim, sunglasses, beach bag or back pack, frisbee, tennis ball, or
beach ball. Island restaurants are informal – no tie or jacket, but bring long
pants. A light sweater in winter is a good idea.

Flying to Kauai: it's all in your connections

The typical travel plan involves a flight first to Honolulu International
Airport on Oahu and then a connecting flight to Kauai's Lihue Airport. This
route can turn into a full day of travel, particularly on the return trip to the
mainland, when the clock can move 3 (or even more) hours ahead of you.
Consider paying a premium for a non-stop flight on United, American,
Alaska, Delta, US Air, or Continental from 7 gateway cities. Airlines with
frequent daily flights give you more options in case someone gets sick, or
you need to go home earlier, or (even better) later!

Hawaiian and *Go! Airlines* fly the twenty-minute flight from Honolulu
to Kauai. Airline regulations require a minimum 70 minute layover in
Honolulu to allow passengers and baggage to be transferred to inter-island
connecting flights. However, if you travel only with carry-on luggage, you
might be able to catch an earlier flight to Lihue, if you are willing to take
your chances as a stand-by. (The computer data is often wrong, and stand-
bys can often get seats). Ever vigilant for a profit stream, inter-island

airlines now charge a change fee, but instead of paying, try this: go directly to the gate and socialize with the attendant who might just want to put you on that earlier flight to clear the gate area. On your inter-island flight, you may be asked to gate-check your carry-on luggage because of size, as some inter-island aircraft have small overhead bins. Keep your jewelry, camera, prescription drugs, and favorite stuffed animals in a small bag you can pull out of that carry on, if necessary.

Hawaiian Airlines 808.835.3700; 800.367.5320 *www.hawaiianair.com*

GO! Airlines   888-IFLYGO2 *www.iflygo.com*

Traveling with kids

If you are traveling with babies or toddlers, you can request bulkhead seating (but not exit rows, which can be assigned only to adults) in advance. Be sure to get an assigned seat in the computer in advance too, so that your seats have priority if the flight is overbooked. If you haven't already done so, enroll everyone in the airline's Frequent Flyer Program.

You should bring along your child's car seat, which can go into the

baggage compartment, as Hawaii state law requires them for children under three. Airlines now permit use of the child's restraint seat on board the aircraft, but usually require the child to have a paid seat on crowded flights.

Families who fly to Kauai from the east coast might consider staying overnight in California to help children make the difficult time adjustment in stages, particularly on the long trip home. After flying from Kauai to California, the kids can run around the hotel, have ice cream, and stay up late in order to push their body clocks ahead 3 hours while they sleep. If you book a late morning flight out of California the next day, the kids can sleep late in the morning, and if you're lucky, wake up fresh for the second day's flight, ready to adjust their body clocks through another time zone.

Kite flying at Hanalei Bay

On that journey home, if bad weather threatens to delay your connecting flight from Lihue to Honolulu, consider taking an earlier flight, before the inter-island flights get backed up. In fact, it's a good idea to get on any earlier flight to Honolulu once you're in the Lihue airport.

To amuse the kids during the long flight, you can pack small toys, crayons, books, paper dolls, and an 'airplane present' to be unwrapped when the seat belt sign goes off. Ask the cabin attendants for 'kiddie packs' or cards right away as supplies are often limited. Snacks and a secret toy can save the day in those awful moments when one child spills coke on another. Keep chewing gum handy to help children relieve the ear-clogging which can be so uncomfortable, even painful, during the last twenty minutes of the descent when cabin pressure changes. Sucking on a bottle will help a baby or toddler cope with altitude adjustment.

To save shopping time, we stuff as many beach and swimming toys into suitcase corners as possible. 'Swimmies' (arm floats) are great for small children to use in the pool, as are goggles and masks, toy trucks for sand-dozing, frisbees, inflatable beach balls, and floats. Boogie boards, by far the best swimming toy, can be brought home in the baggage compartment after your vacation (packed in a pillowcase). Best choices are at the Deja Vu store (Kapa'a), Progressive Expressions (Koloa), or even K-Mart, Wal-Mart, or Costco (Lihue). Boogie boards are better balanced than the cheaper imitations. Caution: they can be hazardous in a pool; small children who tip over in water over their heads can be trapped underneath.

Rent equipment at *Ready Rentals*: 808.823.8008; 800.599.8008 *www. readyrentals.com*. To protect a baby's delicate skin, bring a hat with a large brim, socks for feet, and a strong, waterproof sunblock (re-apply frequently). Beach umbrellas can be bought at Wal-Mart and Costco in Lihue.

Tips for visitors with disabilities

Kauai County provides a 'Landeez' all-terrain wheelchair at lifeguard stations at *Poipu Beach Park, Lydgate Park,* and *Salt Pond Beach Park.* These parks, and *Kalapaki Beach* (parking tips: p 33) have the most accessible facilities and pathways. At *Kalihiwai* and *Anini Beach* (north shore) and *Hanama'ulu Beach* (eastside), parking is flat and close to the water. Some companies make a special effort to help: *Gregg Winston* at Watersports Adventures is a wizard with teaching kids scuba/snorkeling 808.821.1599 *www.watersportsadventures.ws*. *Charlie Smith* works with KORE (a non-profit helping residents and visitors with disabilities) and gives private water-based lessons: *www.blueseassurfingschool.com* 808.634.6979. Also: Kauai Nature Tours's *Chuck Blay*: 808.742.8305;

888.233.8365 *www.kauainaturetours.com*; and *Mary* at Liko Kauai Cruises
808.338.0333; 888-sea-liko *www.liko-kauai.com*.

Equipment rental 24/7, including Landeez chairs and ramps, as well as
helpful advice: *Gammie Home Care*: 808.632.2333 *www.gammie.com*. Also
contact the County ADA Office (*cpilkington@kauai.gov* 808.241.6203 V/
TTY) and the *Kauai Bus*: 808.241.6417 *www.kauai.gov*. Bring your valid
ADA paratransit ID card and parking placard for accessible parking stalls.

Getting Around: It's a two–lane lifestyle

No matter where you stay, you can easily explore most of the island by
car. Except for the wilderness in the northwest quadrant, Kauai is nearly
encircled by a main two-lane highway, with sequentially numbered 'mile
markers' to make tracking easy. You can drive from Lihue to Kapa'a in
about 10 minutes (depending on traffic), from Kapa'a to Hanalei in about 30
minutes (ditto), from Lihue to Poipu in about 20 minutes, and from Poipu to
Polihale in about 35 minutes.

The best places to explore on Kauai are accessible by either paved
roads or established dirt roads in the cane fields maintained as 'rights of
way' to the beaches. So pack a picnic lunch, some beach mats, sunscreen,
your guidebook, Keali'i Reichel music CD, and explore some of the island's
most beautiful hidden beaches. Plan your adventures according to the
weather and the season. In winter, the surf is more unpredictable and
dangerous on the north and northeast, while the safest swimming may be on
the south shore. In summer, the surf may be up on the south and west, with
north shore beaches calm for swimming.

Whatever the season, follow this simple rule for swimming safety:
don't swim alone or too far out at any beach whose currents are unfamiliar.
Read Ocean Safety carefully (p 80). When you park, lock valuables in the
trunk, as you would at home.

Kauai is still rural in infrastructure – just two-lanes, pretty much all
around the island. Traffic has led to establishing contra flow on Rt 56
between Hanama'ulu and Wailua during rush hour, and 4 'bypass roads.'
You'll see the first one, Rt 51, as you leave the airport; it merges with Rt 56
(Kuhio Highway, the main north/south road) near Hanama'ulu. Maps 1, 2

Northbound traffic moves easily until Wailua, where three traffic lights
can cause unbelievable congestion at rush hour. The Wailua bypass winds
through cane fields, then comes out near the center of Kapa'a. You'll see
the turnoff to the west, just north of the light at Brick Oven Pizza and south
of Coconut Plantation Marketplace. It brings you to the center of Kapa'a
about two blocks behind the ABC Store. Maps 1, 3, 4

The Koloa bypass avoids the center of Koloa town and ends at the Hyatt Resort. Turn left off Rt 520 (Maluhia Rd) just before Koloa (the left turn is well marked), and follow signs to Poipu. Maps 6, 7

The Lihue bypass: Take Niumali Rd in Nawiliwili near the small boat harbor to Halemalu Rd; follow it past the Menehune Fish Pond to Puhi Rd which connects with Rt 50; then continue on to Koloa and Poipu. This bypass skirts traffic on Rt 56 as you pass Kukui Grove. Map 2

Best of virtual Kauai

Feeling awash in the sea of Kauai-related websites? Here are some of the best – with the most useful information and few ads.

First stops	www.kauaidiscovery.com
	www.kauai.gov
Garden Island Newspaper	www.kauaiworld.com
Beaches & surf	www.kauaiexplorer.com
Kauai calendar	www.kauaiworld.com/calendar
	www.kauaiexplorer.com
Kauai shows	www.kauaifestivals.com
All-island calendars	www.calendar.gohawaii.com
Kauai Yellow Pages	www.htyellowpages.com
Local Kauai links	www.trykauai.com/Lilikoi_Links.htm
Poipu Beach	www.poipu-beach.org
B & B's, condo rentals	www.kauaivacationrentals.com
	www.vrbo.com
	www.redweek.com
Hawaiian music	www.mele.com
Keali'i Reichel MP3s	www.kealiireichel.com
Hawaiian language	www.hawaiianlanguage.com
Kauai hiking	www.hawaiitrails.org
	www.hawaiistateparks.org
	www.kokee.org
	www.kauaiexplorer.com
Kauai Gardens	www.ntbg.org
	www.naainakai.org
Kauai camping	www.campingkauai.com

Speed limits and seat belt laws are strictly enforced. It's illegal to make a U-turn in a 'business district,' even if it doesn't look to you like much is going on. On Kauai, it's a two-lane lifestyle. Polish your left hand turn skills, avoid driving between 4pm and 6:30pm, load your Keali'i Reichel CD into your car's stereo, and remember— you're on vacation!

Managing Kauai's weather: chasing the sun

Call 808.245.6001 for the weather report on Kauai, and you will probably hear this 'forecast': "Mostly fair today, with occasional windward and mauka (mountain) showers. Tonight, mostly fair, with showers varying from time to time and from place to place." Except for storms, Kauai's normal weather is mostly sunny, with showers passing over the ocean, crossing the coastline and backing up against the mountainous interior.

Like all the Hawaiian islands, Kauai's sunny side varies with the winds. Normal trade winds from the north and northeast bring rainfall to these 'windward' shores and create the 'lee' of the island in the south, at Poipu, and west, at Kekaha and Waimea. When the clouds back up against the mountains and bring showers to the north shore beaches, Poipu and Salt Pond may have sunny skies. However, when the winds blow from south and west, called 'Kona winds,' the lee is in the north and northeast. The north shore may be dry while the eastern and southern shores have rain.

Kauai has 'micro climates' however and a 20 minute drive may take you from rain to sun. Be prepared to drive to the sun – all the way west to Kekaha or Polihale if necessary. If it's clear up north, visit the north shore, for these beaches are by far the most spectacular, and if your stay is only for a few days, you may not get another chance. Rain outside? Drive south to Poipu or west to Salt Pond or Kekaha, where it's usually drier. Only an island-wide storm should send you indoors to rent a movie, so check the weather and surf report. Call 808.245.6001 or call these friendly merchants who have agreed to be your weather tipsters: *Nukumoi Beach Center*, Poipu: 808.742.8019; *Wrangler's Steak House*, Waimea: 808.328.1218; *Pedal & Paddle*, Hanalei: 808.826.9069, or online at *www.kauaiexplorer.com*.

Weather patterns vary with the seasons. Showers are more frequent in winter and spring, while summer months are warmer and more humid, fall months clearer and more dry. Temperatures range between 60's at night & mid-80's most days, and in summer can reach the low 90's.

The beaches also change their moods with the seasons. In summer, the water may be calm and clear, but winter surf at the same beach can foam and crash like thunder. Some north shore beaches disappear entirely under winter surf, and may officially close for safety.

Eastside Beach Adventures

*Kalapaki Beach,
a family favorite for
swimming & playing
frisbee – and
exploring the Marriott
Hotel afterwards*

*Lydgate's rock pools,
great for family swimming*

Beaches

Ninini Beach 35
Kalapaki Beach 34
Hanamaʻulu 35
* Lydgate Park 36
Wailua Bay 37
* Kealia Beach 39
Donkey Beach 39
* Anahola Beach 40
(* Lifeguard)

Hotels

A Beach Resort, Makaiwa
B Kauai Coast Resort
C Islander on the Beach
D Aloha Beach Resort
E Kauai Beach Resort
(Hilton)
F Marriott, Kauai Lagoons

Anahola Bay is great
for beachwalks and
family fun (*Lifeguard*)

For island tastes, visit
farmers' markets in
Lihue and Kapaʻa, 99
Steelgrass Farm
    chocolate tour, 95

Scuba anyone?
Lessons are fun and
can begin a great
adventure, 130

Wailua River, Kauai's
only navigable
waterway: try kayak
explorations, 121
& water-skiing, 143

Zipline, 147
Tubing, 141

Lydgate Park
has snorkel-
ing and
rafting for
the whole
family
(*Lifeguard*)

Long beachwalks along Wailua
Beach south of Lydgate Park

Kauai's main traveled roads:
Rt 56 (Kuhio Hwy) travels north from
Lihue to Wailua, Kapaʻa and Anahola.
Rt 56 then curves to the west towards
Kilauea and Princeville.

Rt 56 also connects in Lihue with Rt 50
heading west (towards Poipu via Rt 520)
and Waimea.

Kayaking on the Huleʻia River
and Alakoko (Menehune)
Fish Pond, 122

Secret Beach

Kilauea Lighthouse
Crater Hill

Kahili ("Rock Quarry") Beach
Kilauea Bay
Beach access

Kilauea Rd
Kolo Rd
❶
❷

To Princeville

Wailapa Rd
North Wailakalua Rd

Pila'a Beach

Larsen's Beach

Ko.O'olau Rd
Beach access
Moloa'a Bay

56

Moloa'a Stream

Pa'a'a Stream
Kuhio Hwy

Moloa'a Rd

Eastern Shore
Kauai

Map 1
Eastside

Aliomanu Beach
Aliomanu Rd
Anahola Bay
Anahola Beach Park
Lifeguard

Anahola
❸
Kahala Point
Anahola Rd

Anahola Stream

Kahena Rd
Kealia Rd
Kealia Stream
Kealia Rd

Donkey Beach

Kawaihau Rd
Mailihuna Rd
Walk/bike trail
Kealia Beach

Kaehula Rd
Kapahula Rd
Kapa'a ❹
❺
Kapa'a Shopping Center ❻
❼
Kapa'a Farmers Market

To Keahua Arboretum

580
Kamalu Rd
Kuamoo Rd
581
Kauai Village Shopping Center
Bypass Rd
❽
❾
Kapa'a Beach Park

Waipouli Town Center
❿
⓫
⓬
Wailua
⓭ A
B Waipouli Beach
⓮
C
Coconut Plantation Marketplace
Wailua Bay

Fern Grotto
⓯
Wailua Falls
Leho Rd
D
Rock Pool

583
Ma'alo Rd

Lydgate State Park

Nukolii Beach

Wailua River
Wailua Golf Course

Hanama'ulu Stream
56
⓰
E
Hanama'ulu Beach
Hanama'ulu
Hanama'ulu Bay

Ahukini Landing

51

Grove Farm Plantation
Ahukini Rd
Rice St
Lihue
Lihue Airport
Lihue Farmers Market

⓴
⓱
22
50
㉑
Nawiliwili Rd
⓳
Kaumuali Hwy
Kukui Grove Shopping Center
⓲
Kauai Lagoons Golf Course

To Poipu

Hulemalu Rd
F
Kalapaki Bay
Ninini Point & Lighthouse

Huleia River & Wildlife Preserve
Menehune Fishpond
Kalapaki Beach

Kalapaki Beach

N

0   1   2
Miles

Activities

Family Fun

Tours

The beautiful Wailua coastline along the 'coconut coast'

Restaurants

Kilauea

1	Lighthouse Bistro	203
2	Kilauea Bakery	201
	Pau Hana Pizza	201
	Kilauea Fish Market	201

Anahola

3	Ono Char Burger	180

Kapa'a

5	Kountry Kitchen	173
	Small Town Coffee	94
6	Eastside	163
	El Café	177
	Mermaids Café	175
	Olympic Café	179
	Ono Family Rest	179
	Sushi Bushido	184
	TNT Steakburger	185
7	Sukothai	182
	Verde	186

Wailua

8	Kauai Pasta	172
9	Lemongrass	175
10	Waipouli Deli	189
	Papaya's Café	180
	Pho Vy	181
	Sweet Marie's	184

	Wahooo Seafood	187
12	Bull Shed	158
	The Oasis	177
14	Hukilau Lanai	171
	Mema Thai & Chinese	175
13	Caffé Coco	159
	Kintaro	172
	Monico's	176
	Brick Oven Pizza	157
	Tutu's Soup Hale	186
	Icing on the Cake	170
15	Wailua Marina	188

Hanama'ulu

16	Hanama'ulu Tea House	167

Lihue

18	Duke's Canoe Club	162
	JJ's Broiler	170
	Kalapaki Beach Hut	171
	Portofino Café	160
	Gingbua	166
19	Garden Island BBQ	164
	Barbecue Inn	156
	Halo Halo Shave Ice	120
	Hamura's Saimin	166
20	Oki Diner	178
21	Deli & Bread Connection	190
	La Bamba	173
22	Gaylord's at Kilohana	156

Eastside It List

• Our favorite swimming beach is Kalapaki Beach, wonderful for swimming, skim boarding, and when the surf is right, boogie boards. The sand is perfect for playing volleyball or frisbee, running, or simply sunning. Rent a catamaran or kayak, or try stand up paddle surfing.

• Lydgate Park in Wailua is perfect for families – an enormous lava rock-rimmed pool offers wonderful swimming and snorkeling, with a smaller rock-rimmed pool just right for toddlers. Lifeguard. Beyond the pools, the beach is great for long walks. Lydgate also offers the best playground on Kauai, the Kamalani Playground, with two sections.

• For water activities, Wailua Beach is popular with local surfers. On the Wailua River, you can water ski, learn to paddle surf (p 140) or explore upstream by kayak (p 121).

• Surfers will love Kealia Beach, where wonderful, even rollers can give great rides when conditions are right. Lifeguard. A paved public walkway/bike path north from Kealia Beach offers beautiful coastal vistas.

• For picnics and beach walks, visit beautiful Anahola Bay. Lifeguard.

• Hungry? For inexpensive, tasty lunch try *Hamura's Saimin, Barbecue Inn* or *Kalapaki Beach Hut* (Lihue), *Monico's, Brick Oven Pizza, Tutu's Soup Hale, Pho Vy* or *Caffé Coco* (Wailua), or *Mermaid's* (Kapa'a). Spend a bit more and enjoy *Duke's Barefoot Bar* or *Gaylord's* (Lihue).

Snapshot: the Eastside

Most visits to Kauai begin (and end) on the east side, at the Lihue airport, roughly the midpoint of driveable roads on the island. When you leave the airport in your rental car, you can head north along the eastern shore to Wailua and Kapa'a, then on to Princeville, Hanalei and Ha'ena. Or you can head west to Poipu, Kalaheo, and Waimea. *Lihue*, the county seat, sits on the right angle of Rt 56 going north and Rt 50 going west. It's home to many of Kauai's original family businesses, the Kauai Museum, and the

Great Days on the Eastside

Day 1: WAILUA/KAPA'A: Breakfast at *Kountry Kitchen* (p 173) or *Ono Family Restaurant* (p 179). Morning: water-ski, learn to stand-up paddle surf (p 140) or kayak on the Wailua River (p 121), or hike Sleeping Giant Mountain (p 117). Lunch at *Monico's* (p 176) or *Tutu's Soup Hale* (p 186). Afternoon at *Lydgate Park*, great for family fun and long beachwalks (p 32). Dinner at *Hukilau Lanai* (fresh fish: 171), *Kintaro* (sushi: 172), or *The Eastside* (Asian Fusion: 163).

Day 2: LIHUE: Breakfast at *Tip Top* (p 185) or *Tutu's Soup Hale* (p 186). Morning: kayak trip up the Hule'ia River (p 122), tour *Grove Farm Homestead* (p 125), or try a *zipline* (p 147) or *tubing* (p 141) adventure. Lunch at *Pho Vy* (p 181) or *Hamura's Saimin* (p 166). Afternoon: relax or sail at Kalapaki Beach. Dinner *Bull Shed* (prime rib: 158) or *Duke's* (steak & seafood: 163).

Kauai Lagoons Marriott Resort. Just outside of town, as you head west toward Poipu on Rt 50, is Kukui Grove Center (Borders, Macy's, Starbucks, Quiznos, KMart, Costco, and Home Depot).

Heading north along the eastern shore takes you through the towns of Wailua and Kapaʻa. You will drive on Rt 56, Kuhio Highway, the most traveled of Kauai's three main roads. You'll come to *Wailua* as you cross the Wailua River, the only navigable river in Hawaii, as it flows into Wailua Bay, a popular local spot for surfing and beachwalking. Brick Oven Pizza (west side of Rt 56), Tutu's Soup Hale and Monico's in Kinipopo Center (east side of Rt 56) offer tasty, inexpensive meals. Next door, browse Goldsmith's Gallery for exquisite jewelry by island goldsmiths and designers. About a mile north, Coconut Plantation Marketplace is a tourist-style shopping center with clothing stores, fast food, and souvenir shops.

Continue north to *Kapaʻa* for small art galleries (Kela Glass), specialty shops (Hee Fat Store, Taj Beach Co, Coconut Coast) and restaurants. Pack a picnic lunch from Mermaid's and head just north of town to Kealia Beach (mile marker 10), a favorite surfing spot. Walk or bike the improved pathway from the parking lot around the rocky point to Donkey Beach. *Anahola*, at mile marker 13, is a quiet residential area designated by law for families of Hawaiian descent. Anahola Beach is peaceful, great for a family picnic or a long, relaxing beach walk. Take out a picnic from Ono Char Burger. Beyond Anahola, the road curves past Moloaʻa Bay and Larsen's Beach towards Kilauea and the north shore.

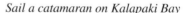

Sail a catamaran on Kalapaki Bay

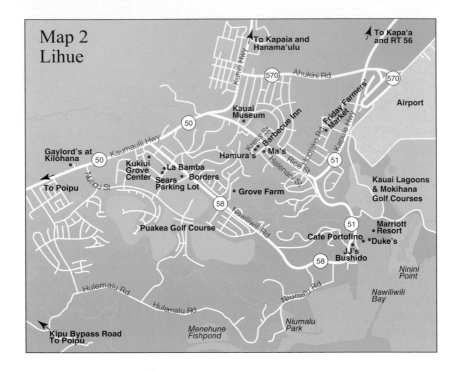

Eastside Beaches

Lihue Area Beaches: Kalapaki Beach

Great family fun: Almost enclosed by craggy green hillsides, Kalapaki Bay's natural harbor has a wide sandy beach with some of the best swimming on the island. The waves roll to shore in long, even swells usually great for swimming and rafting. At times, surf is very rough, but even if you shouldn't swim, you can still enjoy beautiful views. Green mountains with the contours of a giant animal sleeping in the sun face houses on stilts perched precariously on the sheer cliff.

Fronting this beach is the Marriott Resort at Kauai Lagoons, a headline-maker from the time it opened in the late '80's as a Westin because of its lavish design, elaborate collection of far eastern art, and mini zoo of tropical birds and animals. Today you'll still find Kauai's largest swimming pool, its tallest high-rise (set into the cliff, it is technically still 'no higher than a coconut tree'), and its only two-storey escalator.

Kalapaki Beach is a favorite family spot. The firm sand is perfect for games and hard running, and the waves can at times break perfectly for boogie boards. Build sand castles, play beach volleyball, rent a kayak or catamaran, or try your hand at windsurfing or stand-up paddle surfing.

Safety info: Heed high surf warnings. In winter months, waves can break with enormous force, and every so often a really big one seems to come up out of nowhere to smash unwary swimmers. *No Lifeguard.*

Directions: Take Rice St through Lihue, and turn left into the main entrance of the Kauai Marriott. Pass the main lobby, turn right at the first street, follow it down the hill to the beach access parking lot. The hotel maintains an accessible restroom for people with disabilities. Maps 1, 2

Ninini Beach

The drive to this tiny beach, 'Running Waters,' is more interesting than the destination. You wind along a cane road next to the airport runway, so close that the jets taking off and landing almost make you want to duck.

Turn off Kapule Rd just south of the Lihue airport at the marble gates (once the limo entrance to the old Westin), drive through brush and rustling grasses, then through the hotel grounds, always bearing towards the water, until you reach the lighthouse at Ninini Point. You'll have a gorgeous view of the coastline, a great spot to picnic, but *not safe for swimming.*

Hanama'ulu Beach

A perfect crescent of soft shining sand, the beach at Hanama'ulu Bay is perfect for building sand castles and hunting sunrise shells. In summer, waves are gentle enough for children. Rolling to shore in long, even swells only a foot or two high, they break into miniature crests and layers of white foam flecked with sandy gold, like the lacy borders of a lovely shawl. Even occasional 'wipe-outs' are not serious because of the gentle, gradual slope of the sandy bottom.

There is plenty of shade for babies beneath the tall

Hanama'ulu Beach

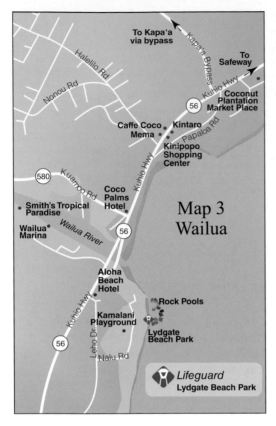

Map 3
Wailua

ironwood trees which fringe the sand. Behind the beach, the Hanamaʻulu Stream forms shallow pools as it winds toward the bay, and kids can hunt for tiny crayfish and other creatures with nets. A picnic pavilion faces the river, and tables look out over the bay. Everything is uncrowded, as this beach is frequented by few tourists.

Unfortunately, it is also in the path sometimes used by helicopters returning to the airport from their scenic tours. Try to ignore the noisy choppers, and plan your visit for the morning, as the mosquitoes get hungry about 4pm.

Safety Info: No Lifeguard.

Directions: Turn off Rt 56 Kuhio Highway towards the sea at Hanamaʻulu, between the 7-Eleven and the school. Bear right at the fork. The road ends at the park. Restrooms, playground. Map 1

Wailua Area Beaches: Lydgate Beach Park

A favorite for the whole family: Lydgate Park features two rock-rimmed pools. A small one provides safe swimming for babies and toddlers, even in winter months. Adjacent is an enormous rock-rimmed pool which breaks the surf into rolling swells excellent for swimming, rafting, and floats of all kinds. The pool is one of the best year–round snorkeling spots on the island, for families of brightly colored fish feed along the rocky perimeter. The rocky wall protects snorkelers and swimmers from surf and dangerous currents. Fly a kite, play frisbee on the wide, sandy beach.

Lydgate's rock rimmed pools

Kids will love the *Kamalani Playground,* 16,000 square feet of fun, with mirror mazes, a suspension bridge, lava tubes, and circular slide. A second section is just south of Lydgate, connected by a paved path.

A beachwalker's delight: The nearly deserted beach past the rocky point in front of Kaha Lani Condominium is one of the best combinations of sand and views on the eastside. Sand is firm, and coastal views spectacular, particularly beautiful at sunrise or sunset.

Safety info: Lifeguard at Lydgate's rock enclosed pools. Outside the pools, swimming can be dangerous due to rough surf and strong currents.

Directions: If you are driving north on Rt 56, turn right onto Leho Rd just past the Wailua Golf Course, then turn right to the park. If you are driving south on Rt 56, turn left onto the Leho Rd just across the bridge over the Wailua River, at the Aloha Beach Resort. Lydgate Park has a lifeguard, picnic tables, and showers. Maps 1, 3

Wailua Bay

Great Walking Beach: Wailua Bay's long, curve of golden sand is perfect for walking. Near the bridge is the mouth of the Wailua River, sometimes shallow enough to ford, but at other times deep and treacherous.

Safety Info: No Lifeguard. Swimming in the brackish, calm water of the river can be fun, although young children who stray from the edges can get into trouble because the water can become deep very quickly. Swimming where the river empties into the bay is not recommended because

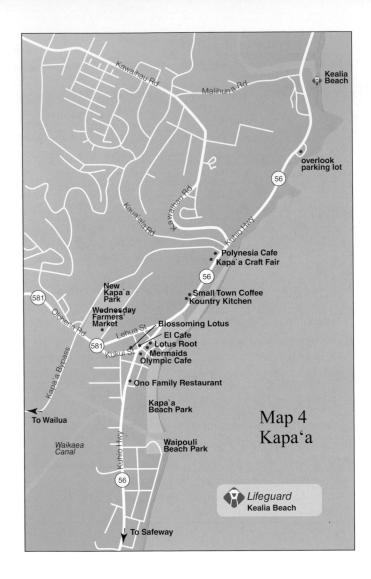

Kawaihau Rd

Malihuna Rd

Kealia Beach

overlook parking lot

56

Kaua`ala Rd

Kawaihau Rd

Kuhio Hwy

Polynesia Cafe
Kapa`a Craft Fair

56

New Kapa`a Park

Small Town Coffee
Kountry Kitchen

581

Olohena Rd

Wednesday Farmers' Market

Lehua St

Blossoming Lotus

El Cafe

581

Kukui St

Lotus Root

Mermaids
Olympic Cafe

Kapa`a Bypass

Ono Family Restaurant

Kapa`a Beach Park

To Wailua

Kuhio Hwy

Map 4
Kapa‘a

Waikaea Canal

Waipouli Beach Park

56

Lifeguard
Kealia Beach

To Safeway

currents can be dangerous and unpredictable, and murky water attracts sharks. In the Wailua River, try water skiing (p 142), kayaking (p 120), stand-up paddle surfing lessons (p 140). Some enjoy Smith's Boat Tours to Fern Grotto: 808.821.6895.

Directions: On Rt 56, just north of the Wailua River bridge. Maps 1, 3

Kapa'a Area Beaches:
Kealia Beach

Surfing and Body Board Favorite: North of Kapa'a on Rt 56 and just past a scenic overlook turnout, you will see spectacular Kealia Beach, a long, wide curve of golden sand ending in a rocky point. When the surf is up, lots of surfers ride the long, even rollers. During summer months, the waves can be gentle enough for children at the far end of the beach where lava rocks extending into the sea create a cove where the water is quieter. Kealia has long been one of Jeremy's and Mike's favorite beaches for surfing and body boarding. The sandy bottom slopes gradually, and you can walk out to catch some wonderful long rides, though at times the waves can be too powerful for children (even adults).

Great for Walking: Firm, level sand makes this a perfect walking beach. Don't miss the improved bike/walking tour to Donkey Beach.

Safety info: Lifeguard. Look for where local folks are body boarding and follow their lead, not hard board surfers seeking the bigger thrill. Be cautious in winter surf. If you see small, blue 'men o' war' jellyfish on the sand, they are probably also in the water. They pack a nasty sting, so head to another beach. Near the river mouth, strong rip currents can make ocean swimming hazardous.

Directions: Drive north of Kapa'a on Rt 56 until you see the parking lot between mile markers 10 and 11. You can walk (or bike) on the paved public pathway around the point to beautiful Donkey Beach. Maps 1, 4

Donkey Beach

Bike/Walk to Donkey Beach: A long curve of sand which ends in piles of rock on both sides, Donkey Beach was once known as a haven for nude sunbathing, but that has changed due to the wonderful new pedestrian bike path and walking path linking it to Kealia. The lasting achievement of former Mayor Maryanne Kusaka, this walkway offers vistas of the east-shore, churning surf below and grassy hills, particulary lovely in early morning or late afternoon. *No Lifeguard;* powerful currents.

Directions: The public bike and walking path follows the cane road from Kealia Beach parking lot. Or park in the additional public lot just off Rt 56 between the mile 11 and 12 markers. Map 1

Anahola Area: Anahola Bay

Family Friendly: The beach at Anahola Bay is so long that to walk from one end to the other may take you nearly an hour. Colors are magnificent, especially at sunrise or in late afternoon as the sun moves west over the mountains, deepening the blue of the water and the gold of the sand while brightening tall white puff clouds until they glow with light.

With lifeguard protection, Anahola Bay is a family favorite, and a good choice on weekends when more well-known beaches are crowded. The county park at the sheltered southern end of the bay is better for snorkeling and picnicking. On the northern end the bay, where the Anahola stream flows into the bay, children can play in shallow pools which sometimes fill with tadpoles and tiny fish for kids to net, or float on body boards. Just north of the Anahola stream is Aliomanu Beach, with sandy 'nooks' along the road perfect for a picnic.

Body board fun at Kalapaki, Kealia, Anahola, Lydgate, and Hanama'ulu.

Safety info: Lifeguard. Swimming can be risky in areas distant from the Lifeguard Tower, which can be up to a quarter mile away. At the center of the bay, surf and currents can be strong most of the year. Watch out for small blue 'men o' war' jellyfish on the sand; they're in the water too.

Directions: Turn off Rt 56 at the Aliomanu Rd just north of Duane's Ono Burger (great burgers: 808.822.9181), drive to the mouth of the stream. To get to the beach park at the southern end of Anahola Beach, which has the Lifeguard, take Anahola Rd (just south of Ono Burger) and head towards the water to the parking area. Map 1

North Shore
Beach Adventures

Kilauea Lighthouse has a bird's eye view of Secret Beach

Lifeguard
Ke'e Beach (Summer Only)
Ha'ena Beach Park
Hanalei

Ke'e Beach
Ha'ena Beach Park
Tunnels Beach
Kepuhi Beach
560
1 C
Ha'ena
Wainiha Beach
Lumahai Beach
Hanalei Bay
Pali Ke Kua ("Hideaways") 7
Pu'u Poa Beach A B 6 5
Honoiki'ino
Liholiho
Hanakapiai Beach
Kalalau Trail
Wet Caves
Limahuli Stream
Manoa Stream
Wainiha Powerhouse Rd
Wainiha River
Lumahai Stream
Waikoko Beach
Wai'oli Beach Park
Kuhio Hwy
Hanalei Pier
Ching Young Village 3 4
Weke Ave
Aku Rd
Hanakapiai Stream
Limahuli Falls
Hanalei Center 2
Wai'oli Stream
Hanalei

Hanakapiai Falls

Lumahai Beach

Hanalei Bay

*Hike the Kalalau trail
to Hanakapi'ai, 115*

*St Regis Hotel
– come for sunset*

*Limahuli Gardens, 92
Na Aina Kai, 92*

Hotels

Beaches

Kilauea Lighthouse. 128

Most Na Pali boat tours now depart from south and westside harbors, 87

Sharing the wave at Kalihiwai

Kauai's main traveled roads: Rt 56 (Kuhio Hwy) travels north from Lihue, becomes Rt 560 at Princeville, continues west to road's end at Ke'e Beach.

Kalihiwai Bay, a jewel on the North Shore

North Shore snapshot

Exploring the north shore takes you to spectacular beaches, magnificent cliffs, amazing vistas. As Rt 56 winds north and then west, you will pass through three main residential areas: Kilauea, Princeville/Hanalei, and Ha'ena. Each has wonderful beaches and opportunities for adventure.

Driving north from Anahola, you will first come to *Kilauea*, passing along the way the turnoff to *Moloa'a Bay* and *Larsen's Beach*, both great spots for quiet beachwalking. Just outside Kilauea town (pick up picnic supplies at Kilauea Fish Market, Kilauea Bakery, or Kilauea Market Deli). Kilauea Bay and Kalihiwai Beach are beautiful places to explore. You can visit the *Kilauea Lighthouse* and nature preserve; tour *Na 'Aina Kai Botanical Gardens* nearby; and shop at Kong Lung and Banana Patch.

Princeville comes next, an ocean bluff community of condos, homes, two famous Robert Trent Jones Jr golf courses, and the spectacular St Regis Hotel, well worth a stop for lunch, afternoon tea, or sunset cocktail, or just sunset. Bring your camera for amazing vistas of *Hanalei Bay*.

As the road winds down the cliffside, you will see one of the loveliest beaches anywhere in the world, Hanalei Bay, and the town of *Hanalei*, with quaint shops and tiny eateries. Stop for a picnic or at least a wonderful beachwalk on firm golden sand at one of the most beautiful places you will ever see.

Continuing west around Hanalei Bay, you will pass *Lumahai Beach* (you'll see all the cars parked on the roadside). We prefer to continue on all the way to the end of the road, crossing scenic one-lane bridges, hugging cliffs, and visit *Ke'e Beach* – a great spot for summertime snorkeling and the starting point for the trail to Hanakapi'ai (and Kalalau).

The north shore – and the drive to the end of the road – are absolute musts! Take extra film/storage media for your camera.

North Shore It List

- Spectacular *Hanalei Bay*, an unforgettable image of Kauai for those rainy evenings back home. Great swimming and surfing, running, walking (p 55), and in summer, kayaking. Sunset views at St Regis.

- Our favorite family beach is *Kalihiwai*, which combines spectacular beauty with wonderful summertime swimming, as well as firm golden sand, perfect for running. In winter, surf is up, to the delight of our boys, and even spectators can have fun watching the surfers catch spectacular rides. Kids will love the brackish pools behind the beach for fishing, swimming, and playing with their boogie boards (p 53).

- Love history and nature? A tour of *Haraguchi Rice Mill* gives you both. Visit *Lumahuli Gardens* and *Na 'Aina Kai* for flowers, fields and trees (p 92).

- *Anini Beach* is gentle enough for children (p 53), and a popular spot for snorkeling (p 132) and windsurfing (p 145).

- For long, solitary beachwalks, try *Larsen's Beach* (p 47); for a peaceful picnic, try *Moloa'a Bay* (p 46).

- Adventurers love hiking to *Secret Beach,* both secluded and spectacular, with magnificent views of the coastline (p 51).

- The best snorkeling, when surf is calm, is at *Tunnels Beach* (p 58). In summer months, *Ke'e Beach* (p 60) has excellent snorkeling as well.
- From Ke'e Beach, you can hike the cliffside trail through the Na Pali wilderness to *Hanakapi'ai Beach* (p 114), magnificently beautiful, though too dangerous for swimming, and further, to *Hanakapi'ai Falls*. Try the first quarter-mile climb to a spectacular point overlooking Ke'e Beach and the Ha'ena reefs.
- For sunset watching, don't miss the view from the St Regis Hotel, or from *Tunnels Beach,* or, in summer months, *Anini Beach* or *Ke'e Beach.*

Great Days on the North Shore

Day 1: Breakfast at *Hanalei Wake Up Café.* Relax on *Hanalei Bay* (p 53), rent a kayak and explore the *Hanalei River* (p 122), or try windsurfing at *Anini Beach* (p 145). Picnic at *Kalihiwai* (p 53) with sandwiches/wraps from *Kilauea Fish Market* (p 201). Or tour *Haraguchi Rice Mill* (p 129). Sunset at *St Regis*; dinner at *Neidie's* (p 206).

Day 2: Breakfast at *Kalypso's* (p 198). Drive to the end of the road to *Ke'e Beach* (summer, p 60). Hike the cliff trail to the Ke'e Beach overlook (p 115) or on to Hanakapi'ai Beach. Or visit *Limahuli Gardens* (p 92). Grab a burrito at *Red Hot Mama's* (p 208) and snorkel at *Ke'e Beach* or *Tunnels*. Listen to a slack key guitar concert at Hanalei Pavilion (p 128). Dinner at *Postcards* (p 206) or *Bar Acuda* (p 195).

Day 3. Breakfast at *Kilauea Bakery* (p 201). Hike to *Secret Beach* (summer, p 51) or trail ride (p 119) or try surf lessons at Hanalei Pier (p 138). Lunch at *Tropical Taco* or in Princeville, *Tamarind* (p 209) or take out from Foodland deli. Lazy afternoon beachwalk at *Larsen's Beach* (p 47) or *Moloa'a* (p 46). Or tour *Kilauea Lighthouse* or *Na Aina Kai Gardens*. Dinner at *Dolphin* (p 197) or *Makana Terrace* (p 203).

Moloa'a area beaches: Moloa'a Bay

Peaceful picnic spot: Just north of Anahola and before you reach Kilauea, you can visit Moloa'a Bay or Larsen's Beach, which though beautiful are more suitable for relaxed beachwalking than swimming. The road to Moloa'a winds through countryside for several miles, and you can hear wonderful sounds – the breeze rustling in the leaves, the chirping of

Moloaʻa Bay

insects, the snorting of horses grazing in tree-shaded meadows. At road's end, you will find a gate attached to an unfriendly looking fence intended to discourage parking along the shoulder. Walk through the gate and cross a shallow stream.

At this point the bay, hidden by the half dozen homes which ring the beach, suddenly comes into view – an almost dazzling half-moon of shining golden sand and turquoise water. The long, sandy beach ends in grassy hills and piles of lava rocks on the left, and a sheer cliff on the right. To the left, the rocks are fun to climb and search for shells and trapped fish, although this windward side of the bay is usually too rough for swimming, and the bottom is very rocky. To the right of the stream, the bay is more sheltered, the water gentler.

Safety info: No Lifeguard. In times of heavy surf, this bay, like all windward beaches, can have dangerous currents.

Moloaʻa Bay is a place of peaceful solitude, filled with the sound of waves. The crystal blue water, traced with the shadowy patterns of the rocks below, stretches out to a horizon where pale clouds fade into a limitless sky.

Turn off Rt 56 about a half-mile north of the mile 16 marker onto Kuamoʻo Rd; turn right onto Moloaʻa Rd and follow it to the end. Map 5

Larsen's Beach

A favorite for Beachwalking and Exploring: Getting to Larsen's Beach is half the fun. A right-of-way-to-beach road wanders by pastureland, where horses grazing peacefully seem sketched into a landscape portrait of silvery green meadows. At the end of the well-graded, sandy road is a small parking area and a gate leading to the top of the cliff, where the beach below seems a slender ribbon of white against the dark blue water. Although a second, smaller gate seems to direct you to the right, walking through it takes you to a steep path ending in rocks. Instead, walk down the hillside to the left on a

Larsen's Beach, a great spot for beachwalking and shell collecting, even if winter surf is too strong for safe swimming.

well worn path with a gentle slope. A five-minute walk brings you to a long, lovely beach curving along the coastline and disappearing around a distant bend – perfect for lazy afternoons of beachcombing and exploring. Although a rocky reef offshore seems to invite snorkeling, Larsen's Beach is extremely dangerous.

Safety info: No Lifeguard. Before you begin the hike down, observe the ocean carefully and locate the channel through the reef, just to the left of the rocky point where you are standing. The churning water caused by the swift current makes the channel easiest to see from this height, and once noted, it can be recognized at sea level. Once you see this channel, you can also pick out the smaller channels which cut through the reef at several other points. Swimmers and snorkelers should avoid going near any of these channels, particularly the large one, because currents can be dangerously strong and even turn into a whirlpool when the tide is going out. Remember, Larsen's Beach has no lifeguard, and help is not close by. *Currents can be treacherous at any time, but particularly in winter months, and experienced local fishermen have drowned here. The watchword is caution: swim in pairs,*

*never go out beyond the reef, try to stay within easy distance of the shore,
and examine the surface of the water carefully to avoid swimming near a
channel.* If you snorkel, don't get so absorbed in looking at the fish that you
lose track of where you are, and don't go out at all if surf conditions don't
seem right. Sorry about all the 'don'ts,' but safety is a key issue at Larsen's.

A trip to Larsen's Beach does not require swimming or snorkeling. If
you bring reef-walking sneakers to protect your feet, you can walk around
in the shallow water and watch colorful fish who don't seem afraid of
people. Or walk for miles along the magnificent coastline of this picture-
perfect beach. Hunt for shells, or simply lose yourself in the spectacle of
nature's beauty. You will probably encounter only another person or two.

The drive back is wonderful, with spectacular views of the rolling hills,
lined by fences and stands of trees, and beyond them the dark and majestic
mountains reaching to touch the clouds.

The turnoff at Kuamoʻo Rd that takes you to Moloaʻa, (just north of the
mile 16 marker on Rt 56) also takes you to Larsen's Beach. After you bear
left at the Moloaʻa Rd turnoff, go about 1.1 miles and look for a dirt road on
the right. The right turn marked 'beach access' will be very sharp and
angled up an incline. Then another beach access sign will mark the left turn
onto the long, straight road to the beach. (From Hanalei, turn left off Rt 56
at the mile 20 marker, and left again onto the beach access road). Park, lock
up, walk towards the cliff, where you will find a gate leading to the top of
the cliff and down the trail on the left. Map 5

Kilauea area beaches: Kilauea Bay ('Rock Quarry')

Fun for exploring: The road to this unspoiled beach tests the mettle of
both car and driver with challenges at practically every turn, and takes you
past sobering reminders of the devastating and deadly flood that caused
enormous destruction when the Ka Loko dam broke. Deeply rutted, even
gouged by ditches and holes, the road can turn into a quagmire in rain, but
in dry weather, it can be navigated without too much difficulty by a careful
driver even in a rented subcompact. Pick a dry day, and the road will add the
zest of adventure and heighten the excitement of discovering, just down the
hill from the parking area at road's end, a bay shaped like a perfect half-
moon, the deep blue water sparkling with light, and the golden sand
outstretched between two rocky bluffs like a tawny cat sleeping in the sun.

At the northern end is the Kilauea stream. One year it may be shallow
enough for small children at low tide; the next, too deep. The width can vary
from a few yards to fifty. To the left, the beach ends abruptly in an old rock

Surfing at Kilauea on a summer day

quarry, a great spot for pole fishing. To the right, the sandy beach extends a long way before ending in piles of lava rocks which are great for climbing and exploring tidal pools. Chances are you'll encounter only another person or two and can watch in solitude as the waves roll towards to the beach in long, even swells, break into dazzling white crests, and rush to shore in layers of gold and white foam.

Safety info: No Lifeguard.

Surf can be dangerously strong and currents treacherous, particularly in winter when the beach may almost disappear beneath the crashing waves. We found the swimming safe enough in summer for our seven and ten-year-olds to surf on their boogie boards in the shallow water, although even close to shore the pull of the current was strong.Tiny blue Portuguese 'men o' war' sometimes wash ashore after a storm. If you see them on the sand, they are probably in the water too. It's prudent to go to another beach, for these small jellyfish pack a giant sting.

Behind the beach, the stream forms brackish pools where children can swim safely, except near the stream's entrance into the bay where the current can be swift, particularly at high tide. One August, the pools were wider than we had ever seen, like a shallow lagoon, and our family had a great time netting tadpoles.

Our children loved this beach because of the variety of things they could do and the challenge of ripping the leaves off the branches that scraped the sides of the car as we maneuvered around gullies. We love the beach because we have had it, sometimes, all to ourselves.

Directions: South of Kilauea town, between mile markers 21 and 22 on Rt 56, take Wailapa Rd towards the ocean. After .4 of a mile, turn left onto a dirt road and follow it (only in dry weather) for about a mile until you reach Kahili Beach at Kilauea Bay. You will see signs of the tragic break in the Ka Loko dam in 2006. Sobering traces of destruction remain. Map 5

Secret Beach

Beautiful and isolated: Nestled at the base of a sheer cliff just north of Kilauea, Secret Beach is well off the beaten track for good reason. You must hike down (and back up!) a rocky trail which zigzags through trees, gullies, and brush. You can drive only to the trail's beginning at the top of the cliff. From here, you can hear the waves crashing below – apparently not very far away – as you look down on a trail which seems to disappear into a tangle of jungle. The path is steep in places – sneakers are a good idea – but branches, roots, and vines offer plenty of handholds, and in a pinch, you can always resort to the seat of your pants!

The walk down will take about seven minutes, and as the path makes the last sharp plunge before leveling off to the sand, you can see, at last, through a screen of trees and hanging vines, a magnificent stretch of golden sand and a shining turquoise sea. In rainy times, this enormous triangle of sand may be partly covered by a lagoon fed in part by a stream winding down behind the beach. Towards the left, you can climb a rocky outcropping and find a small beach ending in a steep cliff. Towards the right, you can see the Kilauea lighthouse and walk a long way across the sand.

Safety info: No Lifeguard. Secret Beach is not a place to come alone, for the obvious reason of its isolation. Swimming is not safe. The surf is rough, and currents strong and unpredictable; There is no Lifeguard if you had trouble. During the winter, this beach, enormous as it is, can disappear almost entirely under huge, crashing waves. Instead of swimming, walk along the water, hunt for shells, and forget everything but the feel of wet sand between your toes.

The walk back up the cliff will give you time to adjust to the world you left behind – just about 10 minutes of mild exertion, with the air cool under the trees and the leaves speckled with sunlight. This would not be pleasant in the mud, though, so don't go after a soaking rain. By the time you reach your car and remember that you have to stop at the store for milk, the peaceful solitude you left behind will be as hard to recapture as a wave rippling on the sand. But for a few moments, you were lost to your working-day world. This may be the secret of Secret Beach, a secret worth keeping!

Note: One reader discovered another secret about this beach, when she and her family reached the bottom of the trail and ran into "a long-haired young man wearing nothing but a guitar!" So be prepared for strange music!

Directions: Approach Secret Beach and Kalihiwai Bay from Kalihiwai Rd, about a half mile north of Kilauea on Rt 56. Turn towards the ocean onto

Kalihiwai—our favorite family beach on the north shore. In summer, the ocean can be calm, almost like a lake (below) while in winter, thundering surf can crash onto the sand (above).

Kalihiwai Rd. Bear left, then turn right onto a dirt road that looks like a broad red gash in the landscape. Follow towards the water till it ends. Park, lock up valuables in the trunk, and walk down the trail. Map 5

Kalihiwai Bay

Our family favorite: You'll catch your first glimpse of Kalihiwai Bay as you drive down the narrow road carved into the side of the sheer cliff which encloses it on one side. From this angle, the bay is a perfect semi-circle of blue, rimmed with shining white sand and nestled between two lava cliffs. Ironwood trees ring the beach. A freshwater stream flows into the bay near the far end, so shallow and gentle at low tide that small children can splash around safely. It becomes deep enough behind the beach for kayak adventuring up-river.

Kalihiwai Bay offers wonderful summertime fun for people of all ages. Little ones will love the shallow pools behind the beach where they can fish or float on rafts, while older kids will enjoy the ocean swimming. At times, the waves rise very slowly and break in long, even crests over a sloping sandy bottom, perfect for wave jumping and boogie boarding. One summer day we watched a dozen children celebrate a birthday with a surfing party.

Safety info: No Lifeguard. In winter, the surf and currents in the bay can become formidable. Even experienced surfers may have difficulty managing the currents which can be particularly strong when a swell is running. If the surf is too rough, Kalihiwai is still a lovely beach for walking or running, with firm sand and magnificent views of the cliffs. There are portapotties, but the nearest public restrooms are in Kilauea at the ball field behind Kilauea Market (next to home plate). Pick up picnic supplies at Kilauea Bakery or Kilauea Fish Market.

A yellow siren atop a pole on the beach road is a reminder of the *tsunami* or tidal wave of 1957 which washed away the bridge originally linking the two roads leading from Rt 56 to Kalihiwai Bay. Both are still marked Kalihiwai Rd at their separate intersections with Rt 56. Either will take you to the bay. If you choose the Kalihiwai Rd just north of the long bridge on Rt 56, you'll have to wade across the stream's mouth to reach the beach. The Kalihiwai Rd just south of the bridge and north of Kilauea is preferable. Map 5

Anini Beach

Great views: This quiet, beautiful beach goes for miles along a coastline protected by an extensive offshore reef. At some places the road is so close to the water you could almost jump in. *The Beach Park* has restrooms, camping, and picnic facilities, although you can turn off the road at almost any spot, park, and find your private paradise. The reef creates a quiet lagoon, great for summertime snorkeling, and for windsurfing lessons year-round.

Safety info: No Lifeguard. During high surf, particularly in winter, the current running parallel to the beach can become strong enough to pull an unwary swimmer out of the lagoon through the channel in the reef at the west end of the park. Stay inside the reef.

Across from the Beach Park, the Kauai Polo Club hosts polo matches on summer Sunday afternoons. Continue along Anini road through a quiet residential area all the way to its western end, where a sandbar extending quite far out invites wading and fishing. Children enjoy the quiet water and the tiny shells along the waterline, and you'll love the amazing combination of sounds – the roar of the surf breaking on the reef far offshore, and near your feet, the gentle rippling of the sea upon the sand.

In summer months, you can watch the sun set into the ocean at Anini Beach, a glorious sight which can be yours in perfect solitude. The tall ironwood trees darken to feathery silhouettes against a pale gray and orange sky, filled with lines of puff clouds. The water shimmers gold as the sun's dying fire fades slowly to a pearl and smoky gray, to the songs of crickets and the lapping of gentle waves.

Just northwest of Kilauea, between mile markers 25 and 26 on Rt 56, turn towards the ocean at the Kalihiwai Rd just north of the long bridge. Bear left at the fork, and follow the road as it winds downhill past the park till it ends at the base of the cliffs at Princeville. Map 5

Hanalei area: Princeville: Pu'u Poa Beach

Tucked beneath the St Regis Hotel's ocean bluff perch is a sandy beach set inside a reef. When you look down from the hotel, you can see the rocky bottom that makes swimming less than perfect. This same reef can make for good snorkeling in calm summer seas, but you must negotiate your way carefully through one of the small sandy channels into the deeper water. In winter, waves crash against the outer reef, a challenging surfing spot.

Public access is by a cement path from the left of the gatehouse hotel entry. On the way down the cliff, you'll have to descend nearly 200 steps (and then come back *up* later on). You can also explore the beach if you visit the hotel for breakfast or lunch. After dining, take the hotel elevator down to the beach level, where lovely gardens frame the sand. Bring a camera.

Directions: Drive Rt 56 north, enter Princeville at the main entrance (pick up a free map) and stay on Ka Haku Rd until the end. Park in the hotel visitor's lot if you're going to the hotel for lunch. If not, try the small public lot just in front and to the right of the hotel entry gate. Map 5

Pali Ke Kua or 'Hideaways' Beach

Hard to get to: At the base of the cliff near the Pali Ke Kua Condominiums in Princeville is a sandy beach set inside a reef, where you can watch the sun sparkle on the waves in near solitude. It is a peaceful spot popular with surfers, secluded and beautiful, actually two beaches connected by a rocky point. Swimming is not the best because of the coral bottom and the offshore rocks, but snorkeling can be very good in calm summer seas.

It's called Hideaways for good reason – access is by a trail down the cliff, (guests at Pali Ke Kua can use the condominium's improved concrete pathway). Initially it's steep steps with a railing, then it dwindles to dirt path. It can be slippery, even treacherous, when wet. The trek down takes about ten minutes, and the way up, as you can imagine, somewhat longer.

Safety info: No Lifeguard. Be cautious. On all north shore beaches, snorkeling and swimming can be risky, advisable only in a calm ocean. When the surf is up, currents can become dangerous. In winter, waves can cover the beach entirely.

Directions: Enter Princeville, drive to the hotel and park in the lot. The hotel staff usually doesn't mind if you take one of the back spaces nearest the cliff, where you'll see the top of the steps down to the beach. Map 5

Hanalei Bay

Simply spectacular: A long half moon of golden sand stretching for miles, set against gorgeous green mountains, Hanalei Bay is perfect for just about anything: swimming (primarily in summer but in winter depending on surf conditions) and surfing (ditto) and walking at any time of year. Several Trans-Pacific Cup Races from California to Hawaii end in this beautiful bay.

The boats tell the story: during summer, gaily colored boats rock gently at anchor, but they are moved out of the bay by mid-October, and by winter, 20-foot waves are not uncommon. In dangerously high surf, the beach is closed to swimming.

Hanalei can be peaceful and calm in summer, but winter waves can reach 20 feet, and boats move to safer harbors on the south shore and westside.

Looking for surfing? The biggest breakers are at 'Pinetrees,' near the center of the bay. During winter months, when the surf can become dangerous, Hanalei Bay is still wonderful – the wide sandy beach is firm and level for hard running. Walk west to where the Wai'oli Stream, icy cold from mountain water, flows into the bay. Sometimes it's shallow, at other times the current is formidable, but at all times it's beautiful and peaceful, waves crossing from different directions in foam glistening with gold.

West of the town, you can explore almost any road turning off Route 560 towards the water. At the westernmost curve of the bay, near the mile 4 marker, you'll find a calm, protected beach where the water is relatively quiet even when most of the north shore is too rough for safe swimming.

Safety Info: There are two Lifeguard Towers at Hanalei Bay, but where you go into the water can be up to 1/2 mile away from them.

After you pass Princeville, Rt 56 curves down the cliffside to the town of Hanalei (mile 3 marker). Aku Rd (or any other right turn) will take you to Weke Rd, which runs along the bay from east to west. Turn right on Weke to go to Hanalei Pavilion Park (showers, rest rooms, *Lifeguard*) or past it to Hanalei pier. Turn left onto Weke, and you can choose several 'right of way to beach' streets leading to the bay. Showers, restrooms and *Lifeguard* Tower are available at Ama'ama Rd, or 'Second Parking Lot.' Map 5

Ha'ena Area Beaches: Lumahai Beach

Beautiful but dangerous: The setting for the Bali Hai scenes in *South Pacific*, Lumahai is stunningly beautiful, a curve of white sand nestled at the base of a dark lava cliff, with a giant lava rock jutting out of the turquoise sea just offshore. Keep in mind that the trek down from the road may take you through slippery mud (showers are frequent on the north), and the trip back up can be worse, especially if you have to carry a tired child.

Safety info: No Lifeguard. Swimming can be very dangerous, particularly during winter months. Without a reef to offer protection from unpredictable currents and rip tides, Lumahai Beach is one of the most treacherous spots on Kauai, and people drown here almost every year. Beware of climbing that spectacular offshore rock for a photograph, as a sudden powerful wave can easily knock you off. No restrooms.

You can also continue to the western end of Lumahai, about a mile further along Rt 560 at the mile 5 marker. Across the street from an emergency telephone is the entrance to a sandy parking area. Here the beach is wide and golden, with breakers and currents which can be strong enough to make swimming dangerous. Children will love playing in the stream flowing into the sea, ice cold from mountain rainwater. No restrooms.

The stream meets the ocean at a huge rocky bluff, a spectacular place to sit quietly and watch the waves crash against the rocks, sending dazzling spray into the air. It is also a beautiful beach for walking although the coarse sand is hard-going near the waterline, and you must cross a vast expanse of hot sand to get from the parking area to the sea, so bring sandals. Hunt for striped scallop shells shining in the sun, or wander all the way to the other rocky bluff that separates this part of Lumahai Beach from the part pictured in all the postcards. Crossing the rocks could be hazardous even at low tide, because an occasional 'killer wave' can come up suddenly out of nowhere and smash you into the rocks. A small cave etched into the base of the cliff, with powder soft, cool sand invites wave-watching.

Pass Hanalei on Rt 560, and you will soon see, at about the mile 4 marker, cars parked on the shoulder just past a 25 mph sign. If you choose to hike down the cliff to Lumahai Beach, park on the right and lock up. Map 5

Tunnels (Makua)

Snorkeler's delight–but no parking: Popularly known as Tunnels Beach, Makua Beach has a large lagoon perfect for swimming because it is protected by two reefs, the outer reef favored by surfers for perfectly formed arcs, and the inner reef filled with cavities and crevices to explore for fish and sea life. Divers love the outer reef for its tunnels, caverns, and sudden, dramatic drop off. Tunnels is about the only beach on the north shore that is usually calm enough for those trying to snorkel for the first time although even here you may find rough surf and treacherous currents during winter.

Listen to the surf reports, and plan any winter visits for times when surf is manageable, and preferably at low tide. In calm conditions, bring the kids and let them paddle about on boogie boards while the older ones try their luck with mask and snorkel. Bring fish food, or even a green leaf, in a plastic baggy and swish it in the water and you'll be surrounded by fish (Just be sure to take the bag back out with you). Swimming through the coral formations of the reef, which is almost like a maze of tunnels, can be great fun when the water is quiet. Enter the reef through one of the small sandy channels or the large one on the right, and dozens of fish in rainbow colors will swim right up to your mask. If the showers which frequent the north shore rain on your parade, you can take shelter under the ironwood

The reefs at Makua Beach, or Tunnels, can be great for snorkeling.

trees – or under your boogie board! If you see a monk seal lying on the beach, give it a wide berth. It's probably exhausted, sleeping before heading out to sea. Seals don't trust humans and need privacy to rest.

Safety Info: The Ha'ena Beach Park Lifeguards work hard, with binoculars and a beach rover, to keep an eye on Tunnels, but be aware that they are stationed 1/2 mile away. *Warning:* Even when the area between the two reefs may look calm enough for safe swimming, watch out for these danger signs: high surf on the outer reef or fast moving ripples in the channel between the reefs. These indicate powerful, swift currents that could sweep you out through the channel into open ocean. Instead of swimming, walk around the rocks to the east and hunt for shells.

Snorkelers at Tunnels

Directions: Continue west on Rt 560, and go 1.1 miles west of the Hanalei Colony Resort. You will pass the mile 8 marker and the turnoff to the YMCA camp. Parking is nearly impossible due to safety issues and also opposition by local residents. Cars parked along Rt 560, a state road, will be ticketed. You can drive ahead to Ha'ena Beach Park, park, and walk back along the beach, or try parking along the county road leading to the YMCA campground (Parking is legal on county roads). No public facilities. Map 5

Ha'ena Beach Park

Past Tunnels is Ha'ena Beach Park, where an icy stream winds across a lovely golden sand beach curving along the coastline. The water is a dazzling blue. Reefs bordering both sides of the beach, named 'Maniniholo' after striped convict fish feeding on the coral, can provide summertime snorkeling, swimming and rafting. During winter months, however, large waves can break right onto the beach, making swimming, even standing, hazardous. Restrooms, showers, picnic and barbecue facilities; camping by permit. *Lifeguard.*

Pull into the Beach Park lot at the mile 8 marker on Rt 560. Map 5

Ke'e Beach

When you can drive no further on the main road along Kauai's north shore, you will discover a beach so beautiful you won't quite believe it to be real. Na Pali cliffs rise like dark green towers behind the golden sand, and a reef extending offshore creates a peaceful lagoon ideal for summertime swimming. As you walk along the shining sand, new cliffs come into view until the horizon is filled with their astonishing shapes. Nearby is Kaulu Paoa Heia'u, said to have among the strongest vibrations of spiritual energy in the world, second only to Egypt.

Safety info: Lifeguard in summer. Like all north shore beaches, surf varies with the seasons. Winter surf can reach 20 feet, with undercurrents far too strong for safe swimming. Even in summer, *unpredictable currents in the channel to the left of the reef can be strong enough to pull a swimmer out of this sheltered area into the open sea.* Avoid the channel.

Ke'e Beach's lagoon (at left in this photograph) is great for summer swimming, but thunders with surf in winter.

Jeffrey Courson   *Mt Namahana beyond Keʻe Beach in Na Pali*

Inside the lagoon, the turquoise water can be perfectly still and so clear that bubbles on the surface cast shadows on the sandy bottom. Summertime snorkeling can be spectacular inside the reef, where the water, though sun-warmed, will feel icy along the surface from rainshowers. If the tide is not too low, you can snorkel on top of the reef itself. Be careful. The coral reef may look shallow enough to walk on, but avoid coral cuts.

Trees provide shade for babies and protection from the occasional rainshowers which cool the air and make the coastline sparkle. The dark sand can be very hot, so you'll need sandals. Small children can play and swim safely in the shallow water. Bring nets and pails for small fishermen.

Sometimes you can walk west across the rocks and around the point. From this vantage point, the Na Pali cliffs are truly magnificent – jutting into the cobalt blue ocean in vivid green ridges, the surf crashing in thundering sprays of foam. This walk can be dangerous in any but the calmest sea; watch the direction of the tide carefully so that your return trip does not involve crossing slippery rocks through crashing waves.

For a spectacular, bird's eye view of Keʻe Lagoon, climb the first quarter-mile of the trail to Hanakapiʻai Beach. Restrooms and showers. If possible come early and come midweek.

Parking is hard to come by, particularly on weekends. We drive all the way to the end of the road, passing the large lots, and hope for good luck. Someone is usually going out. Map 5

Beach Access

By state law, all beaches on Kauai are public. Beachfront hotels and condos along the beaches (but not private homeowners) are required to provide public beach access. That does not always mean convenient access or even parking, unfortunately. While the county has provided for many public beach access points (the sign for access is a waist high silver pole with yellow band), there may not be adequate parking spaces. On the road to Ha'ena and all its lovely beaches, for example, parking is legal only on a few designated shoulders, and not at all near popular Tunnels Beach, where parking has become next to impossible. So look for the pole – and hope for the best!

Some Useful Hawaiian Words

aloha– (a LOW ha) hello, good-bye, love, kindness, friendship

hale – (HAH lee) house

haole – (HOW lee) foreigner white man

heia'u – (HEY ow) ancient Hawaiian temple

hui– (HOO' ee) club or group

kahuna– (ka HOO and) an elder, wise person

kalua– (ka LOO a) to roast underground, like kalua pig

kai – the sea

kama'aina – (ka ma EYE na) a native

kane – (KA neh) man

kapu – (KA poo) forbidden, keep out

keiki – (KAY kee) child

kona– (KOH na) leeward side of the island

lani – (LAH nee) heavens, sky

lomilomi – (low me low me) massage

mahalo – (ma HA lo) thank you

makai – (ma KAI) ocean side

mauka– (MOW ka) towards the mountains

menehune– Kauai's legendary little people & builders

nani – (NA nee) beautiful

ohana – (o HA na) family

ono – (OH no) delicious

pali – (PA lee) cliff, precipice

paniolo – (pa nee O lo) cowboy

pau– (pow) finished, done

puka – (POO ka) hole

wahine – (wa HEE neh) woman,wife

wikiwiki – hurry up

South Shore
Beach Adventures

Maha'ulepu Beach

Restaurants, 210

Rt 50 (Kaumuali'i Highway) heads west from Lihue to Kalaheo, Hanapepe, Kekaha, & Waimea. Turn off Rt 50 at Rt 520 to reach Koloa and then Poipu. The Koloa Bypass Road skirts Koloa and links directly with eastern Poipu.

Map 6
South Shore

Many Na Pali Boat Tours depart from Port Allen, 86

Salt Pond Beach Park, a family favorite, 75

scuba, 130

Beaches

Hotels

The wild beauty of Maha'ulepu.

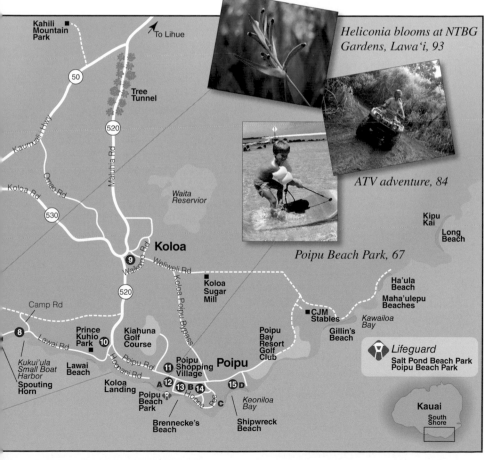

Heliconia blooms at NTBG Gardens, Lawa'i, 93

ATV adventure, 84

Poipu Beach Park, 67

Great Days on the South Shore

Day 1. Breakfast *Tomkats,* Koloa (p 227). Take a boat cruise (p 87) along the south shore to Kipu Kai (winter) or Na Pali Coast (summer). Or head to *Maha'ulepu Beach* for great walking (p 70). Sunset dinner at *Beach House* (p 210). Or watch the sky glow at sunset from Poipu Beach Park and dine at *Brennecke's* (p 212), or try creative fresh fish entrees at newcomer *Red Salt* (p 224). Stroll through the beautiful *Grand Hyatt Resort* after dinner (free valet parking).

Day 2. Breakfast *Joe's on the Green* (p 217). Tour *National Tropical Botanical Gardens* (p 93), or take a zipline tour to *Kipu Falls* (p 147), or trail ride (p 119). Take out lunch from *Koloa Fish Market* (p 221), then snorkel at *Poipu Beach Park.* Before dinner, enjoy Hawaiian music at Hyatt's *Seaview Lounge* (free p 97). Dinner at *Josselin's* (p 218) or *Plantation Gardens* (p 222). Stroll through the *Kiahuna* and *Sheraton* grounds after dinner.

South Shore Snapshot

The south shore extends along the sea from Kipu Kai (nearly inaccessible except by boat) and Maha'ulepu Beach to the Poipu Beaches, and west towards Salt Pond Beach Park, including the inland towns of Koloa and Kalaheo. Rt 50 takes you west from Lihue to the turnoff at Rt 520 (Maluhia Rd) just before the Mile 11 marker; follow it through the 'Tunnel of Trees' to Koloa, then to the new circle taking you either to Poipu Beach (left) or to Lawa'i (right) home of National Tropical Botanical Gardens and the popular blow hole called Spouting Horn. You can also avoid Koloa and take the bypass road that goes directly to eastern Poipu; the left turn is well marked on Rt 520 after you come through the pass.

South Shore It List

When it's raining up north, you may want to travel south (even west) to find the sun. Usually in the island's lee, south shore beaches offer relatively calm swimming conditions all year, except during a south shore 'swell.'

• *Poipu Beach Park* is perfect for families, the rock rimmed pool a safe place for small children. Lifeguard. Snorkeling at the other end of the curving beach is wonderful for older ones and their parents (p 66).

• Learn to surf with lessons (p 98) in front of Kiahuna.

- *Brennecke's Beach* is (nearly) back to pre-Iniki waves, the long rollers legendary for bodyboards and body surfing (p 68).
- Our favorite hidden beach (though increasingly popular) is *Maha'ulepu Beach* east of Poipu. Wild and beautiful (p 70).

Zipline tours, kayak tours, scuba & snorkeling, and garden tours at the Natural Botanical Gardens make fun for all ages.

Poipu Beach Park

Family perfect: You could not imagine a better beach for children than this lovely curve of soft golden sand sloping down to a gentle, friendly sea. The waves, with changing shades of turquoise sparkling with sunlight and dazzling white foam, break gently over a protective reef across the entrance to this small cove.

For babies and toddlers, a ring of black lava rocks creates a sheltered pool where the water is shallow and still. For older children, waves beyond the pool roll to shore in graceful swells perfect for rafts or body boards. Children can explore the long rocky point at the far end of the beach. Bring nets and pails for tiny fish in the tidepools. The park has a lifeguard, restrooms, outdoor showers, barbecues, picnic tables, and shaded pavilions. Sometimes you may see a monk seal taking a sunbath on the sand. Give it a wide berth: it's resting, gathering strength to face another day in paradise.

Poipu Beach, Waiohai

Just around the rocky point, in front of the old Waiohai Hotel (now a Marriott time-share resort), you can enjoy some of the best snorkeling on the island. Hundreds of fish in rainbow colors feed on the coral, so tame they almost swim into your hands. Wave a green leaf around in the water as you swim, and they'll swim right to you.

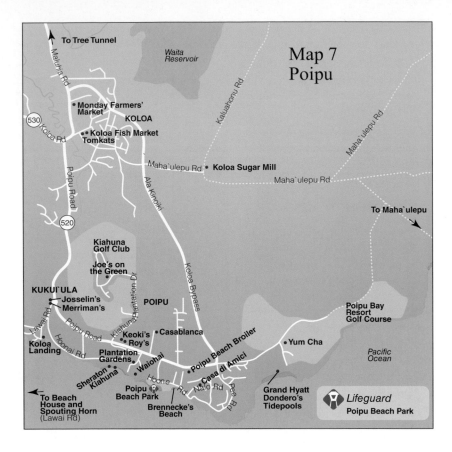

Safety info: Stay inside the reef to avoid being caught in a strong current and carried out. Unwary snorkelers have drowned here. See *Ocean Safety* (p 80). *No Lifeguard.*

Directions: In Poipu, take Hoʻowilili Rd to Hoʻone Rd. Park in the lot. To park near the Kiahuna and Sheraton, turn off Hoʻowilili Rd at the Sheraton's sign, then turn left at Hoonani Rd and continue to the end. Enter the last driveways on the left and on the right for public parking. Maps 6,7

Brennecke's Beach

Famous for body surfing: Adjacent to Poipu Beach Park, Brennecke's Beach was once the best beach for body surfing in Hawaii. Now, it is finally recovering from Hurricane Iniki, which smashed giant boulders into the seawall and washed away most of the sand. Today, as the sand is coming back, the waves are gradually returning to their old pattern, breaking far out for the big kids, and then again closer to shore for younger ones to catch a swift and exciting ride. After Hurricane Iwa caused a similar level of destruction in 1982, the return of the sandy bottom took ten years, and it's taken just about as long after Iniki. Wave riders must still be wary of rocks, and watch out for waves that head towards the sea wall.

Safety Info: *No Lifeguard.*

Directions: Adjacent to Poipu Beach Park, on the eastern side. Maps 6, 7

Shipwreck Beach

Shipwreck Beach along Keoniloa Bay is called 'Shipwreck' with good reason: the surf is powerful, breaking in long, shining arcs which crest slowly, one at a time, with deceptive smoothness, and then crash in thunderous explosions of spray not far from shore.

Safety info: *No Lifeguard.* Local people warn that beyond the break point are dangerous currents and large rocks. A better place for family swimming would be Poipu Beach Park, and novice surfers would be better off at Kealia Beach, where rocks and wind are not a problem, or in surf

Shipwreck Beach – walk along the rocky bluff and explore fascinating rock formations.

lessons in front of Kiahuna (p 138). Be particularly careful during summer months, when a south shore swell can bring big surf.

Instead of swimming, you can climb the cliff to explore strange caves and rock formations. The colors are breathtaking – the deep blue of the water and the gold of the cliffs dazzle the eye, and the view down is a dizzying spectacle of surf crashing against the rocks. Be careful, though. Avoid going close to the cliff's edge, as the footing is slippery with loose sand. It's great for photographers but not for children.

Directions: Take Poipu Rd past the main entrance to the Hyatt Hotel. Turn toward the water on Ainako Rd. Park in the lot. Public access restrooms and showers are by the parking lot. Maps 6, 7

Maha'ulepu

Wonderful walking: At the end of a dusty drive through winding sugar cane roads, you will find a beautiful sandy beach carved into a rocky point. This part of the south shore can be very dry and very hot – and you may soon find a thin red film on every surface inside your car, including you. But it's worth the dust to reach a beach astonishing in its wild beauty, the surf crashing against the rocks and sand, the churning turquoise water almost glowing with sunlight. Beautiful it is, but very often not safe enough for swimming. Unless surf on the whole south shore is flat, you may find the

Solitude at Maha'ulepu

waves crashing with enough force to knock you down, and currents powerful enough to make local people wary.

Maha'ulepu is a lovely beach for exploring. On the eastern end, a lovely half-moon of golden sand nestles at the base of a rocky cliff. A long walk to the west takes you past a rocky reef which at low tide juts out of the sand in fascinating formations. As you reach the end of the curve, the tip turns out to be a point, and on the other side, you'll find another, even longer stretch of beach. Here the water ripples in toward shore, protected by an offshore reef where the waves roll in long, even swells. You might see a fisherman casting his line or colorful windsurfers. At the western most end, sun-warmed tidal pools are shallow and still; kids can catch tiny fish in nets.

At the far eastern end of Maha'ulepu is a rocky bluff. After a moderate uphill climb, you will come to a promontory with spectacular views of the coastline. Rock formations are amazing, and a tiny beach set into the cliffside shelters interesting pools of tiny sea life.

Safety Info: No Lifeguard.

Directions: Take Rt 50 to Rt 520 (Maluhia Rd), and follow signs to Poipu. Take Poipu Rd past the Hyatt Regency, continue on to the unpaved road, and pass the golf course and the quarry. When you come to a stop sign, turn right and head toward the water. This is sugar company land; at road's end, park or turn left to another lot. Maps 6, 7

Kipu Kai

Unspoiled beauty: The best way to get to Kipu Kai is by boat, for the rugged private road crossing the gap in the mountains between Rt 50 and the south shore is suitable only for sturdy 4-wheel-drive vehicles. Some boat tour companies offer day trips to this lovely section of Kauai's coastline (p 86). On a rocky peninsula shaped like an alligator, Long Beach stretches out in the shape of a half moon, nearly enclosed by outcroppings of rocks at each end. Set at the base of the rocky mountains behind Kipu Kai, Long Beach combines the favorable weather of the south with a rugged beauty more characteristic of the north shore. As if this weren't enough, the ocean is relatively gentle due to the rocky points which embrace the beach, breaking the surf and creating a protected lagoon.

A wonderful old rambling ranch house sits atop Turtle Beach, built in the last century by the Waterhouse family and destined to be a state park at end of the next generation.

Map 8
Westside

Miloli'i State Park

Nu'alolo Kai State Park

Kalalau Lookout ■

■ Pu'u o Kila Lookout

■ Koke'e Lodge & Museum

550

■ Pu'u Hinahina Lookout

Koke'e State Park

Waimea Canyon (1 mile wide and 3657 feet deep)

■ Waimea Canyon Lookout

Polihale State Park

Pokale Rd

Nohili Point

■ Barking Sands

Kao Rd

Mana

Old Mana Rd

Waimea River

Mana Point

Military Airfield

50

Pacific Range Missile Center

550

Koke'e Rd

Waimea Canyon Rd

Kokole Point

Kekaha Beach Park

Kekaha

Waimea

Kikiaola Small Boat Harbor

6 A

5

Lucy Wright Beach Park

Russian Fort Elizabeth ■

50

Pakala Beach ("Infinities")

Kaumuali'i Hwy

Olokele Rd

Hanapepe

Eleele

4 3 2

Lolokai

Lele

1

Port Allen

Salt Pond Beach Park

Port Allen Airport

Hanapepe Bay

Drive Waimea Canyon, 142 and hike at Koke'e, 117

Na Pali Boat Tours depart from Port Allen, 87

Kauai

Westside

N

0   1   2
Miles

Westside Beach Adventures

Salt Pond Beach Park – great for families, and often a sunny spot when other parts of the island are cloudy.

Restaurants & Hotels

Beaches

Salt Pond Beach tidepool — perfect for kids!

Westside Snapshot

Kauai's Westside is still small town rural, and the weather is often sunnier than the windward shores. Port Allen is headquarters of many boat tours companies and also *Kauai Chocolate Co.* In HANAPEPE, Kauai's 'biggest little town,' check out the swinging bridge, visit art galleries (like *Arius Hopman Photography* and *Banana Patch Studio*) and sample *Taro Ka chips* at the factory. *Hanapepe Café* is great for lunch or a mid-afternoon coffee. Stop at *Kauai Kookie Factory* on Rt 56 for flavors like lavender shortbread; it's set back from road. Visit beautiful *Salt Pond Beach Park*.

Next is WAIMEA, with a black sand beach perhaps less appealing than the beautiful long white sand beach a few miles farther at Kekaha. For lunch and free wireless, stop at *Waimea Plantation Cottages*, or choose *Wrangler's*, or try poke at *Ishihara's Market*. Waimea is the gateway to *Waimea Canyon* and beautiful *Koke'e State Park* and its wonderful hiking. Beyond is Kekaha and then Polihale at the end of the road on the westside.

Westside it list

- *Salt Pond Beach Park* offers great swimming, protected by a reef, as well as usually sunny weather. Kids love the tidal pools (p 75).
- At *Kekaha*, you'll find firm sand and miles of beach perfect for beachwalking and running, as well as surf for body boards (p 77).
- Drive all the way to the end of the road to magnificent *Polihale Beach*, the western most part of the island (p 78).
- Hike in *Koke'e,* for a taste of the island's wild beauty (p 117).

- On trips west, stop for a tasty lunch at *Wrangler's* in Waimea (sandwiches and salads, p 231), or in Hanapepe, *Hanapepe Café* (vegetarian delights, p 229) or *Grinds* in Ele'ele (sandwiches on fresh baked bread).

- Stop for pie and treats at *Auntie Lilikoi*, or step back in time in *Ishihara's Market*. Try shave ice at *JoJo's Anueanue Shave Ice* (on side street next to Bucky's Liquor 808.338.9964) where there are 60 flavors!

Great Days on the Westside

Day 1: Drive to *Kekaha* or *Polihale Beach*. Stop in Waimea at *Yumi's* for a hot apple turnover; pack a picnic lunch with poke from *Ishihara's Market*. Or take *Waimea Canyon* Rd to *Koke'e* (p 142), and explore the forest preserve (p 117). Try *JoJo's* shave (original) in Waimea (p 120). Dinner at *Wrangler's* (p 231).

Day 2: Tour the *Na Pali Coast* by boat (p 87), or visit quaint *Hanapepe*, test its swinging bridge, browse art galleries and have lunch at *Hanapepe Café* (p 229) or a sandwich at *Grinds* (Ele'ele). Afternoon: *Salt Pond Beach* (p 75) or *Kekaha* (p 77) and shave ice afterwards at *JoJo's* original shop. Dinner at *Waimea Brew Co* or at *Kalaheo Steak & Ribs* only a short drive away in Kalaheo.

Hanapepe area beaches: Salt Pond Beach Park

Family friendly: The beach at Salt Pond is a semicircle where sand slopes downward like a golden bowl to hold the sea. A reef near the mouth of this sheltered cove breaks the surf into slow, rolling swells that break again gently near the shore so that children can raft and swim inside this natural lagoon most of the year. At both ends of the beach, tidepools can be calm enough at low tide for babies and toddlers, and great fun for older kids when the incoming tide splashes over the rocks to make waterfalls.

Walk along the beach and explore tidal pools and the ancient salt ponds where local people still harvest sea salt. The park is spectacular, especially when brightly colored windsurfers race out across the reef, and particularly favored in terms of weather. Even when clouds and rain prevail elsewhere,

Miles of golden sand at Kekaha

this little point of land seems to escape them, and in winter, the water seems a few degrees warmer and more friendly. Showers, rest rooms, picnic tables, barbecues make Salt Pond popular on weekends with local families, although the beach never seems crowded.

Safety info: Lifeguard. Be careful in periods of high surf as unpredictable currents can create hazardous swimming, and stay inside the lagoon, where the Lifeguard can see. For lunch, stop at the *Hanapepe Café*, or take out a picnic lunch from *Grinds* in Ele'ele, just a few miles east of Hanapepe on Rt 50, or stop in Kalaheo at *Kalaheo Deli*.

West of Hanapepe on Rt 50 at the mile 21 marker, turn left at Lele St; take the first right onto Lokokai Rd; drive until you see parking. Map 8

Pakala's Beach or 'Infinities'

For experienced surfers and even newbie sun seekers: Just west of Hanapepe on Rt 50, past the mile 21 marker, you will see cars parked along the road next to a low concrete bridge. They belong to surfers, who head for Pakala's by way of an overgrown path. Wear shoes or sturdy sandals, and avoid the thorny kiawe which grows near the beach. You can hear the crash of the waves before the path takes you through the trees to the curving beach. The sand and sea are deep gold because of red volcanic soil flowing through the A'akukui stream.

The bay is divided by a rocky point where local fishermen try for pompano. If you cross the stream and climb the rocky ledge, you come to a sandy beach dotted with shells, sea glass, and coral. Beyond the reef is a surfing spot famous for long, perfectly formed waves that surfers can ride on to 'infinity' (see Surfing, 137). Paddling out over the shallow reef takes a long time, but the ride can be special. Be careful at low tide, when shallow water over the reef can expose an unwary surfer to spiny sea urchins.

To the right of the rocky point, the beach stretches a long way before disappearing around a bend. The firm golden sand is perfect for walking, This western spot is good to try when other parts of the island are in rain.

Safety info: No Lifeguard.

Just west of Hanapepe on Rt 50, watch for the mile 21 marker and then the low concrete bridge. No facilities, but about 1 mile further on Rt 50 you'll find public restrooms and showers at the Russian Fort, just across the Waimea River. Bring sandwiches from Grinds in Ele'ele. Map 8

Kekaha area beaches: Kekaha Beaches

Gorgeous and usually sunny: Stretching for miles along Kauai's western coast, the Kekaha beaches combine swimming, surfing, and walking with the predominantly dry weather of the island's leeward side. As Rt 50 curves toward the sea at the small town of Kekaha, the beach is narrow, but a mile or two north, it widens and becomes more golden, with long, rolling waves breaking evenly in brilliant white crests.

At times, the waves can break perfectly for surfing and body boarding, although, as everywhere on Kauai, surf and currents can be dangerous and unpredictable, and you may find high surf and rip currents. Watch where local people are swimming and follow their lead – especially if they are not going into the water!

Safety info: Lifeguard, restrooms are located by the most popular swimming section.

Even if swimming is not advisable, the sand is firm and flat, one of the finest beaches on Kauai – or anywhere – for walking, running, or playing frisbee or football. We recommend driving the full length of this stretch of beach so that you can select the most favorable spot and then double back to park. Despite its clear, sunny weather, the western side of the island has not yet been developed as a tourist area, and so these beaches are frequented primarily by local residents and are not very crowded. You can walk for miles along the sand, with beautiful views of Ni'ihau, purple on the horizon.

Directions: Drive northwest of Waimea on Rt 50 until the road curves towards the water near the mile 25 marker. Map 8

Barking Sands

The beach from Kekaha to Polihale extends about 15 miles. Post September 11, security requires an application for an annual pass. The completed application must be submitted in person with a photo ID. Processing then takes approximately 2 weeks. Contact *thomas.h.clements@ navy.mil* for info, or call 808.335.7936.

Safety info: No Lifeguard. Like Polihale Beach, surf and currents can be extremely strong; a sudden drop-off make swimming hazardous.

Directions: Main entry gate is northwest of Kekaha on Rt 50. Map 8

Polihale Beach Park

Beautiful but not for swimming: From the time you leave paved road behind to jolt north through a maze of sugar cane fields, you know you're in for something special. Gradually, beyond the tall sugar cane rustling in the breeze, a dark ridge of jagged peaks appears on the right. These giant cliffs reveal splendid colors – trees and bush in vivid greens against the black rock slashed with the deep red of the volcanic soil.

When you can drive no further, the beach at Polihale emerges from the base of the cliffs – an enormous stretch of brilliant white sand more immense, it seems, than the cliffs which tower above and the band of deep blue sea beyond. Only the sky seems the equal of this vast expanse of glaring sand, so wide that walking from your car to the ocean on a sunny day will burn your feet. 'Beautiful' is too small a word for this awesome place. Polihale – home of spirits – is more appropriate, not only because the majestic cliffs and beach dwarf anything human to insignificance, but also because here man's access to the western coast really ends. Beyond lies the Na Pali wilderness, unreachable except by boat or helicopter, or by the handful of hikers who dare to climb the narrow and dangerous trails. Polihale is the threshold between the known and the unknown, the tamed and the untamed, the familiar and the wild.

Swimming is treacherous; the rolling, pounding surf even at its most gentle is only for strong, experienced swimmers. No reefs offer protection from the powerful ocean currents.

Come instead for the spectacle, to picnic and walk, to gaze at the grandeur of cliffs above the endless sea and sand, to listen to the silence broken only by the crashing surf, to appreciate in solitude the splendor of nature's power. A feeling of awe lingers even after you return to paved road and a world of smaller proportions.

After a severe storm in December, 2008, the community helped repair the road and park facilities, despite steep cuts in the park budget.

Safety info: *No Lifeguard.* Nearest Lifeguard or First Responder Fire Station is several miles away.

You'll find the turn onto the 5-mile dirt cane road to Polihale, marked by a state park sign, just before Rt 50 ends. Restrooms, showers, roofed picnic tables, barbecues. Camping by permit only. Be careful with your rental car on the cane roads. If you get mired in mud, or stuck in sandy dunes, the rental car companies won't cover the damage. Map 8

Beware the Hawaiian Sun

Hawaii lies close to the equator and the sun is exceedingly strong, so choose a strong lotion protecting against both UVA and UVB rays. Even *waterproof* lotions wash off in salt water and should be reapplied freuently, as we do every two hours. To be most effective, most lotions need a few minutes to dry and adhere to skin before swimming.

Children need special care. For spots they rub often, like right under the eyes, you can try sticky gels like Bullfrog or a sunscreen in chapstick form. We make a rule that kids get 'greased up' in the room or parking lot before heading out as they hate to stand still once the sand is in sight. Hats and tee-shirts are the most reliable sun-protection for after-swimming sandcastle projects. We plan family beach visits for the early morning or late afternoon, and meals, naps, or drives during the noonday sun (11:30-2:30). Sunburns are often not visible until it is too late, but you can check a child's skin by pressing it with your finger. If it blanches dramatically, get the child a shirt or consider calling it a day.

Keep a spare lotion in the car, for if you don't have lotion on, beaches can be hazardous to your health. Babies need a complete sunblock, a hat to protect the scalp, and protection for feet. To give babies shade, an umbrella (KMart, Wal-Mart, Longs) would be a wise purchase for the beach.

Ocean Safety

People have drowned on every beach on Kauai. Plan your beach trips according to surf conditions, which vary by day and season. For the daily surf report, call 808.245.6001 or visit *www.kauaiexplorer.com*.

Surf varies with seasons. From mid-October to mid-April, surf and currents are unpredictable and dangerous on windward beaches (north and northeast), and some north shore beaches nearly disappear under crashing waves. In summer months, the 'swell' can come in on the south and west, while Hanalei on the north may be calm enough for small boats.

Beaches with lifeguards are safest: Lydgate Park, Kealia, Anahola (eastside); Poipu Beach Park (south shore) Salt Pond Beach Park and Kekaha (westside); Hanalei, Ha'ena Beach Park and Ke'e (north shore).

Don't swim alone at an unguarded beach; swim with a buddy.

Never turn your back on the ocean; keep your eye on the waves.

Don't fight a strong current; go with until it weakens, then wave your arms for help, or swim back in where there is no current.

Observe the water carefully before swimming. Waves come in sets, and so what may look like calm water may be only a calm period between sets, which can be separated by up to a half hour. Fast moving water running laterally indicates a strong current you will want to avoid.

Watch out for occasional oversize waves or wave sets. Don't try to ride it (or worse, run from it); dive through it or drop down under it.

Be particularly careful when snorkeling when you can easily get

distracted by the fish and lose your sense of direction. Stay close enough to shore so you can swim in. The safest snorkeling is in the rock-enclosed pool at Lydgate Park (eastside). Waiohai (Poipu) can have dangerous currents.

Beware of walking or even standing close to the edge of cliffs or rocks. Waves vary in size, and a huge one may come up suddenly and wash your camera away – and maybe you along with it – particularly on north shore and westside beaches without reefs to protect against strong ocean currents.

Avoid swimming in murky water where sharks like to feed: water churned up with sand after rain or near where a stream flows into the sea.

Queen's Bath is *exceptionally hazardous*; numerous unsuspecting tourists have drowned there when sudden huge waves crashed over the rocky perimeter.

Kipu Falls has dangerous hidden boulders; licensed tours are the safest way to visit.

Be careful when surfing. Watch local surfers who know where to avoid strong currents, rocks, and dangerous wave breaks. Watch the interval between wave sets (as much as 30 min). Best beaches for learning are Kealia (Lifeguard), Poipu, and Hanalei in summer (Lifeguard and surf school).

Locate the red Rescue Tube at unguarded beaches. But read the instructions (also mounted on the post) carefully before trying to use a rescue tube to save someone, and if you yourself are not a strong swimmer, find someone who is. Use fins if possible.

Avoid Portuguese 'men o' war,' small blue jellyfish with trailing stinging tentacles. Don't step on

RESCUE TUBE

WARNING: Do NOT use this device if you are unsure or unable to respond to a drowning emergency (solid swimming skills required). Call 911 and keep an eye on the victim from the beach. **HOW TO USE:** Wear fins if possible. Wear the shoulder strap across your chest. Drag tube behind you until you are near the victim. Extend the tube to them. Rest and wait for help or kick to shore.

RIP CURRENTS: KEEP CALM. Go with the flow. It will release you just offshore. Rest, and swim perpendicular to shore and back to the beach. People who continue to fight against rip currents usually drown. **Conserve your energy.**

CPR NEEDED? Call 911. If the victim is unresponsive, open the airway and check for breathing. If not breathing, give 2 breaths and begin CPR with 30 chest compressions followed by 2 breaths. Continue until help arrives. Roll victim on side if they vomit. Recheck them.

This rescue tube has been placed here for public use. Please use it to help save lives when there is no lifeguard present. Please do not remove the tube–people have drowned shortly after a previous tube went missing.
If missing please call 822-3695 • Free rescue tube training call 635-7052 • beach and safety info at Kauaiexplorer.com
With Aloha and Love, Kauai Rotary Clubs, Kauai Lifeguard Association and The S.W. Wilcox Trust

Drownings 2008-2009

North Shore

Queens Bath, 2008 (2)
Ha'ena: 2008, 2009
Kalihiwai, 2008
Kilauea: 2008, 2009
Anini: 2009
Hanalei: 2008
Secret Beach: 2009 (2)
Larsen's: 2009

South Shore

Lawa'i Beach : Jan, July, Aug
Poipu (Waiohai): 2008 (2), 2009 (2)
Maha'ulepu: 2008

East Shore

Wailua: 2009
Kalapaki: 2008
Anahola: 2009
Opaeka Falls: 2009
Kipu Falls: 2008, 2009

them or pick them up. If stung, scrape the tentacle off with sand (try not to use fingers), rinse with warm water, or better vinegar or meat tenderizer. The best medicine is prevention: if they're on the sand, they're in the water too. Head to another beach!

The bacterium causing leptospirosis has been found in Kauai's rivers and streams, so avoid freshwater swimming with open cuts or sores. Infection can causes dangerous, flu-like symptoms. Seek medical attention if you develop flu-like symptoms after a possible exposure.

Pack wisely for the beach: antibiotic ointment and bandaids for coral cuts, meat tenderizer (or cortaid) in case you meet a man o' war.

Lock valuables in the trunk; keep a spare sun tan lotion there too, and avoid walking alone at night in unlit, deserted areas – including beaches.

"Although we advise against swimming at unguarded beaches, we realize our visitors enjoy exploring. Before swimming at a beach with no lifeguard, take some time to discuss conditions with a local person who knows where strong, unseen currents can pull you out. If this happens to you, avoid exhaustion and go with the current until it weakens, then signal for help or swim back in where there is no current. Local people also know when water is too rough, even for tumbling around. Eleven families lost someone to drowning on Kauai in 2009, almost all because they underestimated conditions and overestimated their ability."

"If in doubt, don't go out." Monty Downs, MD, Head of Kauai Water Safety Task Force

Monk Seals

You may see a monk seal lying on almost any Kauai beach. Give it a wide berth – it's probably exhausted, resting before heading back out to sea. State law requires you to keep a 'safe distance' of 50 feet. Any closer, and you run the risk of provoking a nasty bite, or perhaps frightening the animal into the water prematurely. The Hawaiian Monk Seal is an endangered species.

Adventures & Discoveries

ATV

An exciting way to tour Kauai's wilderness areas is by ATV. *Kipu Adventures* leads tours through Kipu Ranch, a 3,000 acre cattle ranch between Lihue and Poipu. On wide wheel-base Honda 350s, you maneuver up and down grades, bounce into streams, cross valleys and forest areas, go through pastures with cattle and climb the rocky road to the Ha'upu mountain pass – a spectacular lookout to gorgeous Kipu Kai beach. You may see Nene geese, wild pigs, pheasant, turkeys, amazing trees, as well as locations for *Raiders of the Lost Ark, Jurassic Park, Pirates of the Caribbean 4*, and others. You must be 16 to drive; 2 seater ATVs and a 4-passenger 'Rhino'– are available. Long pants required, and anything you wear will soon become an original red dirt shirt! ($125/3 hrs; $150/4 hrs; passengers about $25 less than drivers) 808.246.9288 *www.kiputours.com*.

Kauai ATV's motto is 'do something dirty' – and for good reason. On tours over cane roads and through cane fields on Kauai's south side, you'll splash through plenty of mud, climb over rocks, cruise through cane fields, and wade into a waterfall (on foot) for a photo. The company provides head lights to go through an old cane tunnel (great fun!). Choose a 4-hour 'waterfall tour' with picnic ($155); a 3-hour 'Koloa tour' ($125); or the 'mudbug tour' on a 2-seater mud cruising machine, which includes kayaking at the Waita Reservoir, the largest inland body of water in the state ($175). Rent mud gear (recommended), but be prepared to get filthy. Two-seaters are available, as well as a specially designed 4-seater for families. Tours include an image CD. Visit the outdoor gear store, unique on Kauai: 808.742.2734; 877.707.7088 *www.kauaiatv.com*.

On the westside, *Gay & Robinson* (2nd largest landholder on Kauai) offers a 4.5-hour tour of scenic areas of the Robinson family's private 18,000 acre Makaweli Ranch and uplands, with views from Polihale to Poipu: $145 for the 'mountain pool adventure' which includes a 'paniolo barbecue,' or $100 for a tour with snack (M-Sat). 808.335.2824.

Artists, Artisans, & Art Tours

For information about artists and artisans on Kauai and where to buy their work, visit *www.kauaimade.net*. At *Kauai Museum's* shop you'll find quilts, native wood boxes, Ni'ihau shell leis, jewelry: 808.245.6931. For pottery, visit *Kilohana Clayworks* in Lihue: 808.246.2529 *www.clayworksatkilohana.com*. In Kapa'a, don't miss *Kela's Glass Gallery* for beautiful colors and shapes: 808.822.4527; 888.255.3527 *www.glass-art.com*.

In Hanapepe's art colony visit *Banana Patch Studio* for pottery and beautifully illustrated books: 808.335.5944 *www.bananapatchstudio.com* and *Kama'aina Koa Wood Gallery:* 808.335.5483. For lovely watercolors, fine art prints, try *Arius Hopman:* 808.335.0227 *www.hopmanart.com*. The *'Art Walk'* is on Friday nites, when you can find pie by *'The Right Slice.'*

In Waimea, *Wrangler's Steakhouse* shop features local crafts, and nearby *Waimea Cottages* has a small museum shop where you can see Gramsy's patchwork art. Stay for lunch and share free wireless.

Craft fairs offer bargains in hand crafts (some local, some imported). SOUTH SHORE: In Poipu, daily at Spouting Horn. WESTSIDE: Waimea, on Rt 50 (Wed - Sun). EASTSIDE: daily opposite Otsuka's in Kapa'a.

For info about Kauai's artists, exhibitions, and open studios: *Kauai Society of Artists,* PO Box 3344, Lihue HI 96766 *www.kauaisocietyofartists. org*. For the schedule for music, art shows, dance, and poetry, contact *Garden Island Arts Council:* 808.245.2733 *www.gardenislandarts.org*.

Artists who love to paint can try a 'Paint for the Day Tour.' Paints, brushes, canvas, easels, transportation are provided. You work on location at one of Kauai's beautiful beaches: 808.823.1263 *www.hawaiianphotos.net*.

Bakery treats

Sweet Marie's across from Safeway in Wailua bakes gluten-free treats like delicious chocolate coconut macaroons, tropical fruit muffins, cookies and cakes at 4-788 Kuhio Hwy (W-Sun 7am – 2pm) 808.823.0227 *www. sweetmarieskauai.com*. Nearby, in Kinipopo Center, Andrea Quinn at *Icing on the Cake* bakes cookies, delicious bran muffins (sweetened with raisin purée), scones, and serves interesting teas and Blue Bottle coffee at 4-356 Kuhio Hwy (opens 8am; closed Mondays) *www.icingonthecakekauai.com* 808.823.1210. In Kapa'a, *Country Moon Rising* (across from Olympic Café) has Hawaiian sweet pineapple bread, taro bread, excellent mango turnovers, macadamia nut biscotti (go early) at 1345 Kuhio Hwy (3am - 8pm S-Th; 8am - 5pm F-S) 808.822.2533. At farmer's markets, look for Sandy's homemade pies with local fruits (our favorite is chocolate coconut macadamia nut): www.therightslice.com.

In Waimea, visit *Yumi's* bakery at 9691 Kaumualii Hwy for a coconut or apple turnover still hot from the oven. Stop at *Aunty Lilikoi's,* 9875 Waimea

Road, for one of the best lilikoi pies on Kauai, rich and custardy (only $12). Frozen, it will stay fresh in the car all the way home: 808.866.LILIKOI. *www.auntylilikoi.com*. The classic, more chiffon version of lilikoi pie is found at *Omoide Bakery,* 13543 Kaumualii Hwy, Hanapepe 808.335.5066. *Hamura's Saimin* is a local favorite (we pick up a frozen pie on the way to the airport and carry it home in a cooler): 2956 Kress St, Lihue 808.245.3271.

Beachwalking & Running

Our favorite running beaches, with firm sand and just the right slope, are Hanalei Bay and Kalihiwai on the north shore, Kalapaki on the east, and Kekaha to the west. For long meandering walks, we like Moloa'a and Larsen's Beach in the north, Maha'ulepu on the south, and on the eastern shore, Anahola Beach or Lydgate Park along the Wailua Golf Course, beautiful at sunrise or sunset. The Kapa'a – Kealia bike/walk trail follows the coastline. Park at Kealia Beach and walk north to Donkey Beach. Remember the sun. Fluids, sunscreen, even a hat are a must.

For info on the annual Kauai Marathon, contact PO Box 573 Koloa, HI 96756 *www.thekauaimarathon.com*.

Bikes & Motorcycles

Kauai's roads do not have bike lanes, but they do have a lot of auto traffic, and so guided bike tours are a prudent choice. On a comfortable cruising bike (wide saddle, hi-rise handlebars), you can try a 'downhill adventure' over 12 miles of winding smooth blacktop from Waimea Canyon, at an elevation of 3,500 feet, to the coast. *Outfitters Kauai* leaves daily at dawn in beautiful early morning light or in late afternoon for sunset. Tours from $94 include helmet: 808.742.9667; 888.742.9887 *www.outfitterskauai.com*. *Outfitters* also rents bikes.

Bike Rentals: EASTSIDE: Try the beautiful, mostly level walking and biking path, *Ala Hele Makalea* ('the Path that Goes by the Coast') from Kapa'a north past Kealia Beach, or bike south of Lydgate Park along the ocean. For bike path info, try *www.kauaipath.org*. Rentals: Kapa'a *Kauai Cycle & Tour:* 808.821.2115 *www.bikehawaii.com/kauaicycle*. Also *Coconut Coasters:* 808.822.7368 *www.coconutcoasters.com*.

NORTH SHORE: tour Hanalei and Ha'ena with *Pedal & Paddle:* 808.826.9069 *www.pedalnpaddle.com*. SOUTH SHORE: *Outfitters Kauai:* 808.742.9667 *www.outfitterskauai.com*. Repairs? *Bicycle John:* 808.245.7579 *www.bicyclejohn.com*. Rent a Harley? *Kauai Harley:*

808.241.7020; 877-A-1-CYCLE *www.kauaiharley-davidson.com*. Or try *Kauai Motorcycle* at *www.kauaimotorcycle.com*.

Boat Tours

The spectacular cliffs of the Na Pali coast are off limits to most visitors – unless they dare to hike the wilderness on narrow and slippery trails. Coastal boat tours provide a way to see these amazing cliffs up close, and enjoy a sometimes rough and ready adventure at the same time. Explore sea caves, watch sparkling waterfalls and pods of spinner dolphins, and marvel at how tenaciously plants can cling to inhospitable rock. You'll see an enormous change in landscape, from the dark, rich green of Ke'e Beach, where rainfall measures nearly 125 inches a year, to the reds and browns of Polihale on the west side, where it's only 20 inches. During winter months (November till March), if seas off Na Pali are too rough and currents too

strong, tours may cruise Kauai's south shore to Kipu Kai, where humpback whales frequent Hawaii's warm waters from December to April.

In choosing a tour company, consider the size of the boat: only smaller boats can enter Na Pali's sea caves and snorkel at protected Nuʻalolo Kai, while larger boats can offer a smoother ride. Also consider onboard amenities (restrooms, shade, and food/beverage selection); length of the tour (how much you see and whether there is a snorkel break); activities offered (snorkeling, scuba, lunch, pu pus, cocktails), and the season (rougher winter seas mean you can't get as close to the cliffs). Snorkeling on any of these trips depends on weather and surf, but most companies try to get you get in the water even if there is nothing much to see.

Small power catamarans: In calm seas, these boats (fewer than 18 passengers) combine a comfortable ride with the agility to go into the sea caves along Na Pali; these companies may close down in winter's rough seas. Twice daily from Waimea, *Makana Tours* takes 12 passengers on a 32-ft power catamaran with bathroom. Captain Mike De Silva, a Kauai native, makes sure everyone gets a bird's eye view of the amazing scenery. You may frolic with a pod of dolphins, even play in a waterfall, and see amazing fish while snorkeling at protected Nuʻalolo Kai. Flotation devices for snorkelers, excellent equipment, a buffet lunch with fresh-baked bread for sandwiches, even a warm fresh water rinse after snorkeling make a difference. Mike's knowledgeable crew describes history, natural history, and local lore ($139/adult) 808.335.6137; 888.808.335.6137 *www.makanacharters.com.*

Liko Kauai offers an excellent 4-hour morning or afternoon snorkeling and sightseeing tour which goes into some of the caves, as well as fishing cruises. The 49-ft power catamaran, 'Na Pali Kai III,' has all forward seating, shade, plus bathroom. Liko's policy is to go as far up Na Pali as weather permits, so you can see everything, occasionally pods of whales in winter ($140/adult) 808.338.0333; 888.SEA-LIKO *www.liko-kauai.com.* *Catamaran Kahanu* tours Na Pali on a 40-ft power catamaran, 18 feet wide

Small Power Catamaran Tours
(fewer than 18 passengers) 808 area code

North Shore:

Captain Sundown	808.826.5855
Na Pali Catamaran	808.826.6853

Westside:

Makana Tours	808.822.9187
Liko Kauai Cruises	808.338.0333
Catamaran Kahanu	808.335.3577
Kaulana Kai	808.337.9309

Large Catamaran Tours
(more than 18 passengers)

Westside:

Blue Dolphin	808.742.6731
Holo Holo Charters	808.335.0815
Kauai Sea Tours	808.826.7254
Captain Andy's	808.335.6833

Zodiacs

Westside:

Na Pali Explorer	808.338.9999
Z-tours	808.742.7422
Kauai Sea Tours	808.826.7254
Captain Zodiac	808.335.6833

with a 'flying bridge' for hanging over the waves to watch for spinning porpoises and humpback whales ($144/adult) 808.645.6176; 888.213.7711 *www. catamarankahanu.com.* On Kaulana Pali Kai, *Keith Silva* takes a 27-ft power boat (up to 6 passengers), ideal for families or small groups: 808.337.9309.

Zodiacs: If you crave a bigger thrill, consider zodiacs, whose 'rough and ready' ride often takes you up and over waves and head on into the surf. These rigid-hull ocean rafts are not for the weak of heart – or back. The ride can be bumpy, so ask right away for gloves to hold onto the rope, especially if you want to sit towards the front. A waterproof camera is a good idea for when the boat goes under waterfalls and through the ocean spray. On the ride home, the boat may feel as if it is hurling into the waves at top speed, so less adventurous passengers might prefer the back, in what is called the 'cadillac seat.' *Z Tours* offers scheduled tours to the south shore, including Kipu Kai (from $94) 808.742.7422; 888.9ZTOURZ *www.ztourz.com.*

Kauai Sea Tours takes 15 passengers on a full-day tour that includes a guided hike ($149/adult), or a half-day tour that includes snorkeling but not landing ($139/adult). Seasonal sightseeing and whale watching raft tours are also available ($69-99) 808.826.PALI; 800.733.7997 *www.kauaiseatours.com.* Now owned by Captain Andy's, *Captain Zodiac* operates a 24-ft motorized rigid hull craft. The 6-hour Na Pali snorkeling adventure includes

(weather permitting) landing at Nu'alolo Kai for lunch ($159/adult) 808.335.6833; 800.535.0830 *www.capt-andys.com*. *Na Pali Explorer* operates 2 boats out of Waimea and one out of Hanalei ($149/4.5-hr tour). A 3-hour south shore whale watching tour goes out in winter months ($100/adult) 808.338.9999; 887.335.9909 *www.napali-explorer.com*. Leaving from Kekaha, *Na Pali Riders* tours the entire Na Pali coast all the way to Ke'e Beach or, if you're lucky, Tunnels Beach. It's long, but you see everything ($109/ morning tour) 808.742.6331 *www.napaliriders.com*.

Larger catamarans: For those who tend to get seasick, these boats offer a smoother ride, particularly in winter months when seas are rougher. *Blue Dolphin Charters* tours Na Pali on the 'Blue Dolphin,' a 63-ft sailing catamaran, and the 'Blue Dolphin II,' a 65-ft catamaran, both of which have top decks with row seating ($58/5-hrs). It begins, as most tours do, with a continental breakfast and safety briefing, and it is the only Na Pali tour company that offers a diving option – both for certified divers and first timers ($35). After the snorkel/scuba break, a make-your-own sandwich lunch is served, and the bar opens with beer, wine, and mai tais. On our last tour, owner-operator Captain Terry took us close enough to the cliffs for a waterfall shower (not possible in rough winter seas). Sunset cruises are also offered ($62/3-hrs) 808.335.5553; 877.511.1311 *www.kauaiboats.com*.

Captain Andy's 55-ft sailing catamarans, 'Spirit of Kauai' and 'Akia-loa,' also sail from Port Allen to Na Pali ($139/adult) 808.335.6833; 800.535.0830 *www.capt-andys.com*. Both boats have 'trampolines' which provide front row seats – if you don't mind getting occasionally soaked with spray. If the wind is right, the captain may hoist the sails and turn off the engine for a quiet, smooth ride. A large, partially covered area offers shelter and beverages (after snorkeling, beer and wine). Morning Na Pali cruises include muffins and fruit, and later a make-your-own sandwich lunch. Four-hour sunset dinner cruise is $105.

On its 60-ft sailing catamaran, 'Lucky Lady,' *Kauai Sea Tours* offers an excellent Na Pali tour ($145/adult) with snorkeling, as well as a sunset dinner cruise ($109/adult), and on longer summer days a snorkel sunset dinner cruise ($145/adult). The crew is friendly, knowledgeable, and courteous. Breakfast and lunch are served, with mai tais, wine, and beer after you get out of the water: 808.826. PALI; 800.733.7997 *www. kauaiseatours.com.* Also from Port Allen, *Holo Holo Tours* goes along Na Pali on 'Leila,' a comfortable 50-ft sailing catamaran with little side-to-side rolling motion, including breakfast, lunch, beer and wine ($139/adult) 808.335.0815; 800.848.6130 *www.holoholocharters.com.*

Snorkeling stop at Nu'alolo Kai

Eastside: *True Blue Sailing* sails a 42-ft trimaran out of Nawiliwili Harbor near Lihue year round, with picnic & snorkel tours to Kipu Kai, snorkel tours off Nawiliwili, and charters. They specialize in small groups (20 or less) 808.246.6333 *www.kauaifun.com.*

NORTH SHORE: The longest operating tour boat captain on Kauai, *Captain Sundown* sails each tour personally, taking 15 passengers in his 40-ft sailing catamaran, 'Ku'uipo,' from Hanalei out along the Na Pali coast ($173/6-hrs) 808.826.5585 *www.captainsundown.com.* His family-owned company has been in business since 1971– that's the record on the island – and the bearded, friendly captain knows just about all there is to know about the island, its stories, and its waters. Choose either a Na Pali snorkel sail with a stop at Nu'alolo Kai, a Na Pali sunset sail, or a whale watching trip. Na Pali tours include a lunch of deli-made sandwiches (vegetarians can bring their own for a discount).

Ni'ihau: If you have the time, consider a tour to Ni'ihau, the 'forbidden' island largely off limits to tourists, except on boats which can come close enough to snorkel and dive but not to land. The crossing can be rough in winter. For skilled divers, *Seasport Divers* offers an outstanding all-day 3-tank dive trip with a knowledgeable and friendly crew. On Tuesdays and Fridays, *Blue Dolphin Charters* takes a comfortable 65-ft sailing catamaran ($196) for snorkeling or diving ($35 extra), and *Holo Holo Charters* offers daily snorkeling-only tours ($164). See Scuba, p 130.

Tour tips: Ask about cancellation policies for weather and surf conditions. You can check the weather report yourself at 808.245.6001 or *www.*

kauaiexplorer.com. Companies may claim they never go out in rough seas, but a lot depends on the definition. Rocking, rolling swells are fun for some, not so much fun for others, especially if there's no shelter from wind and spray, so think twice if your tour is ready to head out in marginal weather. Compare the number of passengers with the overall boat capacity, keeping in mind that the more crowded the boat, the less comfortable you may be. Inquire about your captain's experience on Kauai; every captain must be coast guard licensed, but some have more experience than others. Keep in mind that your young tour guides appreciate a modest tip.

Bring sunscreen, especially if your craft doesn't offer shade, perhaps a hat and sunglasses for glare, a towel, a long sleeved shirt for early morning check ins, and if possible, your own snorkel mask (and anti-fog) that fits properly. Protect your camera in a heavy duty zip lock plastic bag, and bring a dry shirt for the long ride home when you may be soaked with spray and dreaming of a hot shower.

Botanical Gardens

EASTSIDE: Above Wailua, the spectacular *Kadavul Temple* gardens have been developed for more than 20 years around a Hindu monastery. Twenty monks practice near a gorge with waterfalls and plants from all over the world. Self-guided visits 9am – noon daily at 107 Kaholalele Rd, Kapa'a *www.himalayanacademy.com*. Guided tours: 808.822.3012 or email *iraivan@hindu.org*. About 3 miles farther up Kuamo'o Rd is the *Keahua Arboretum*, a 30-acre preserve of grassy meadows and trees. Follow the signs, and don't get discouraged when the road gets bumpy. You'll cross a stream and come to a grassy spot for a picnic and hiking trails beneath ancient trees. From the Arboretum, *Aloha Kauai Tours* can take you by 4x4 van to the base of Mt. Wai'ale'ale, where spectacular waterfalls converge into a river: 808.245.6400. Map 1

NORTH SHORE: In Ha'ena, a walking tour of *National Tropical Botanical Gardens Limahuli Gardens* takes you on a 3/4 mile loop trail through 17 acres of rain forest and gardens lush with native plants to an ocean lookout. An ancient terrace for growing taro is nearly a thousand years old. Guided tour: 10am ($30/adults; $15 kids); self-guided stroll ($15/adults; kids free). Open Tues-Sat: 9:30am - 4pm. Tour reservations: 808.826.1053 *www.ntbg.org*. Rt 560, 1/2 mile past mile 9 marker. Map 5

Na'Aina Kai in Kilauea, a remarkable botanical garden and 'sculpture park,' combines formal tropical gardens, intricate Poinciana maze, a 'wild forest,' carnivorous plant habitat, desert garden, lagoon with fountains and a plunging waterfall, even an oceanfront gazebo overlooking the spectacular north shore coastline. Various guided tours range from 1.5 – 5-hrs on foot and by tram to explore gardens, waterways, and groves (T-F from $30). For families, special tours include a children's garden, gecko maze, rubber tree treehouse, a kid-sized train and other delights ($30/adults; $15/ kids) 808.828.0525 *www. naainakai.com*. Bring your camera. For lunch afterwards, try *Kilauea Fish Market* or *Kilauea Bakery*. Map 5

Allerton Gardens NTBG in Lawai

SOUTH SHORE: *National Tropical Botanical Gardens Lawai* is a unique 186 acre preserve of tropical fruits, spices, trees, rare plants, and flowers of astonishing beauty – e.g. 50 varieties of bananas and 500 species of palm. Instead of a formal garden, plant collections are designed into the natural landscape of the Lawai Valley and irrigated by an ingenious water system of fountains, streams, waterways, and rocky pools. Almost a botanical ark of tropical flora, the gardens preserve the largest collection of native Hawaiian flora anywhere. Stroll at a leisurely pace under spreading, giant trees to pavilions where a statue reflects a graceful image in a pool speckled with fallen leaves. The 'cutting garden' has brilliantly colored heliconia. The popular 2.5 hour guided tour of the Allerton Gardens (about 1 mile of walking) Mon - Sat at 9am requires reservations: 808.742.2623 *www.ntbg. org* ($45/adult; $20/kids who must be at least 10 yrs old). Or choose a self-guided tour of McBryde Gardens (allow 1.5 hours) departing daily by van from Spouting Horn parking lot every hour from 9:30am till 2:30pm ($20/adult; $10/kids; under 5 free). Admission is first come first served. Bring a camera (no tripods), comfortable walking shoes, mosquito repellent, hat (for shade) and bottled water (important). Map 6

Further west in Kalaheo, flower photographers will love *Kukuiolono Golf Course*'s plumeria grove, a rainbow of colors in summer. Turn south on Papalina Rd (the town's main intersection, at the traffic light); after .8 miles, turn into the entrance on the right. Free. Map 6

Camping

Camping is permitted at Anahola, Ha'ena, Anini, Salt Pond, and Polihale Beach Parks, as well as in specified areas of the Na Pali region and other wilderness preserves. For *state parks*, the camping limit is 5 nights in a 30 day period per campground (less on some stopovers on the Kalalau Trail). For info, permits, reservations contact *Department of Land and Natural Resources,* Parks Division, State of Hawaii, 3060 Eiwa St, P.O. Box 1671, Lihue, HI 96766; 808.274.3444 (or reserve online at *www. hawaii.gov/dlnr*). You can also download permit forms at *www.kauai.gov* (click on licenses and permits). For Alakai Swamp or Waimea Canyon, contact *Division of Forestry*. Use the address and phone above. At *Kauai County Parks* the camping limit is 4 days per park, or 12 nights total. Contact 808.241.6670 *www.kauai.gov*. Allow 30 days to process permits.

WESTSIDE: *Koke'e: YWCA Camp Sloggett* in spectacular *Koke'e State Park* has access to 45 miles of hiking trails leading to the Kalalau Lookout and its amazing views of the Waimea Canyon and Na Pali coastline. Group and hostel accommodations include tent camping and a bunkhouse with kitchenettes, shared bath facilities, and hot showers (from $20/pp/night). Reserve at least two months in advance: YWCA of Kauai, 3094 Elua St, Lihue HI 96766; 808.245.5959 *www.campingkauai.com* Map 8

Those who want to be close to nature – and to a shower and refrigerator at the same time – can try *Koke'e Lodge*'s cabins, which have a stove, refrigerator, hot shower, cooking and eating utensils, linens, bedding, and wood burning stove; bargain rates from $65/night (maximum stay of 5 nights during a 30 day period). Reservations: *The Lodge at Koke'e*, Box 367, Waimea HI 96796; 808.335.6061 *www.thelodgeatkokee. com*. Koke'e Lodge serves breakfast and light lunch 9am - 3:30pm. Bring warm clothes for cold nights, and remember to lock valuables in your car's trunk. Be sure to visit *Koke'e Museum*. Koke'e info: *www.kokee. org* Map 8

NORTH SHORE: *YMCA Camp Naue* in spectacular Ha'ena on the north shore offers beachfront camping in bunk houses (or your own tent). It's popular with local clubs and families, but tourists are also welcome to stay in the bunk-house ($15/night; children half-

Wai'oli Mission Church, Hanalei

price); bring your own tent and it's only $10. YMCA Kauai, Box 1786, Lihue 96766; 808.246.9090 *www.ymcaofkauai.org*. Map 5

Camping equipment rentals: *Pedal & Paddle* in Hanalei: 808.826.9069 *www.pedalnpaddle.com*. *Kayak Kauai* in Hanalei: 808.826.9844; 800.437.3507, and also in Kapaʻa: 808.822.9179 *www.kayakkauai.com*. In Poipu, try *Outfitters Kauai:* 808.742.9667. Buy camping equipment in *Long's Drug Store, K- Mart, Wal-Mart, Costco* in Lihue, as well as small variety stores like *Waipouli Variety* (Wailua), *Discount Variety* (Koloa), *Village Variety* (Hanalei), or *Ace Hardware* (Hanalei).

For a camping retreat combining spectacular places with education, yoga and spiritual growth, contact *Encounter Kauai:* 808.634.6812 *www.encounterkauai.com*.

Chocolate and Chocolate Tours

As Kauai shifts from monocropping sugar cane to diversified agriculture, chocolate is developing into a tasty option. Hawaii's climate is perfect for growing cacao, and at *Steelgrass Farms* in Kapaʻa, the Lydgate family (which for generations since 1860 has contributed to education and preservation of Hawaiian culture) is a leader in promoting cacao tree production. The farm provides seedlings free to island farmers to encourage diversified, sustainable agriculture, and also hosts a multidisciplinary educational center for agriculture, music and the arts. Kauai's cacao trees are still too young for large production, but you can tour Steelgrass Farm's beautiful gardens, bamboo forest, fruit trees, and flowers, and sample dark chocolate ($60; mention this book for $10 discount) 808.821.1857 *www.steelgrass.org*. On the north shore, *Garden Island Chocolate* in Kilauea also offers tours and tastings: 808.634.6812 *www.gardenislandchocolate.com*.

In the Port Allen Marina, try *Kauai Chocolate Company's* homemade ice cream – macadamia nut, dark chocolate, coconut, and island fruit flavors – or chocolates created while you watch by Don and Marlene Greer and their family at 4341 Waialo Rd, Hanapepe (12pm - 5pm daily) – a great treat after a long boat ride: 808.335.0048 *www.kauaichocolate.us*. *The Right Slice* makes sensational custom pies with chocolate/coconut/macadamia nut. Call Sandy at 808.212.8320 *www.therightslice.com*.

Churches & Temples

The *Kapaʻa Missionary Church* welcomes visitors of any denomination with a shell lei and warm greeting: 808.822.5594 *www.kapaamissionary. com*. In Hanalei: *Waiʻoli Huiʻia Church* conducts services at 10am Sundays, and the family friendly atmosphere is evident: "Our keikis are apt to wander during church. They do this because they feel at home in God's house. Please love them as we do." 808.826.6253 *www.hanaleichurch.org*. Many lovely old churches on Kauai are on back roads in Koloa, sides streets in Kilauea, cane fields on the west side. Stop and visit.

The *Kadavul Hindu Temple* in the Wailua valley draws thousands of Hindu followers each year, as well as tourists fascinated by the botanical gardens, stone temple, and 300-kg crystal *Siva Lingum*. Visitors to the temple and monastery may be invited to join a *puja* (cleansing) ceremony. Open 9am – 11:30am;107 Kaholalele Rd, Kapa'a; 808.822.3012 *www. himalayanacademy.com* Map 1

Lawai International Center, a temple site of 88 Buddhist shrines, was built over 100 years ago in a beautiful valley known as a place of healing. A tranquil place for meditation, it celebrates Hawaiian, Japanese and Chinese traditions: 808.639.4300 *www.lawaicenter.org* for info on tours (2nd and last Sundays/month or by appointment). Donation appreciated. Map 6

Coffee & Coffee Bars

DRINKS: *Small Town Coffee* in Kapa'a serves great coffees. In fact, owner Anni Caporuscio won the 2006 Hawaii Barista Championship with her unique coconut coffee drink. Try carrot bran muffins from the local organic bakery, free wireless in her blue storefront at 4-1495 Kuhio Hwy, Kapa'a. In Wailua, Southern California favorite *Coffee Bean and Tea Leaf* is next to Foodland; *Starbucks* is next to Safeway and in Lihue's Kukui Grove next to Jamba Juice (try the only-in-Hawaii 'tropical mocha' with coconut). *Icing on the Cake* in Kinipopo Village is one of only two places outside San Francisco Bay Area serving *Blue Bottle Coffee:* 808.823.1210. *Java Kai* sells drinks and beans in Lihue, Hanalei, Kapa'a, and Koloa: 866.JAVA-KAI *www. javakai.com*. On the north shore near Ha'ena, stop at *Na Pali Coffee House* for great mocha frappuccino (in Hanalei Colony Resort).

BEANS: *Kauai Coffee* plantation grows beans free of insecticides on 4,000 acres where Hawaii's first coffee plantation was founded in 1836. Sample at the visitor's center (9am -5pm daily) in Lawai: 808.335.0813; 800.545.8605 *www.kauaicoffee.com*. Near Waimea, *Black Mountain Premium Hawaiian Coffee* is an outstanding local producer. Buy at Wranglers, or order at *www.tropicislemusic.com*. *Kalaheo Coffee and Deli* sells fragrant beans along with tasty deli choices at 2-2560 Kaumualii Hwy, Kalaheo: 808.332.5868. Other home-brew favorites: *Lapperts*: *www. lappertshawaii.com,* and *Lion Coffee*: *www.lioncoffee.com*.

Family Beaches

With a plastic pail and an inexpensive net ($9 for an 8 inch net at Long's), children can have fun trying to catch fish trapped in tidal pools. Net fishing is fun at the rivers behind the beaches at *Anahola, Kalihiwai*, and *Moloa'a*, and at the tidal pools at *Salt Pond* and *Poipu Beach Parks.*

> **Lifeguards** are very important and present only at certain beaches:
> EASTSIDE: *Lydgate Park, Anahola, Kealia.*
> SOUTHSHORE: *Poipu Beach Park.*
> WESTSIDE *Salt Pond Beach Park, Kekaha.*
> NORTHSHORE: *Hanalei Bay, Ha'ena Beach Park, Ke'e Beach (summer).*

Family Fun

For family picnics, beachwalking, swimming, and wading, we like *Kalihiwai* and *Anini* on the north, and on the east, *Kalapaki* in Lihue. At Lydgate Beach Park you'll find *Kamalani Playground* – a 16,000 square foot playground with mirror mazes, a suspension bridge, lava tubes, and circular slide. A half mile paved walkway/bikeway takes you to the playground's newer section just south of Kaha Lani Condominium.

A family favorite: Kids can dress up in their aloha finery and watch the keiki hula show at the Hyatt in Poipu (between 6 and 8pm, Tues and Sat) at Seaview Terrace: 808.742.1234; free valet parking.

Netting tadpoles at Moloa'a

Free hula shows are sponsored at shopping centers and hotels. Times vary, so call ahead or check *www.kauaifestivals.com.*
EASTSIDE: Coconut Plantation Marketplace 808.822.3641;
                   The Hilton 808.245.1955; Marriott in Lihue 808.245.5050;
                   Harbor Mall, Nawiliwili 808.245.6255;
                   Kukui Grove, Lihue 808.245.7784.
NORTH SHORE: Princeville St Regis Fridays at sunset in the lounge;
                   dinner show Wednesdays: 808.826.9644.
SOUTH SHORE: Kuku'iula Village M & W 5-7pm: 808.742.0234;
                   Poipu Shopping Village on T and Th at 5pm: 808.742.2831.

For family-friendly fun, 'Stand Up Paddle Surfing' is a great adventure. First lessons are taught in smooth river water by two outstanding teachers who are great with kids: *Nephi Kalani Quereto*: 808.826.7612 *www. learntosurfkauaihi.com* and *Charlie Smith*, who will take the whole family for customized lessons: 808.634.6979 *www.blueseassurfingschool.com.*

Try *Kauai Backcountry's* tubing adventure, fun for all the family: 808.245.2506; 888.270.0555 *www.kauaibackcountry.com.* Call Gregg at *Watersports Adventures* for scuba lessons (he's terrific with kids) 808.821.1599. For first-rate, kid-friendly windsurfing lessons, call *Celeste Harvel*: 808.828.6838.

Ride the steam train at *Kauai Plantation Railway* through the fields, stopping to feed 'wild' pigs: 808.245.7245 *www.kilohanakauaiplantation-railway.com.* Kids under 18 play golf $1/hole or free after 4pm (one per paying adult) at *Puakea Golf Course:* 808.245.8756 *www.puakeagolf.com.* At *Clayworks at Kilohana*, Keith Tammarine helps young artists have fun: 808.246.2529 *www.clayworksatkilohana.com.*

The whole family will enjoy the dinner theater production of '*South Pacific*' with local performers (Wednesdays 5:30pm) at Hilton Beach Resort: 808.356.6500 *www.southpacifickauai.com.* Great children's books: Joanna Carolan's beautifully illustrated *Kauai Good Night Moon* at *Banana Patch Studio* in Kilauea and Hanapepe. Child equipment rentals: *Ready Rentals*: 808.823.8008; 800.599.8008 *www.readyrentals.com.* Looking for a babysitter? Try *Babysitters of Kauai*: 808.632.2252 or *Kauai Babysitting Company:* 808.652.5373 *www.kauaibabysittingcompany.com* (from $18/hr).

Farmers' Markets

On each day of the week farmers' markets are great spots to talk to local people and enjoy a kaleidoscope of tastes and colors. From truck beds,

cardtables, or the trunks of cars, local farmers sell their fruits, vegetables, and flowers at reasonable prices. Manoa lettuce, as little as $5 for a half-dozen small heads, will be fresh and taste of Kauai's sunny skies and salt air. You may find find tomatoes and avocados; fresh basil, oregano, chives or marjoram; a shiny dark purple eggplant with just the right sound when you thump it, bananas of all kinds – Williams, Bluefield, and apple-bananas which taste like bananas laced with apples and look like golden sand at sunset.

Come early for the best selection – so the starting time is important to know. At the Koloa market, a rope tied across the parking lot drops with a shrill whistle at noon on the nose, when the fun begins.

Sellers quickly become friends who may offer you a slice of their best wares. Papayas will be the local sunrise and strawberry variety, with a red-orange center even tastier with a local lime. Even if you aren't cooking, you'll be tempted by string-beans as long as shoelaces, squash with squeaky skins, all kinds of vegetables with odd shapes, fresh coconuts. You may find leis of pakalana or plumeria for $5 a strand. Take home tropical flowers by the bunches – bird of paradise, parrot colored heliconia blossoms, stalks of fragrant white or yellow ginger. Be ready to bargain if you are buying in quantity, and take advice about trying new tastes. Most sellers price in $2 or $5 packages, so bring lots of bills. For info, visit *www.gardenkauai.com.*

Farmers' Markets

Monday	noon	*Koloa*, Ball Park on Rt 520 next to the ball field off Mahulia. Maps 6, 7
	3pm	*Lihue*, Kukui Grove by Sears. Maps 1, 2
Tuesday	2pm	*Hanalei*, Rt 560 west of town. Till 4pm. Map 5
	3pm till 4:30.	*Kalaheo* Neighborhood Center, 4480 Papalina Rd at Rt 50. Till 4:30pm. Map 6
Wednesday	3pm till 4:30.	*Kapa'a,* Take Kukui Rd off Rt 56, turn right at the end, then the next right onto Kahau Rd and park on the left. The bypass road from Wailua to Kapa'a ends close to Kahau Rd. Map 3
Thursday	3pm	*Hanapepe*, Town Park. Till 4pm. Map 6
	4:30pm	*Kilauea*, Kilauea Neighbor Ctr. 460 Keneke St off Lighthouse Rd. Till 5:30pm. Map 5
Friday	3:00pm	*Lihue*, Vidinha football stadium parking lot, Hoolako Rd near airport. Till 5pm. Maps 1, 2
Saturday	9am	*Kekaha* Neighborhood Center, 8130 Elepaio Rd off Rt 50. Till 10am. Map 8
	11:30am	*Kilauea*, Christ Memorial Church. Till 1pm. Map 5
	10am	Kauai Community College. Till 1pm. Map 1

Bouquets of heliconia and ginger for $5.00

The largest markets are in Kapa'a, Koloa, and Lihue. On Fridays, the *Lihue market* is in the parking lot behind the Vidinha football stadium just south of the airport. Enter off Kapule Highway (Rt 51) at the small street leading to the stadium, or turn off Rice St at Holoko Rd. Map 2

The Wednesday *Kapa'a Market* is opposite the armory on Kahau Rd. Turn off Rt

56 onto Kukui Rd and follow to the end of the street. Turn right, then take the next right onto Kahau Rd. The bypass road from Wailua to Kapa'a comes out just at the end of Kahau Rd. Map 3. Mondays the market is at noon in *Koloa*, at the ballfield, just outside of town. Map 4

Just missed the market? You'll find roadside produce stands all over the island. Look for low acid, 'Sugar Loaf' pineapples from Kahili Farms, strawberry papayas, bananas of all kinds. Sample fresh goat cheese (tour the dairy) at *Kauai Kunana Dairy:* 808.651.5046 *www.kauaikunanadairy.com.* You'll love fruit 'frosties,' a tasty confection of frozen fruit whipped smooth like soft ice cream. Try combinations of mango, banana, papaya, pineapple – whatever is in season – at the *Moloa'a Sunrise Fruit Stand* on Rt 56 north of Anahola and *Banana Joe's* in Kilauea next to the new Kauai miniature golf. Local tropical fruit smoothies are made at lots of places, including *Moloa'a Sunrise, Banana Joe's; Coconut Cup* and *Killer Juice Bar* (Kapa'a); and the mainland version, *Jamba Juice.*

Fitness, Pilates & Athletic Clubs

EASTSIDE: *Kauai Athletic Club* next to Kukui Grove Center in Lihue offers daily, weekly, and monthly visitor rates, classes, weight machines, swimming pool, squash courts: 808.245.5381 *www.kauaiathleticclub.com.* *Kauai YMCA's* new facility at 4477 Nuhou Street, Lihue, has a weight room, Olympic-size lap pool. YMCA members (any state) pay $5: 808.246.9090. *Curves* is also in Lihue: 808.245.9790 *www.curvesinformation.com.*

NORTH SHORE: *Princeville Health Club*, in the Prince Golf Course clubhouse, has views of fairways and ocean, visitor rates for classes, personal training, massage, and yoga: 808.826.1105 *www.princeville.com.* In Kilauea, try *Pilates Kauai:* 808.639.3074 *www.pilateskauai.com.*

SOUTH SHORE: In Poipu, *Hyatt Resort* offers classes, fitness equipment, outdoor pool, as well as massage: 808.240.6440 *www.anaraspa.com.* Use the spa and you can enjoy the lap pool, gym, and health facility all day.

WESTSIDE: Try *24hrFitness* in Port Allen: 808.335.0049.

Fresh Island Fish

You can sometimes find locally-caught fresh fish at roadside stands or farmers' markets. Big stores like *Costco* in Lihue, and *Cost-U-Less* and *Safeway* in Wailua have the high volume which usually means a fresh selection. Exploring small local markets, however, is more fun:

EASTSIDE: Try *Fish Express,* 3343 Kuhio Hwy, Lihue for filets of shibiko (baby yellow fin tuna), ono, ulua, and snappers of all hues – pink, grey, red. Prices and selection vary with the weather, the season, the tides, even the moon, and are higher in winter when fishing boats face rougher seas. The adventurous can try opihi (limpets) raw in the shell with seaweed or smoked marlin. Fish can be vacuum sealed for shipping: 808.245.9918.

In Hanama'ulu, stop in at *Ara's Sakana-Ya* for homemade ahi poke (raw fish, onions, Hawaiian salt and shoyu) and sushi platters: 3-4301 Kuhio Hwy. 808.245.1707. In Kapa'a, try inexpensive *Pono Market*, a local favorite for poke, at 4-1300 Kuhio Hwy. 808.822.4581.

NORTH SHORE: Don't miss *Kilauea Fish Market* for highest quality fresh catch and prepared dishes, 4270 Kilauea Rd. 808.828-MAHI. In Hanalei, *Hanalei Dolphin*'s fish market is next to the Dolphin restaurant. 5-5016 Kuhio Hwy. 808.826.6113.

SOUTH SHORE: *Koloa Fish Market's* seared ahi is a must try; also stand out poke as well as really fresh local fish. 5482 Koloa Rd. 808.742.6199. WESTSIDE: *Ishihara's Market*, 9894 Kaumualii Hwy in Waimea, is a local favorite for varieties of poke: 808.338.1751. Go early!

Flowers & Flower Leis

The fragrance of pikake or white ginger — the cool, silky touch of petals — the delicate yet rich colors of orchids and plumeria — no vacation

is complete without a flower lei, especially on your last night. Safeway, Longs, Wal-Mart offer ready-made leis in a refrigerated case, but imported carnations cannot compare with a local lei which reflects the traditions of the island and the artistry of the lei maker. Order a day in advance, and pick up your lei on the way to dinner.

The *Mauna Loa lei* is a wide woven band of small purple orchids popular at graduation (about $20). *Ginger lei* is a spectacular creation of white, sometimes pink buds tightly threaded like feathers, fragrant enough to turn heads as you walk by. Other fragrant leis: green *pakalana* ($10/strand of 100 flowers), or small, white *stephanotis* ($10), or *pikake,* a tiny, delicate white flower for weddings ($10/strand). *Plumeria* leis are common in summer; large white, yellow, pink, or deep red blossoms have a lovely perfume. The fragrance lingers even when petals turn brown. Dry it for a Hawaiian potpourri. You can wear your lei onto the plane, though petals quickly turn brown in air conditioning. Preserve it in a plastic bag to keep it fresh to cheer your morning coffee back home. On the way home, you may be able to pick one up at the small florist at Lihue airport.

Lei in ti leaf wrap

At farmers' markets and roadside stands, you can sometimes find leis for $7 (even less in summer). Flowers wilt, so sure they are refrigerated. In Anahola, *Aunty Kuini* sells plumeria leis ($7) from a stand opposite Ono Char Burger: 808.821.1514. *Linda Pitman* grows her own flowers and will create a lei just for you: 808.828.1572. In Lihue, try *Flowers Forever:* 808.245.4717. In Wailua, stop at *JC's Flowers & Minimart,* 4-369 Kuhio Hwy: 808.822.5961. JC will ship to the mainland. Talk to Avery Kano at *Pua Lei:* 808.822.1200 *www.pualeiaflowershop.com.* In Kapa'a, check *Pono Market* at 4-1300 Kuhio Hwy: 808.822.4581. For friends at home taking care of the dog, say thanks with a flower assortment arriving fresh and gorgeous in any mainland city. *Hawaii Tropical Flower & Foliage Associations* lists members: *www.htffa.com.*

Orchid lovers will love Kauai. In Hanapepe, visit *Mackie Orchids:* 808.335.0240 *www.mackieorchids.com.* In Kilauea, visit *Kauai Orchids* for many varieties; buy plants to carry home on the plane (carry your plant in a

plastic bag so it can easily be inspected at agriculture to be sure the pot contains only bark and no dirt) 808.828.0904 *www.kauaiorchids. com.*

Geocaching

An electronic treasure hunt activity, geocaching involves searching for ingeniously hidden 'treasure' containers using a handheld GPS unit. Nearly 400,000 'geocaches' are hidden around the world, about 80 on Kauai. You download the longitude/latitude coordinates at *www.geocaching.com* where you can register (free) for a nickname under which to log finds. Some finds involve solving puzzles, or you may locate an item in one cache which is on its 10th stop on an around-the-world journey, and you can help it along. You can swap your own treasure for what's in the cache.

No matter where you stay on the island, there are geocaches nearby, often by points of interest you might not otherwise discover.

Gifts from Kauai

For a listing of Kauai artisans with contact information, consult *www.kauaimade.net*. In Lihue visit the *Kauai Museum Shop*: 808.245.6931 *www.kauaimuseum.org. Kong Lung* and *Banana Patch* in Kilauea have wonderful island-style collections: *www.bananapatchstudio.com. Island Soap* (in Koloa and Kilauea) makes soap and lotions fragrant with coconut, pikake, or plumeria: *www.handmade-soap.com.*

For handmade clothes and wonderful fabrics, stop at *Kapaia Stitchery* just north of Lihue on Rt 56 (Don't take the Rt 51 bypass road, or you'll miss it) where seamstresses still make quilts, dresses, and aloha shirts like their grandmothers did: 808.245.2281.

Buy a doll-size 'mu mu' for your special 'American Girl' back home from *Melody Pigao:* 808.822.4231 *www.kilohanaclothingco.com.* She also makes beautiful bags in vintage cloth. In Koloa, look for hand made tents for Barbie at *Pohaku T's* which has locally designed and created clothing, gifts, and crafts: 808.742.7500 *www.pohaku.com.* In Lihue, *Hilo Hattie's* has a huge selection of Hawaiian style clothing: *www.hilohattie.com.* Directly across the street, *Discount Fabric Warehouse* has the largest selection of Hawaiian fabrics on the island; join the mailing list for special offers: 808.246.2739 *www.gotfabric.com*. At *Vicky's* in Kapa'a you'll find lovely fabrics and old fashioned personal attention: 808.822.1746.

Bargain hunters will enjoy *Kauai's flea markets* daily at Spouting Horn in Poipu; daily in Kapa'a opposite Otsuka's, and in Waimea on Rt 50. Wares may be imports however. *Hawaiian Trading Center* (Rt 50 and 560) has a large selection. See *Sweets & Treats* (p 140) for edible gifts.

Golf Courses

Makai Golf, Princeville. After a remarkable, multimillion dollar re-design by Robert Trent Jones, Jr, the *Makai Course* re-opens with seashore paspalum turf grass, reconfigured complexes and greens surrounding reshaped bunkers. The world-class championship course has 3 challenging nines: Lake, Woods, and Ocean, famous for spectacular views and the dramatic 141-yard seventh hole, where the ocean, foaming like a cauldron, separates tee and green. Ranked 6th in the state, this course has been one of Golf Digest's top 25 resort courses for more than 20 years (Par 72; Slope 133). Fees $175 ($125/Princeville Hotel guests; $140/Princeville Resort guests; $95 after 1:30pm). Enter Princeville at the main gate. For virtual views, tee times: 808.826.1912 *www.makaigolf.com* Map 5

The Prince Course, Hawaii's number-one rated course (*Golf Digest*), is now under reconstruction. The 18 hole, 6,521 yard course, designed by Robert Trent Jones, Jr., (Par 72; Slope 145), is set in 390 acres of pastureland, with rolling hills, deep ravines, tropical jungle with streams and waterfalls. Located just east of Princeville on Rt 56. 808.826.5001; 800.826.1105. Check for updates: ptee@princeville.com. Map 5

Kiahuna Golf Club in Poipu, designed by Robert Trent Jones, Jr, is an 18 hole, links-style course, with smooth, fast greens and tradewind challenges. At 6,925 yards and five sets of tees, this course is geared for all levels of playing ability (Par 70; Slope 134). Fees, with cart, are $99/18 holes or $65 after 2pm. Ask about the bounce back rate for multiple rounds. 808.742.9595 *www.kiahunagolf.com* Maps 6,7

Poipu Bay Resort Golf Course, Poipu, designed by Robert Trent Jones, Jr., home of the Grand Slam of Golf since 1994, completed a greens renovation in December 2010. This Scottish links-style course, 6,845 yards from the blue tees, is set in 210 acres of sugar plantation land along the ocean (Par 72; Slope 132). Discounts for guests at the Hyatt and neighboring hotels: 808.742.8711; 800.858.6300 *www.poipubaygolf.com* Maps 6, 7

Wailua Municipal Golf Course, adjacent to Rt 56 in Wailua, was ranked in the top 25 US municipal courses by *Golf Digest*. This popular 18 hole,

Kauai's Golf Magic by Robert Trent Jones, Jr.

I have played golf all over the world, and I keep coming back to Kauai! The island has unique courses, offering both challenges and enjoyment. With the north shore's spectacular landscape to work with, I laid out the original Princeville Resort course in three distinct nines to take advantage of the dramatic cliffs and breathtaking ocean views. The Ocean nine have great vistas and the sounds of the sea off the cliffs; the Woods thread through the trees, with a wonderful Zen-influenced bunker, an idea from my many trips to Japan.

Ranked first in Hawaii by *Golf Digest*, The Prince Course is more bold and dramatic, and I designed it to retain some of the wilderness character of its site. Carved out of heavy vegetation, it meanders through valleys, with panoramic views. It's a tough course (I'm told the beverage cart driver sells more golf balls than drinks) but from the proper set of tees, I guarantee you'll enjoy this golf nature trek!

On the south shore, the Kiahuna Plantation Course is a fun, yet memorable test with rolling fairways, sweeping bunkers, and small, traditional greens. Our newest creation, Poipu Bay Resort adjacent to the Hyatt Regency, is the site of the PGA's Annual Grand Slam of Golf. The back nine border the ocean, where the almost constant yet variable wind is the challenge. You have to make precise shots, judging both distance and the wind, or it will blow the ball off the green. Many holes hug the cliffs, and special attention has been given to ancient Hawaiian sacred grounds.

On the east side, the Wailua Golf Course is one of the best public courses in the country. Many holes flank the ocean and are protected by palm trees. This course is a must! I am also a fan of the Kiele Course. The finishing holes really get your attention, particularly the par-three 15th, requiring skill and a brave heart to tame.

No matter which course you choose, you really can't go wrong on Kauai. The people are friendly, temperatures comfortable, the pace slow – and a nice surprise around each corner! There's something magical about Kauai that brings people back. I know. I'm one of them!

6,658 yard course is built along the ocean on rolling terrain amid ironwood trees and coconut palms. Small greens and narrow fairways make this a real challenge (Par 72, Slope 125). Unbeatable fees: $44/weekends (and it gets crowded); $32/ weekdays; half-price after 2pm; $16/cart/18 holes): 808.241.6666 *www.kauai.gov/golf* Map 1

Kukuiolono Golf Course, Kalaheo. 9 holes, par 35 with spectacular views over 178 acres and a lovely Japanese garden. Located on a bluff with challenging tradewinds. Greens fee: $7; carts available. It's a local secret most don't want to share. Turn south off Rt 50 in Kalaheo at Papalina Rd (the stoplight) and drive .8 mile. Enter gate on right. 808.332.9151. Map 6

Kauai Lagoons Kiele course (Kauai Marriott, Lihue) on Kalapaki Bay designed by Jack Nicklaus is undergoing renovation. Upon completion, the new Kiele Course will have more ocean holes than any course in Hawaii. Currently golfers enjoy an 18-hole layout combining the Kiele holes, including the entire front 9 (with the signature 16th that plays along the ocean's edge, the par 3 17th and the island green 18th that Jack Nicklaus named the Golden Bear), plus holes from the Mokihana Course. Even before the renovation, the *Kiele Course* was named one of the Top 100 in America by *Golf Digest.* Fees in peak season, including cart, are $175 ($95 after noon; $140/Marriott guests). Call for updates: 808.241.6000; 800.634.6400 *www.kauailagoonsgolf.com.* Map 2

Grove Farm's *'Puakea' Course* located near Kukui Grove Center in Lihue, designed by Robin Nelson, winds through 200 acres of former sugar plantation land with sheer ravines, freshwater streams and views of Mount Hau'upu and the Hule'ia Stream. Ranked 13th Best Course in Hawaii (2009), Puakea offers fun and challenges to golfers of all skill levels (Par 72; Slope 129; 6,954 yards) $99/before 11am; $85/after 11am; $65/after 2pm; 9 holes anytime after 11am/$65. Kids play for $1/hole, and free after 4pm with paying adult: 808.245.8756 *www.puakeagolf.com.* Map 2

The *'Kauai Golf Challenge'* combines one round at different courses. Your hotel or condo may have arrangements with pro shops, so ask about a *'resort discount.'* Visit *www.teetimesamerica.com* for info and discounts.

Helicopter Tours

Many of the most beautiful places on Kauai are inaccessible by car. For this reason, a helicopter tour is an unforgettable way to see this spectacular island. Kauai is breathtakingly beautiful from the air, almost like an America in miniature, with rolling hills and valleys on the eastside and majestic mountains on the west. The island has a flat, dry southland as well as a forested wilderness to the north, and, on the west coast, wide sandy beaches where the setting sun paints the sky with gold before slipping silently into the enormous sea. There is even a 'Grand Canyon' on a small scale, where pink and purple cliffs, etched by centuries of wind and rain into giant towers, seem like remnants of a lost civilization. So much variety is amazing on an island only 32 miles in diameter.

And what you'll see is beyond your fantasies – a mountain goat poised in a ravine, a white bird gliding against the dark green cliffs, a sudden rainbow in the mist, incredible, tower-like mountains of pink and brown in the Waimea 'Grand Canyon,' a glistening waterfall hanging like a slender silver ribbon through trees and rocks, a curve of white sand at the base of the purple and gold Na Pali cliffs, white foam bursting upon the rocky coast.

Then, like the unveiling of the island's final mystery, you fly into the very center of Mt. Wai'ale'ale's crater, where in the dimly lit mists of the rainiest place on the earth, waterfalls are born from ever falling showers. You have journeyed to the very heart of the island, the place of its own birth from the volcano's eruption centuries ago. From your hotel room, you would never have believed that all this splendor existed.

Because of the expense, we worried about picking the 'perfect day.' We began on what seemed in Lihue to be only a partly sunny day, but once in the air, we saw that the clouds would be above us rather than in our way and enhanced the island's beauty with changing patterns of light.

The helicopter touring industry was started more than 30 years ago by an extraordinary pilot, Jack Harter, who became a legend for his extraordinary flying skill and intimate knowledge and love of Kauai. People lucky enough to fly with Jack saw and learned more in their 90 minute flight than they could have imagined. Jack had a perfect safety record, and accomplished rescues in weather other pilots would not–or could not–dare to face.

Following Jack, who has retired to his north shore farm, younger pilots started companies, piloting all the flights personally, and then, as their companies added aircraft and brought in and trained even younger pilots to fly them, the 'owner piloted' company became an economically unworkable business model. The Bell Jet Rangers, which accommodated 4 paying passengers, were gradually replaced by more economical '6-pac' A-STARs.

The typical tour goes in a clockwise direction from the Lihue Airport. A unique option: *Ni'ihau Helicopters* offers a half-day tour including a 3-hour beach landing for snorkeling and picnic ($365), as well as hunting expeditions: 877.441.3500 *www.niihau.us.*

Fixed Wing Air Tours: *Wings Over Kauai* offers a tour, with fewer passengers (3 people not counting the pilot) in a Cessna 172, as well one in a larger 6-passenger G-8 'Air van.' Bruce Coulombe, an FAA rated instructor, can give student pilots a piloting experience while he handles the radio and uses his extensive local knowledge to supervise the flight. (If you have ever wanted to be a pilot, you try an intro lesson for only $50/35 minutes). His Cessna tour offers a small party (up to 3 but most often just 2 passengers) a non-shared experience. However, unlike a helicopter, a fixed-wing

Then and now: The eastside seen in 1995 with fields of sugar cane and more recently (below).

Na Pali Coastline

aircraft cannot hover, or penetrate the interior mountain regions. Part 135 certification: 808.635.0815 *www.wingsoverkauai.com*

Looking at our images and videos back home almost brings back the magic of that hour, when we seemed suspended in a horizon so vast as to seem limitless, and any effort to confine it within camera range was impossible. It is always the best day of the trip.

Helicopter Tours & Safety

Beautiful as Kauai is from the air, accidents have focused everyone's attention squarely on safety. The island's mountainous terrain, occasionally turbulent winds, and rapidly changing cloud conditions can pose real challenges for the pilot. In a review of 8 weather-related accidents statewide since 1994, the National Transportation Safety Board found that half involved pilots relatively new to air tour operations in Hawaii. The reality is that a pilot with sufficient hours to be licensed may not have extensive experience on Kauai, where judgment calls are often crucial.

In 2005, a *Heli USA* helicopter crashed during a 'microburst' or sudden wind and rainstorm in the waters off Ha'ena, killing 3 people. According to an NTSB report (3/26/2007), "the decision by the pilot to continue flight into adverse weather conditions" contributed to the accident. In 2004, a *Bali Hai Helicopters* pilot flying below the recommended SFAR minimum altitude made the decision "to continue flight into an area of turbulent, reduced visibility weather conditions" rather than deviate from his tour route, and crashed into a ridgeline; all 5 on board died (NTSB 3/26/2007). Both pilots had been flying on Kauai for only a few months.

NTSB recommends pilot training that specifically addresses local weather phenomena and in-flight decision-making, and also that the FAA increase surveillance of pilots to ensure compliance with minimum terrain clearance requirements. The Honolulu FAA recommended in August, 2006 that pilots not perform 'non-flight' duties such as operating videography, sound systems, or two-way intercoms which may distract attention from primary flight responsibilities.

Two more accidents took place in March, 2007, when four people died in a *Heli USA* crash at the Princeville Airport after the pilot reported hydraulic problems; NTSB found the probable cause to be failure to "ensure its maintenance program was being executed" (NTSB 1/14/2009). In 2007, an *Inter-Island Helicopter* crashed near Ha'ena with one fatality, due to a manufacturing defect in its tail rotor system (NTSB 7/30/2008). Recently, a NTSB final report attributed a 2003 crash with 5 fatalities involving *Jack Harter Helicopters* to pilot error (NTSB 9/14/2007).

Key questions to ask:

FAA certification: Not all companies are certified under Part 135 of Federal Aviation Regulations, which requires a company to perform a more rigorous (thus more expensive) maintenance program than other certification categories, as well as annual flight tests of its pilots. This certificate

Tunnels Beach as the rain moves in

2007	Inter-Island Helicopters	1 fatality
2007	Heli USA	4 fatalities
2005	Heli USA	3 fatalities
2004	Bali Hai Helicopters	5 fatalities
2003	Jack Harter Helicopters	5 fatalities
1998	Ohana Helicopters	6 fatalities
1994	Inter-Island Helicopters	1 fatality
1994	Papillon Hawaiian	3 fatalities

must be displayed in the company's office. Ask to see it. You also have a right to know whether the company, or *your* pilot, has been involved in accidents during the past three years. You can check with NTSB at *www. ntsb.gov*. You should also ask if the company's FAA certificate has ever been revoked or suspended, and whether it is currently under FAA investigation for accidents or maintenance (as opposed to record-keeping) deficiencies.

Pilot experience: How long has your pilot been flying over Kauai? Will you be told who your pilot will be?

Exact length of the tour: Actual in-flight time for the around-the-island tour should be no less than 60 minutes, or Kauai will appear to whiz past your window, limiting your opportunities to explore the more remote terrain inside the island's perimeter, or to take satisfying photographs. Ask for the daily flight schedule, subtract 5 minutes for landing and changing passengers, and draw your own conclusions. In this area, in our opinion, economy is not always the best policy. Operating costs for helicopters are high;

companies may try to speed up tours to squeeze as many into the day as possible. Cheaper tours will almost certainly be short, possibly too short, and the extra dollars you spend for a longer tour will be well spent.

Aircraft and window configuration: Seating depends on balancing the passenger weight load for safety. The air-conditioned, 6-passenger ASTAR seats 2 passengers next to the pilot in front and 4 passengers in the rear. For passengers in the center rear seats, the view can be obstructed by passengers seated next to the windows as well as those in front. The new oversized windows are essential. Since windows are sealed, wearing darker colored shirts will cause less reflection in the glass and give you better photographs.

The Hughes 500-D helicopter seats two passengers in the rear and two in front next to the pilot, with a narrow middle seat. *Jack Harter Helicopters* offers a 'doors off' option on its Hughes to put passengers even closer to the scenery. The FAA has no objection, but it's not for everyone. Some will like the unique experience of being almost inside the landscape; and some, like photographers, will appreciate the absence of windshield glass for capturing the light and the vivid colors. Others may not enjoy being so close to the weather, when clouds, and the moisture they carry, can drift inside.

Cancellation policy in case of bad weather: When rain and clouds sock in the interior mountains, tours often simply go around the island's perimeter, and you miss all that gorgeous interior scenery. Even in a rainstorm, we often see choppers flying. You will want a refund if you can't see very much – once you're in the air. (*Jack Harter Helicopters* will cancel and try to reschedule your flight if visibility is below par.)

We consider helicopter tours a unique and special way to see Kauai. We wouldn't go ourselves, or let our children fly, if we thought they were

The Kalalau trail from Keʻe Beach to Hanakapiʻai winds along the rugged Na Pali coastline, through dense vegetation, along switchbacks and over rocks, sometimes only inches away from a sheer drop. Views are incredible! Mud from the frequent rain showers can create slippery conditions, so good footgear is a must.

unsafe. But we make careful decisions about the pilots we fly with. We think you should do your homework carefully and have all pertinent information when making your choices as well.

Hiking

Hiking can be a spectacular way to see Kauai, for more than half of the island's 551,000 square miles is forestland, and many of its most beautiful regions are inaccessible by car. However, hiking Kauai can also be dangerous. Many trails can become treacherous from washouts and mudslides, and in the Na Pali coastal region, where trails are often etched into the sides of sheer cliffs, hikers must be wary of waves crashing over the rocks without warning, as well as vegetation which masks the edge of a sheer drop.

Stick to clearly marked trails, heed posted warnings, and avoid getting too close to any cliffedge – even those overlooking beautiful waterfalls or spectacular coastlines. In December 2006, two young visitors fell to their deaths on an 'off the beaten path' trail, leading, so they thought, to a waterfall. Hiring an experienced guide may be a wise idea.

Careful planning is a must. For maps, directions, and detailed trail information, start with *www.hawaii.gov/dlnr* and *www.hawaiitrails.com.* Order a paper recreational map of hiking trails in the forest preserves (scale 1:50,000) from *Na Ala Hele*, a non-profit helping with trail improvement, by sending $6 (cashier's check or money order please) to *Division of Forestry*, Kauai District, 3060 Eiwa St, Room 306, Lihue, HI 96766 808.274.3433), or pick it up at the office. For specific questions about the Na Pali region, contact 808.274.3446. For maps of Kauai's geological, archeological, and topographical profiles, visit *www.teok.com.* Review Bob Smith's *Hiking Kauai*, the original guidebook to hikes on Kauai, Kathy Morey's *Kauai Trails*, or *Kauai Trailblazer* by Jerry and Janine Sprout. Request a catalog of books and maps for hiking and camping on Kauai from *Hawaii Geographic Society*, PO Box 1698, Honolulu, HI 96806.

Kauai's most famous trail, the *Kalalau trail,* is a spectacular but strenuous 11-mile hike through the Na Pali cliff region, though even recreational hikers can enjoy the first few miles. This subsection, the *Hanakapi'ai trail*, has breathtaking views of the coast along switchbacks which take you into forest and back out to the ocean. About a quarter-mile of uphill walking brings you to a magnificent view of Ke'e Beach and the Ha'ena reefs. Two more miles of rigorous up and down hiking will bring you to Hanakapi'ai Beach, nestled in a picturesque, terraced valley. Unfortunately, this beach has currents far too dangerous for swimming; rip currents can be so powerful that more than one unwary hiker standing in the surf at knee level has been swept up in a sudden, large wave, pulled out to sea and drowned. On a recent hike, we helped some folks stranded on the sand bar

The Kalalau Trail into the Na Pali wilderness begins where paved road ends, at Ke'e Beach on the north shore.

Reward: The view after climbing the first quarter-mile.

by high surf; fortunately we had a rope and a tall, strong friend, otherwise they would have been in trouble. Beyond the beach, you can take the trail to Hanakapi'ai Falls. It's very strenuous; the path crosses the river in several places and at times you may have to hold onto trees to keep your balance on rocky, wet footing. Allow 6 hours for the round trip from Ke'e Beach to Hanakapi'ai Falls, with a rest stop for a picnic. Carry plenty of water and fill up your bottles at Ke'e Beach, the last source of safe drinking water. For detailed trail info: *www.hawaii.gov/dlnr* or *www.kauaiexplorer.com*

Important safety information: When it rains, this narrow trail gets muddy – and dangerously slippery, a fact we appreciated when we saw a woman slip over the steep edge and disappear down into the slick vegetation. Fortunately, her quick-thinking companion had managed to grab her hand so that we could pull her back up. In many places, the trail is actually a stream bed and fills with water after heavy rains. Essential items: shoes with good traction for slippery rocks and mud (instead of jogging shoes or slippers), sunscreen, water, strong insect repellent, a hat, perhaps a nylon poncho, and a walking stick (perhaps a telescoping stick that can double as a monopod: *www.rei.com)*. For an update on trail conditions in Na Pali, contact *Pedal & Paddle*: 808.826.9069 *www.pedalnpaddle.com* in Hanalei or *Kayak Kauai:* 808.826.9844 *www.kayakkauai.com* which offers guided hikes of the Kalalau Trail. Helpful trail info: *www.kauaiexplorer.com.*

EASTSIDE: In Wailua, we like the *Mount Nounou Trail* on Sleeping Giant Mountain. This semi-strenuous 1.75-mile hike takes you to the Ali'i Vista Hale picnic shelter on the 'chest' of the Sleeping Giant. From this vantage point, you can see the inland mountains to Mount Wai'ale'ale and the Wailua River winding to the sea. The trail head is on Halelilo Rd in Wailua. From Kuhio Hwy (Route 56), take Halelilo Rd for 2 miles and park on the right near telephone pole #38. After a moderate ascent over switch-backs, about an hour or less, with some climbing over boulders, through dense guava and eucalyptus, you'll come to a junction marked by multiple-rooted hala trees. The trail to the left leads to another fork, and either of these paths will lead to the shelter. Avoid trails leading south towards the giant's 'head' which are hazardous.

WESTSIDE: The *Koke'e Forest* region has a different kind of beauty. Within this 4,345 acre wilderness preserve are 45 miles of trails, from pleasant walks to rugged hikes, as well as fresh water fishing streams, and the 20 square mile highland bog known as Alaka'i Swamp. From Koke'e Lodge, day hikers can choose from three trails which explore the plateau

Hanakapi'ai Beach – beautiful but hazardous in anything other than truly flat calm conditions as in this photo. At any time, however, sudden strong waves can crash across the sandbar and pull swimmers out to sea.

and Waimea Canyon rim, ranging from the half-mile 'Black Pipe Trail' to the 1.5 mile 'Canyon Trail' along the north rim of Waimea Canyon, past upper Wa'ipo'o Falls to the Kumuwela Overlook. From this perch you can see the canyon's 3,600-foot depth and 10 mile stretch to the sea. Contact *Koke'e Museum:* 808.335.9975 *www.kokee.org* for guides, maps, brochures, and reservations for guided Sunday walks (summer). Sign up for an e-newsletter that brings Koke'e news to you all year long. For hunting and fishing licenses contact *Koke'e Lodge* at 808.335.6061.

Hiking tours: The *Sierra Club* sponsors hikes on Kauai each month. Popular destinations: the Kalalau Trail to Hanakapi'ai on the Na Pali; Sleeping Giant Mountain trails on the eastern shore; Shipwreck Beach to Maha'ulepu on the south shore; on the west, the first few miles along the coast beyond Polihale. Send a stamped, addressed envelope to PO Box 3412, Lihue, HI 96766 *www.hi.sierraclub.org/Kauai.*

Guides: An excellent local guide is *Jeffrey Courson*, a Kauai resident for more than 30 years, who knows more than most about remarkable places and how to reach them. Jeffrey is keen to share the spiritual as well as the physical dimension of hiking Kauai, emphasizing safety and conservation. For a custom itinerary, suggestions, rates: 808.639.9709; jcourson@mac. com; *www.consciousjourneys.com.*

Princeville Ranch Adventures offers an excellent group recreational hike through pastureland and along a secluded stream, with a picnic lunch at a hidden waterfall before the return trip (4 hrs/$79). Great views, peaceful quiet, and healthful lunch. A variation on the hiking trip includes a kayaking segment through one of Kauai's 'jungle' streams (4 hrs/$94) 808.826.7669; 888.955.7669 *www.adventureskauai.com.*

You can hike to spectacular *Kipu Falls* with *Outfitters Kauai* ($155), explore a hidden but previously inaccessible gem on private land, even soar over the treetops on a zipline: *www.outfitterskauai.com* 808.742.9667; 888.742.9887. Guides are knowledgeable; the group (up to 20) proceeds at a leisurely pace on foot and by kayak to the falls. *Kauai Nature Tours* features naturalist guides and hikes at all skill levels: 808.742.8305; 888.233.8365 *www.teok.com*. *Aloha Kauai Tours* explores the back country by 4x4 to hike into the 'blue hole' at the base of Mt. Wai'ale'ale (3 hrs/$75) 808.245.6400; 800.452.1113 *www.alohakauaitours.com*.

Horseback Riding

North shore scenery is breathtaking, but weather can be more uncertain than on the south, where the ride can be warmer and more dusty. A morning ride avoids the heat of the day. Take sunglasses and a hat which won't blow off. (Once you're on board, it's hard to climb down and chase it.)

EASTSIDE: *Esprit de Corps* in Kapa'a gives lessons and trail rides (you can canter on the advanced ride) in the lush Sleeping Giant Mountain area. Tour rates range from $130, including a 6-hour 'spiritual' meditation ride overlooking Mt Wai'ale'ale ($270). Owner Dale Rosenfeld enjoys working with children (she offers ponies) and visitors with disabilities: 808.822.4688 *www.kauaihorses.com* Map 1

NORTH SHORE: *Princeville Ranch Stables* offers rides across the ranch lands and towards the mountains – some including a hike to a waterfall for a picnic, another a 'Ride 'n Glide' zipline tour (tours from $145): 808.826.7699 *www.princevilleranch.com*. Closed Sundays. *Silver Falls Ranch* in Kilauea escorts groups along the beautiful Kalihiwai Ridge with lunch and swim at a waterfall. Tours from $95/1.5 hr: 808.828.6718 *www. silverfallsranch.com* Map 5

SOUTH SHORE: Near Maha'ulepu Beach, *CJM Stables* offers a 2-hr beach tour ($98) and a 3-hr picnic beach ride ($125) 808.742.6096 *www. cjmstables.com*. Closed Sundays. Tour guides are very friendly and provide historical information as well as photo-opportunities. Map 6

Ice Cream, Shave Ice, & Gelato

In addition to traditional flavors (pistachio or Belgian chocolate), newcomer *Papalani Gelato* features tropical treats (mango or papaya), local Kauai flavors (kulolo and macadamia nut), and chocolates made with Hawaiian grown chocolate. In Kiahuna Center, 2360 Kiahuna Plantation Rd; 808.742.CONE (2663) *www.papalanigelato.com*. *Paradise Ice Cream* in Kilauea has unique tropical flavors.

Walter Lappert's ice cream factory serves island flavors like 'Kauai pie' in Koloa town, Hanapepe, Wailua in Coconut Marketplace, and Princeville Center. *Coldstone Creamery* is now in Lihue's Kukui Grove Center and next to Safeway in Wailua. Hawaiian made *Meadow Gold* ice cream, available in

Foodland and Big Save Markets, makes our favorite version of Macadamia Nut. The more calorie conscious can try *Zack's Frozen Yogurt* in the Coconut Marketplace.

Shave Ice is a special island treat. EASTSIDE: *Halo Halo Shave Ice* next to *Hamura's Saimin* is one of the originals: 2956 Kress St, Lihue. *Ono Family Restaurant*, 4-1292 Kuhio Hwy, Kapa'a has a stand just outside.

NORTH SHORE: The *Wishing Well* (the trailer by Kayak Kauai in Hanalei) has some of the best flavors and textures. The owner is a local legend for establishing the first shave ice in Hanalei, and for her sometimes less-than-sweet attitude. The shop next to Bubba's is more conventional.

WESTSIDE: On the way to Waimea Canyon or Kekaha, stop at *JoJo's Anueanue Shave Ice* in Waimea. This is the new location for the original owner of the *JoJo's* store on Main Street (now under new management). It's a tiny room with barely enough space to turn around, located on a side street, next to Bucky's Liquor: 808.338.9964. Try all of JoJo's 60 flavors! and ask for macadamia nut ice cream on the bottom of your paper cone.

Internet & Cyber Cafés

They change all the time. Find free wireless in the food court in *Kukui Grove* and *Borders* (Lihue); *Waimea Cottages* (Waimea); *Small Town Coffee* (Kapa'a) where there's great coffee, pastries, old-fashioned friendliness, public Macs to download your images, burn CDs: 9am - 7pm (M-Sat) at 4-1495 Kuhio Hwy (Rt 56) Kapa'a: 808.821.1604. *Akamai Computers* rents PCs 9am-5:30pm M-F at 4-1286 Kuhio Hwy, Suite A, next to Ono Family Restaurant, Kapa'a: 808.823.0047. *Java Kai* in Lihue, Kapa'a, Koloa, and Hanalei has T-Mobile. In Hanalei, *Discount Activities Internet Portal* is at 5-5156 Kuhio Hwy, across from Kalypso's, 8am - 8pm daily: 808.826.9117.

Jewelry

Goldsmith's Kauai in the Kinipopo Shopping Village, Wailua, is a must stop for original designs crafted of gold, silver, precious gems, or lustrous pearls. Dana Romsdal and her award-winning designers create beautiful pieces like a *humu humu nuku nuku apu a'a*, or a butterfly fish, or a plumeria on a gold chain. Check photographs of their designs, or let them create something just for you. Seashell designs in gold are lovely, gem settings are exquisite, yet prices are reasonable. We worked with Dana to create a pearl birthday pendant, watching the design develop on its own page at *www. goldsmiths-kauai.com* 808.822.4653; 800.692.7166. In Kapa'a, *Jim Saylor* works with fine gems and can create a special setting for a loose gemstone, or help you select a design from his portfolio: 808.822.3591.

Ni'ihau shell leis can be found at *Kauai Gold* in Wailua's Coconut Marketplace. The *Kauai Museum Shop* offers certificates of authenticity and a guarantee of workmanship: 4428 Rice St, Lihue 808.245.6931 *www. kauaimuseum.org*. *Hawaiian Trading Post* at 3427 Koloa Rd, Lawai (Rt 50 and 560) has a large selection. Without certificates, prices are lower.

Kayaking

Exploring Kauai's rivers by kayak can be fun, but increasingly contro-versial as rivers become more crowded. The problem is most acute at the Wailua River, Hawaii's only navigable river, which offers various water sports. You may see powerboats zipping by the Smith's boat tour barges lumbering along in the middle, sending waves toward canoes and kayaks hugging the shore.

EASTSIDE: WAILUA RIVER: *Rainbow Kayaks* has an excellent trip upriver to the waterfall (about a mile) in two person kayaks ($96/adult). Knowledgeable guides describe local wildlife, history, and legends. After hiking another mile, you reach the waterfall for a swim and excellent picnic lunch. Since the trail can get muddy, shoes with some sort of sole are recommended

(not slippers). Tour guides will take family photos: 808.826.9983; 866.826.9983 *www.rainbowkayak.com*. *Outfitters Kauai* also offers a Wailua River tour and waterfall hike ($98 with lunch) 808.742.9667; 888.742.9887 *www.outfitterskauai.com*. Both *Outfitters* and *Kauai Water Ski & Surf Company* will rent kayaks ($40/day/double) 808.822.3574.

SOUTHSHORE: HULE'IA RIVER, where *Raiders of the Lost Ark* was filmed. *Island Adventures* has a one-way guided paddle through the Hule'ia National Wildlife Refuge and Hawaii State Conservation District to the Alakoko or 'Menehune' Fish Pond, made, according to legend, by the 'Menehune,' Kauai's magical 'little people.' After a short hike, where you

After all the paddling, the waterfall!

observe birds, waterfowl, and exotic plants, you reach Papakolea Falls for a swim and picnic before a van ride to your car ($89): 808.246.6333 *www. kauaifun.com*

Hule'ia River tours ($98) are also offered by *Outfitters Kauai*. They can take you to *Kipu Falls*, a beautiful spot on private land, by guided kayak tour (or a separate zipline tour, p 147) – the only safe and legal way to visit Kipu Falls. On the kayak tour, a group of up to 20 proceeds at a leisurely pace on a two-mile paddle upriver, then a hike along trails (often muddy) and a 275-ft zipline ride. After a brief wagon tour of Kipu Ranch and lunch, you spend an hour at Kipu falls for swimming and trying out the 25-ft rope swing ($178). It's great for recreational hikers and kayakers who want to enjoy inaccessible places, but not those who like to push ahead: 808.742.9667; 888.742.9887 *www.outfitterskauai.com*

NORTH SHORE: *Princeville Ranch Adventures* offers a wonderful hike (45 min) combined with kayaking on a secluded stream (1/2 hour) and a picnic lunch at a hidden waterfall before the return trip (4 hours total). Great views, peaceful scenery, and healthful lunch: 808.826.7669; 888.955.7669 *www.adventureskauai.com*. *Kayak Kauai* offers tours and rents 2-person and 1-person kayaks (2-hour minimum). Travel upriver, or venture downriver to Hanalei Bay. In summer, when Hanalei Bay is calm, you can paddle along the bay's edge and pull up on the St Regis Hotel's beach: 808.826.9844; 800.437.3507 *www.kayakkauai.com*. Rent also from *Pedal & Paddle*: 808.826.9069 *www.pedalnpaddle.com*.

Sea Kayaking: Sea kayaking in the right conditions can take you into sea caves and up close to marine life. Strong currents and sudden weather, however, can get novice renters into trouble, and folks have to be rescued each year. A guided tour is a wise idea. *Kayak Kauai* offers a day-long kayak excursion between Ha'ena and Polihale State Beach on the westside. Views are spectacular, but be forewarned: be ready for a strenuous six hours of hard paddling, and sudden squalls and choppy water may punctuate the ride ($206) 808.826.9844 *www.kayakkauai.com*. When Na Pali waters become too rough (October through April), whale-watching tours go along the south shore to Kipu Kai ($148). Poipu-based *Outfitters Kauai* also offers guided sea kayak tours along Na Pali (summer: $225) and the south shore (winter: $145) 808.742.9667; 888.742.9887 *www.outfitterskauai.com.*

Tips: If you are taking a tour, review the cancellation policy carefully, or you may wind up being charged if you change your mind. Remember the sun. A hat, sunscreen, and drinking water are a must. Bring a towel and spare shirt. Everything in the kayak can get wet, so protect your camera in a waterproof bag. We are often asked about the other kind of tips; if you are so inclined, about $5/pp would be really appreciated by your local guides.

Rentals: Go early for the best selection and check the kayak before-hand for patches and leaks.

Great spots: In summer, rent in Hanalei and load the kayak onto your car and go to the boat pier, to Anini Beach, or Kalihiwai Bay (about 10 minutes). Eastside, rent at Kalapaki Bay or the Wailua River. When winter surf and currents are too strong, your best options will be the Hanalei, Wailua, or Kalihiwai Rivers. Remember: don't drink river water, and be cautious if you have any open cuts or wounds. The bacterium causing *leptospirosis* found in all of Kauai's rivers can cause serious, even fatal, flu-like symptoms. Seek medical help immediately if this happens to you.

Luaus

For centuries, Hawaiians have celebrated festive occasions with a luau feast, usually a whole pig roasted in an imu (underground oven), island fish, chicken cooked in coconut and taro, tropical fruits, and salads. Today you can see shows with (or in some cases) without the feast, and some shows are free. See *Music on Kauai* (p 128) and *Family Fun* (p 97). For info on shows check *www.kauaifestivals.com* and also *www.northshorekauai.com*

EASTSIDE In Wailua, a good value is *Smith's Tropical Paradise* with Asian/Polynesian dances, presented in a natural amphitheater ($65 with buffet or $15 just for the show) 808.821.6895 *www.smithskauai.com*

Smiths has re-started Wailua River Boat Tours up to *Fern Grotto* and back, with some musical entertainment (1.5 hrs). The grotto has been restored by the state although visitors can no longer go inside. *Kilohana Plantation* near Lihue has Tahitian, Maori, and Polynesian dances ($50 or $100 with buffet) 808.245.9593 *www.luaukalamaku.com.* Map 1

Major hotels offer luaus or musical shows. At the *St Regis Hotel,* dancers perform in the lounge (Fridays) or in a dinner show (Wednesdays) 808.826.9644. In Poipu, *The Grand Hyatt* Luau all Polynesian show is Sunday and Thursday 5:30pm ($94/$84/$57) 808.240.6546 *www.tihati.com.*

Massage, Kauai Style

For something truly special, try an unforgettable *Hawaiian lomi lomi* massage at *Mu'olaulani* in Anahola. This unique massage experience, developed by Aunty Angeline, begins in a wood-paneled steam room, with a 'sea salt scrub' to cleanse your skin in preparation for the amazingly soothing lomi lomi performed by a team of two with fragrant oils. Angeline, her family and staff consider lomi lomi sacred to the Hawaiian tradition of healing. This extraordinary, incredibly relaxing two-hour experience costs a reasonable $150. Since the steamer is shared, specify if you prefer being with your own gender (though steam makes a nice curtain). Mornings only. Closed weekends: 808.822.3235 *info@auntyangelines.com*.

A tranquil retreat facility, *Kahuna Valley* in the hills above Kapa'a offers massage, hot stone work, Watsu water-based therapy, and instruction in the Chinese healing experience of Qigong. Contact Daisy or Francesco:

Man in gourd mask by John Weber, artist with Captain Cook

808.822.4268 *www.kahunaval-ley.org*. At *Tri Health Ayurveda Spa* in Kilauea, try Samvahana, a traditional healing oil massage, with two therapists (from $130) 808.828.2104.

Day Spas: Spa Makaiwa in the Kauai Coast Resort, 520 Aleka Loop in Wailua offers wraps, facials, manicures, and massage, including a 'Hot Stone Raindrop Therapy': warm essential oils drip gently onto your back and are then massaged into the skin with smooth, hot rocks: 808.821.2626.

Private practitioners offer a reasonable price, flexible hours/locations. EASTSIDE: the exceptional *Bonnie Morris* in Anahola: 808.639.3459 and *Carol Launch* in Lihue: 808.245.7005. Local companies include *Waipouli Massage*:

808.821.0878 and *A Touch in Paradise:* 808.639.0389. *Aloha Day Spa* in Lihue near the Marriott: 808.246.2414 *www.touchofalohaspa.com.*

Resorts: In Poipu, at the *Hyatt's Anara Spa,* a massage (from $160) or even a pedicure allows you to use spa facilities, including lap pool, steam room, sauna, weight room: 808.240.6440 *www.anaraspa.com.* The new *St Regis Halele'a Spa* takes massage luxury to a new level, with steam, dry sauna, or deluxe 5 nozzle rain shower available before or after (from $165) 808.826.9644.

Museums & History Tours

The story of Kauai is in many ways the story of sugar—the plantations which shaped the island's multi-ethnic culture as much as its agriculture and economy. *Grove Farm Homestead* in Lihue offers a fascinating glimpse into the island's past. Grove Farm was founded in 1864 by George Wilcox, son of Protestant missionary teachers at Wai'oli Mission in Hanalei. Planting and harvesting Grove Farm's sugar crop, which grew from 80 acres to more than 1,000, ultimately involved hundreds of Hawaiian, Chinese, Korean, German, Portuguese, and Filipino laborers, who brought to Kauai a rich cultural heritage. A two-hour tour of Grove Farm's cluster of buildings, gardens, and orchards shows you the gracious Wilcox home, where large rooms are cooled by verandas and furnished with oriental carpets, magnificent koa wood floors and hand crafted furniture of native woods. You'll see the 'board and batten' cottage of the plantation housekeeper, who came to Kauai as a Japanese 'picture bride.' Buildings are covered by traditional 'beach sand paint' (sand thrown against wet paint) to protect them against both heat and damp for as long as 20 years. Grove Farm was established at a significant point in the island's history, the 1850's, when the monarchy began to sell land and Hawaii entered the age of private property. Before this time, land was not sold but given in trust to subjects in pie-shaped slices, from the interior mountains to the sea, so that each landhold would include precious fresh water as well as coastline.

The leisurely, friendly tour includes a stop in the kitchen for cookies and mint ice tea. The library's collection of Hawaiiana and plantation records is available by appointment. Tours: Mon, Wed, Thurs at 10am and 1pm. Reservations (in advance): PO Box 1631, Lihue HI 96766; 808.245.3202 *www.grovefarm.net.* Map 1

In Hanalei, make an appointment for a fascinating Wednesday morning tour of *Ho`opulapula Haraguchi Rice Mill,* the only rice mill left in Hawaii, including parts of the *Hanalei National Wildlife Refuge* off limits to most visitors. Built by Chinese laborers and purchased by the Haraguchi family in 1924, the mill closed in 1960 with the collapse of Kauai's rice industry and the introduction of taro. The 4th generation Haraguchi family offers tours of the mill and taro fields sheltering many endangered species of birds. The tour begins with a taro smoothie, adds a snack of hand pounded taro and freshly grated coconut, and ends with lunch (family taro recipes such as chicken lau lau, macaroni and taro salad, and coconut taro mochi). Profits help education, restoration. Tours Wednesday mornings by reservation: 808.651.3399 *www.haraguchiricemill.org* Map 5

Also in Hanalei, visit the 1837 missionary home and grounds, *Wai'oli Mission House*. Tours: T, Th, Sat 9am - 3pm; 808.245.3202. Map 5

If these tours don't fit into your schedule, visit the *Kauai Museum* on Rice St in Lihue. The Rice Building exhibits the *Story of Kauai* – the volcanic eruptions which shaped the land; the Polynesians who voyaged to the island in canoes and left behind marvelous petroglyphs; the missionaries who altered its culture; and the sugar planters who defined much of its agricultural destiny. The adjacent Wilcox building features local artists and rotating exhibits (e.g. 'Year of the Tiger,' or Japanese, Chinese, Hawaiian, and Filipino wedding dress and traditions). The museum shop sells books, maps, crafts (free admission to shop). You can ask for a free pass for the next day if you run out of time. Mon - Sat 10am - 5pm. Families free the first Saturday of the month: 808.245.6931 *www.kauaimuseum.org*.

History buffs will enjoy online history of Kapa'a at *kauaihistoricalsociety.org*. For a catalog of books on Hawaii as well as hard-to-find Hawaiian authors, check Basically Books: 808.961.0144 *www.basicallybooks.com*.

Movie Tours

Kauai Movie Tours guided van tour of the island's movie locations is, at press time, no longer offering tours (though you can always call for an update (800-628-843). *Kipu Ranch Adventures* offers a 4-hour 'waterfall tour' by ATV that includes the spectacular settings in the Kipu area of the south side. So while you won't see the north shore's gorgeous *South Pacific* Bali Hai mountain settings, you will scout the forest and river locations of *Raiders of the Lost Ark, Outbreak, Six Days & Seven Nights, Mighty Joe Young, Hook, Jurassic Park, Pirates of the Caribbean 4; The Descendants*, and other box office hits. Tour includes two waterfall stops and picnic lunch. ($156/driver adult and $125/passenger adult). Single rider vehicles and also up to 4 passenger vehicles for families (children 5 - 15 yrs). You roll through streams, into the forest, over rocks, following the Hule'ia River where Indiana Jones took off in his seaplane: 808.246.9288 *www.kiputours.com*.

Music

Hawaiian music has a contemporary sound, thanks to Keali'i Reichel's wonderful original compositions in the Hawaiian language. Keali'i's first album, *Kawaipunahele*, exploded onto the music scene in 1994 and has become the bestselling album of Hawaiian music, earning a gold record in 2007, the first gold for a Hawaiian language album. *Lei Hali'a, E O Mai,* and *Melelana* should be in your rental car's CD changer, at home too. *Ke'alaokamaile* ('The Scent of Maile') is a beautiful tribute to family, especially his grandmother. The Keali'i Reichel Collection, *Kamahiwa* (a CD of music and one of chants) is a must-have, and his Christmas album, *Kamahiwa,* is a delight (p 240): *www.kealiireichel.com.*

Keali'i Reichel
Ke'alaokamaile

The classics include the Brothers Cazimero (*Hawaiian Paradise* and *The Best*), The Makaha Sons of Ni'ihau, whose album *Na Pua o Hawai'i* features some of Hawaii's singing greats like Robert Cazimero, Cyril Pahinui, and Dennis Pavao. Also listen to Israel Kamakawiwo'ole's albums *E Ale E*, and *Facing Forward*, and Hapa's *Namahana* and *Collection.* Slack key guitar music brings you haunting melodies. Listen to Keola Beamer's album, *Island Born*, featuring his original music and lyrics. *Great Grandmother-Great Grandson* is Kapono Beamer's instrumental tribute to the songs of Helen Desha Beamer. Don't miss *Makana*, an up and coming star, and *Hahani Mai* by female vocalist and songwriter, Kekuhi Kanehele. On the re-release of Gaby Pahinui's 1972 album, *Gaby*, this legendary performer sings with his 4 talented sons; the first track is his original 1947 recording of 'Aloha 'Oe.'

Find the newest releases, sample tracks, links to musicians' home pages, on *www.mele.com* and *www.hawaii-music.com.* Listen to Hawaiian music radio at home while you surf: *www.alohajoe.com.*

Musicians of Kauai

Kauai's own Norman Ka'awa Solomon has recorded what is becoming the island's 'signature' album, *Na Mele O Kauai*, a unique collection of favorite Kauai songs that is a real must for your rental car. Norman devotes the profits to help children on Kauai. His earlier album, *Aloha Ke Kahi,* has wonderful original compositions including one of our favorites, 'Kalapaki.' 808.651.8386 *kaawa_music@hotmail.com.*

For more than twenty years, *Doug & Sandy McMaster* have delighted audiences with traditional slack key guitar music. Each evening they serenade sunset at Hanalei Pavilion Beach Park and on Fridays at Hanalei Community Center from 4-8pm ($20). On cold winter evenings, their hauntingly beautiful music will call you right back to Hanalei; order CDs *Hanalei Sunset, Kauai Homecoming,* and *In A Land Called Hanalei* with a slack key 'Puff the Magic Dragon' at *www.hanaleisunsets.com* and enjoy slide shows of Hanalei sunsets. *Pacific Tunings* by the Kauai group Na Pali collects the group's vocal numbers, accompanied by steel guitar, acoustic bass, and ukulele. Find CDs at Borders (you can listen before you buy) or *Paradise Music* at Coconut Marketplace, Koloa Big Save, and Princeville Center *www.hawaiianparadisemusic. com.* On Kauai, KKCR (91.9), north shore public radio, plays Hawaiian music (listen at home on *www. hawaii-music.com).* KSRF (95.9) features local musician DJs. For show calendar, check with *www.northshorekauai.com.*

Natural History Tours

Halfway between Kapa'a and Princeville, the *Kilauea Lighthouse*, built in 1913, once warned mariners away from Kauai's rugged north coast until technology replaced light flashes with radio transmissions. Come for spectacular views of the coastline and Mukuae'ae island, and if you're lucky, a glimpse of spinner dolphins or humpback whales on winter vacation in the waves. This is the northernmost point of Kauai, indeed of all the Hawaiian islands, and changes in weather are often first detected by the weather station here. Best of all, you will see a tiny part of the *Hawaiian Island National Wildlife Refuge*, which shelters more than 10 million seabirds in a chain of islands scattered over 1200 miles of ocean. One amazing story: 4 tons of French prisms were carried up a sheer cliff for the giant clam shaped light (10am - 4pm daily except federal holidays) 808.828.1413 *www.kilauealighthouse.org*.

More of Kauai's rare birds and plants can be seen at the *Koke'e Natural History Museum* in *Koke'e State Park* (10am - 4pm daily) 808.335.9975 *www.kokee.org*. Donations welcome. Interested in birds? Go to *www. kauaibirds.com* for photos and facts. Arrange tours near Koke'e with *Kauai Nature Tours*: 808.742.8305; 888.233.8365 *www.teok.com*.

Tour *Ho`opulapula Haraguchi Rice Mill*, the only rice mill left in Hawaii, and visit parts of the *Hanalei National Wildlife Refuge* off limits to most visitors. See many endangered species of birds and sample taro treats. Reservations: 808.651.3399 *www.haraguchiricemill.org*. Map 5

Night Life

Check *www.kauaifestivals.com* or *www.northshorekauai.com*.

* EASTSIDE: *Rob's Good Times Grill* 808.246.0311; *Caffé Cocco* 808.822.7990; *Duke's Barefoot Bar* 808.246.9599; *Kauai Beach Resort* 808.254.1955; *Oasis* 808.822.9332; *The Eastside* 808.823.9500; *Wahooo* 808.822.7833; *Kauai Pasta* 808.822.7447

* NORTH SHORE: *Tahiti Nui* 808.826.6277 (a great local experience); *Hanalei Gourmet* 808.826.2524; *Bouchon's* 808.826.9701; *St Regis* 808.826.9644. *Mediterranean Gourmet* 808.826.9875. *Hanalei Bay Resort* 808.826.6522

* SOUTHSHORE: *Keoki's* 808.742.7534; *The Point* (Sheraton) 808.742.1661; *Seaview Terrace & Stevenson's Library* (Hyatt) 808.742.1234; *Joe's on the Green* 808.742.9696; *Casablanca* 808.742.2929

* WESTSIDE: *Kalaheo Steak & Ribs* 808.332.4444

Photographing Kauai

* *Shoot in early morning or late afternoon light*. Strong sunlight can wash out colors and shadow your subjects' faces. Light is best coming from the side rather than over the photographer's shoulder.

* *Vary your composition*. Combine something in the foreground, like a palm tree, with the middle-ground and background. Try vertical shots, great for people and flowers; a vertical composition of sky, ocean, surf and sand can look like a "slice of Kauai."

* *Horizons should be level* or the sea might look like it is 'dumping water.' Placing the horizon across the middle of the picture cuts it in half. A higher horizon emphasizes the foreground; a lower one is a better 'sky shot' for great sunsets or cloud scenes.

* *A polarizing filter can enhance color*, darken sky to whiten clouds, but it slows your shutter speed. Brace the camera (on tree, building, friend).

* *Protect your camera* from salt and sand with a lens cap or lens filter, zipper case, even zip lock bag. Download images/burn CDs: *Small Town Coffee* 4-1495 Kuhio Hwy, Kapa'a.

* *Move in close for people pictures*; fill the frame with the person. To better show the location, place the person towards one side. Don't let a palm tree appear to be growing out of your subject's head.

* *Great spots for great shots*: Sunsets & rainbows from St Regis terrace; Na Pali cliffs from Ke'e Beach (or first mile of Kalalau trail); Allerton Gardens, Kukuiolono Park plumerias, Limahuli Gardens, Na Aina Kai; farmer's markets; sunrise at Lydgate Park; sunset menehune fish pond.

Photo Tours

A 5-hour photography and sightseeing tour with *Kauai Photo Tours* is a great way to explore beautiful secluded places, benefit from professional camera advice (no matter your level of expertise), make the best use of your island time. Choose an EZ Tour (drive and stroll); a Drive and Light Hiking Tour; or let Vince Tylor design a private tour of favorite places only a resident photographer knows about. You can rent equipment and see the gallery of his beautiful images: 808.823.1263 *www.hawaiianphotos.net.*

Vince's wife Michele Tylor leads an Art-for-a-Day Tour for painters (equipment provided).

Scuba

You can dive Kauai's reefs and play with sea turtles on the south shore near Poipu or, weather permitting, on the north shore near the Ha'ena reefs. More than a dozen companies offer introductory and refresher lessons, 3-5 day PADI certification, shore and boat dives, full or half-day charters, as well as free introductory pool lessons.

Contact Gregg Winston at *Watersports Adventures* for professional, careful, yet friendly scuba instruction, PADI certification, even refresher classes for 'rusty' divers. He has a perfect safety record, and reserved parking at Tunnels Beach. The company specializes in educational 'naturalist' dives, and night dives (even night snorkeling) when the sea lights up in colors, the coral comes alive, and you can see glowing fish and eels, turtles hunting for a place to rest: 808.821.1599 *www.watersportsadventures.ws.*

Never tried diving? Gregg will make it special. In a free introductory lesson, you learn about diving equipment and safety and have a chance to practice with the gear in a swimming pool. Your first real dive ($105) will probably be at sheltered Koloa Landing (winter) or Tunnels (summer). Gregg is terrific with beginners. If you feel nervous, he may ask you to swim next to him and hold onto his arm. Gregg is a very strong swimmer, so when you swim next to him,

holding on to his arm, you actually cover a lot of territory. You are soon absorbed in the amazing sights – magnificent arrays of red and green coral, schools of silver or brilliant yellow fish swimming in geometric precision. You may see a ray gliding along in the shimmering water, possibly an eel hiding in the rocks, maybe even an octopus. Before you know it, you are swimming along quietly and comfortably, relaxed on your adventure. Gregg makes sure you have a good time and develop confidence.

Certified divers appreciate Gregg's extensive knowledge, careful planning, well-maintained equipment ($85/one tank and $135/two).

Seasport Divers in Poipu offers boat dives along Kauai's south shore as well as off Ni'ihau. The two-storey dive boat is spacious, the largest on the island, with 2 hot water showers, perfect after the chill of a 90 foot dive. Dive masters are friendly, extremely knowledgeable about Kauai's reefs, and very resourceful (2 wetsuits may help with cold ocean temperatures). In winter months, the captain may take passengers whale watching during the

surface interval. Excellent equipment includes computers to gauge depth and bottom time: 808.742.9303; 800.685.5889 *www. seasportdivers.com.*

Among the other companies, the longest established on Kauai, *Ocean Odyssey* in Lihue: 808.245.8681 offers lessons, shore and boat dives, certification classes. EASTSIDE: *Dive Kauai* in Kapaʻa: 808.822.0452; 800.828.3483 *www.divekauai.com. Nitrox Tropical Dives:* 808.245.NX5-DIVE; *SeaFun Kauai* in Lihue: 808.245.6400; 800.452.1113. NORTH SHORE: *North Shore Divers:* 808.828.1223.

SOUTH SHORE: *Fathom Five Divers* in Poipu offers classes in a new fully loaded multi-media classroom, certification, boat dives, night dives and trips to Niʼihau: 808.742.6991; 800.972.3078 *www.fathomfive.com.* To see fish without carrying scuba gear, *Snuba of Kauai* offers tours with your air source attached on a flotation raft: 808.823.8912 *www.snubakauai.com.*

The best diving in all of the Hawaiian islands can be found off Niʻihau, the privately owned, largely undeveloped island preserved by the Robinson family as a place for Hawaiian people and culture. It's a unique opportunity to explore untouched reefs. Surf is often too rough in winter months, however. *Seasport Divers* does an incredible all-day boat dive to Niʻihau for experienced divers ($265/3 tanks): 808.742.9303; 800.685.5889 *www.seasportdivers.com.*

Snorkeling

On the south shore, *Poipu Beach Park* offers excellent and relatively safe snorkeling most of the year. Just west of the rocky point dividing the park from the new Marriott (old Waiohai), you can find yellow tang, striped manini fish, butterfly fish, parrot fish, and silvery needle fish feeding on the coral. More than once, we have met a spotted box fish (Lauren has nick-named him 'Fred') curious enough to swim right up to our masks. Be extremely careful of the current at the edge of the reef, which can pull you out and has caused drownings (see *Ocean Safety* p 80). Stay well inside the reef.

Fred

Our family also enjoys *Tunnels* on the north shore, so named (in part) for the intricate 'tunnels' along the edge of the reef where the water seems to plunge to unfathomable depths (Lifeguard). In summer, we like *Keʻe Beach*, where we find *humu humu nuku nuku apu aʻa*, Hawaii's state fish. At all seasons, *Lydgate Park* has friendly schools of fish in its huge, sandy bottomed, rock-rimmed pool (*Lifeguard*).

Plan snorkeling with an eye to the tides, the weather, and the season. North shore is best in summer, when the ocean is relatively calm – even pancake flat. In winter, when surf is up on the north, Poipu Beach Park and Lydgate Park will probably have calmer water.

If you are not at a beach with a lifeguard, snorkel where others are snorkeling so you can get help if you need it – avoid deserted beaches. Try not to lose track of where you are in the water, and stay dry if the surf looks rough or a rippling wave pattern indicates strong current.

Feeding the fish can be fun, but packaged snorkel fish food is not really necessary and can cause a problem when the plastic film casing begins to disintegrate in the water. Instead, bring something to stimulate the fish's curiosity. Try a green leaf or piece of seaweed – it attracts the curious, rather than the ravenous, fish. Tuck a leaf ot two securely into your suit, then once you are in the ocean, swirl the leaf around as a 'visual display.' You'll be amazed at the interest it creates.

Tours: *SeaFun Kauai* at 808.245.6400 and *Watersports Adventures* at 808.821.1599 offer shore-based snorkeling tours, where shallower water shows you a different kind of sea life than the deep waters you may find on a boat tour off Na Pali. *Watersports* emphasizes education and reef restoration. Some boat tour compa- nies can take you to Niʻihau, whose age and remote- ness create unique

opportunities for exploring (*Boat Tours*, p 86).

A well-fitting mask is important. To test the fit, place the mask on your face (without using the straps) and breathe in; a well-fitting mask will stay on by itself. Pack your own mask if you can. A dilute solution of detergent and water – even spit – coats the lens to avoid fogging. Gregg Winston's tip: find a Naupaka leaf, crush it and rub it into the mask, then rinse. Or try toothpaste, even baby shampoo, then rinse. The Pentax Optio W80 is waterproof to 5 meters and even takes underwater HD movies.

Coral cuts can be dreadful. Keep bandaids and antibiotic cream in your bag and avoid touching coral with any body part. Don't walk on it or try to pick it up. Even fins won't completely protect your feet.

Sport Fishing

Kauai's warm tropical waters offer great fishing for big and medium to light tackle game fish. No fishing license is required, and you can depart from ports all over the island, depending on surf and season. The north shore is beautiful, though too rough during winter months. From Port Allen on the west side, you have the advantage of being close to the spectacular Na Pali coastline and its amazing cliffs – fishing with a view.

Most companies equip their boats with sonar, and help to pair you up with other anglers to share the cost. Expect to pay upwards of $100 for a half-day shared rate, or as much as $875 for an all-day exclusive.

EASTSIDE: Kapaʻa: *Hawaiian Style Fishing*, owned by a seasoned commercial fisherman, takes only 4 passengers on a 25-ft Kauai-built Radon, emphasizing reasonable prices and personal attention. People have a great time, and the catch is shared generously ($182/8 hrs or $125/4 hrs as well as charters) 635.7808.335.

Renting Snorkel Gear

$5/day or $15/week for a good quality mask, fins, snorkel.
$8/day for a body board (be safe; rent fins too). $25/day surfboard.

Lihue

Kalapaki Beach Boys at the Kauai Marriott	808.246.9661

Wailua

Kauai Water Ski & Surf	808.822.3574
Kayak Kauai, Coconut Plantation Marketplace	808.822.9179

Hanalei

Pedal & Paddle	808.826.9096
Snorkel Depot	808.826.9983

Poipu

Nukomoi Surf Co.	808.742.7019
Snorkel Bob's	808.742.8322

Snorkel Tours

SeaFun Kauai	808.245.1113 800.452.1113	www.alohakauaitours.com
Kauai Snorkel Tours	808.742.7576	www.kauaisnorkeltours.com
Watersports Adventures	808.821.1599	www.watersportsadventures.ws

Hana Pa'a Sport Fishing Charters offers a larger craft, a 38-ft Bertram with fly bridge, full tuna tower, main cabin, 2 bunk rooms, and full head. Fish are filleted and shared on 4, 6, and 8 hr private and split charters: 808.823.6031; 866.PRO-FISH *www.fishkauai.com.*

True Blue Charters operates the 42-ft trimaran, 'Rainbow Runner,' for fishing and snorkeling charters, or touring Kipu Kai, specializing in smaller groups and shorter tours: 808.246.6333 *www.kauaifun.com. Captain Don's Charters* offers charters and/or Na Pali cruises: 808.639.3012 *www.captaindonsfishing.com.*

NORTH SHORE: *Anini Charters:* 808.828.1285 *www.kauaifishing.com* departs from Anini Beach; Captain 'Honeybear' Bob shares the catch. Also try *Kai Bear Sportfishing*: 808.652.4556.

WESTSIDE: *Kauai Fun Tours* represents 5 small companies: 808.335.5555 *www.kauaifuntours.com*. Also try *Open Sea Charter:* 808.332.8213; 877.332.8213. Captain Scott Akana of *La hala Ocean Adventures* is considered one of the best on the island ($219/4hrs; spectators 1/2 price) 808.635.4020 *www.sport-fishing-kauai.com*. Captain Harry Shigekane has 30 yrs experience with *Happy Hunter Sport Fishing* ($625/6 people/4 hrs) 808.639.4351 *www.happyhuntersportfishing.com*.

Sunset Watching & Sunset Drive to Hanalei

Watch spectacular sunsets from the lanai at the *St Regis Hotel* (better in summer when the sun sets into the water on the north) and enjoy cocktails and music, or try *Beach House* on the south shore (better in winter when the sun sets into the water on south). Or go to the beach with a blanket, possibly beach chairs, CD player with headphones, a *Keali'i Reichel* CD, an ice chest with drinks and snacks. *Doug & Sandy McMaster* serenade sunset each evening with traditional slack key guitar music (at Hanalei Pavilion Beach Park) and Fridays (at Hanalei Community Center 4-8pm ($20).

If your accommodations are on the eastside, consider a drive north for sunset, which may occur earlier than you expect because Hawaii never changes to daylight savings time, so check the exact time before you head out. Hundreds of clouds, already tinged with peach and gold, float in an azure sky above a shimmering sea. Rt 56 winds along the coast, and the colors of land and sky change almost mile by mile as the declining sun deepens the greens and blues and touches everything with shades of pink and gold. At Kilauea, where the road curves to the west, a line of tall Norfolk pines stands starkly silhouetted against the blazing sky, and near Princeville, clouds luminous with reflected golds and pinks seem enormous, dwarfing cliffs whose great jagged peaks have turned an astonishing purple.

We never tire of this drive, as each sunset is different. The gleaming expanse of ocean, sharply angled mountains, and masses of clouds are blended each night by the sun's magic into a composition of colors that will never occur again in exactly the same way. A sunset in the rain is most amazing of all. Mountains are shrouded with grey, yet above the sea, the sky is brilliant with color, with sunny clouds stretching along the horizon, rimmed with pink. Dark showers move across the horizon like 'legs of the rain,' blurring the line between ocean and sky, reaching for the sun as it slowly descends, then disappears.

If the clouds are not too thick, you can enjoy the sunset less than a mile past the entrance to Princeville; park at a scenic overlook on Rt 560 and see most of Hanalei's western side. But you have to contend with traffic and car radios as well as conversations of other sunset seekers ("Rita! I *told* you we

Sunset in the rain near Bali Hai Restaurant

were going to miss it!"). For a more panoramic view, with greater privacy, enter Princeville and follow the signs to Pali Ke Kua, park in the lot, and enjoy the view discreetly from the lawn between the buildings.

The drive home after dinner is another sensuous experience of cool evening breezes you can almost taste as well as feel. As you drive south, you can hear wonderful sounds – the chirping of crickets, the leaves rustling in the breeze – and see the different shades of darkness in the landscape, lit by the moon against an enormous star-filled sky and the shimmering waves of the wide ocean beyond.

Surfing

Surfing, like everything on Kauai, depends on the tides, the winds, and the season. In winter, the ground swell is mostly on the north and west shores, and experienced surfers look for surf on the north from Kilauea to

Ha'ena, and on the westside from Kekaha to Polihale. In the summer, the surf is 'up' on the south shore, and experienced surfers look to the south from Kalapaki Bay to Poipu. The eastside picks up tradewind swell year round. At any season, and no matter your skill level, be careful: wave pattern varies at each beach, and some spots are safer than others. Hawaiian swells rise more quickly than mainland swells, and Hawaiian waves are more powerful. Avoid going out alone, respect local surfers, and as always: **When in doubt, do not go out.** Channel 15 on local cable TV recycles National Weather Service buoy readings on water, surf and wind conditions. Check *www.hanaleisurf.com* or *www.kauaiexplorer.com* for surf info and links.

Lessons: Surfing pro Charlie Smith offers lessons island-wide. He will drive you to wherever he thinks he'll find the island's best surf, and his personalized 1.5 hr lessons can expand to family picnics and snorkeling. Experienced surfers can learn the island; he knows the best breaks, has high performance boards: 808.634.6979 *www.blueseassurfingschool.com*. At *Learn to Surf*, Nephi Kalani Quereto has a friendly, supportive manner, and with a limit of just 3 students per instructor, he offers a great rate ($45). He also gives private lessons and can take you all over the island. His guarantee is: stand up or lesson is free: 808.826.7612 *www.learntosurfkauaihi.com*.

SOUTH SHORE: Next to the Sheraton Poipu, surf conditions are usually relatively safe, with waves less than four feet and winds moderate. With *Aloha Surf Lessons*, run by Kauai-born surfing pro Chava Greenle and his father Danny, his first teacher, a first-rate lesson combines one hour of personalized instruction followed by one hour of surfing on your own. One instructor works with up to six students. Skilled and supportive, Chava and Danny make sure everyone gets 'up,' and they love making that happen

Lupe & Gaby Godinez

Hanalei Bay near lifeguard station

Sharing the wave at Kalihiwai

($75; also private lessons) 808.639.8614; email *soongalohasurf@aol.com*. Also in Poipu, *Margo Oberg*, 7-time world title winner, has a school for all skill levels, 6 students per instructor ($75/1.5 hr, as well as private lessons) 808.332.6100 *www.surfonkauai.com*.

NORTH SHORE: Hanalei Pier is the best spot for beginners, with several companies for lessons and rentals. *Titus Kinimaka* has walk-up lessons at Hanalei Pier and by appointment: 808.652.1116 *www.hawaiianschoolofsurfing.com*. *Celeste Harvel* teaches surfing and windsurfing: 808.828.6838. *Brando Wattson* teaches surfing and kitesurfing: 808.639.WAVE *surf.www.kauaistyle.com*. Elite coach Russell Lewis offers advanced coaching (he's coached Bethany Hamilton): 808.346.5710.

EASTSIDE: *Kayak Kauai:* 808.826.9844 *www.kayakkauai.com*.

Rentals: (about $25/day): EASTSIDE: *Tamba Surf Company* is the choice of local folks at 4-1543 Kuhio Hwy, Kapa'a: 808.823.6942. Also try *Kauai Beach Boys* in Lihue: 808.246.6333 and Poipu: 808.742.4442. NORTH SHORE: You can usually find rental boards at Hanalei pier. *Hanalei Surf Co*: 808.826.9000. *Kayak Kauai:* 808.826.9844. *Kai Kane*: 808.826.5594.

SOUTH SHORE: *Nukumoi* in Poipu: 808.742.8019 and Waimea: 808.338.1617 *www.nukumoisurf.com*. In Koloa, try *SeaSport Divers:* 808.742.9303, and *Progressive Expressions:* 808.742.6041, which also arranges surfing lessons with *Garden Island Surf School:* 808.652.4841.

Outrigger Canoeing: Hawaiian Surfing Adventures in Kilauea: 808.482.0749 *www.hawaiiansurfingadventures.com.*

Surfing: Body Boards and Body Surfing

When they were small, our kids loved to take their boogie boards to Poipu Beach Park. Then they grew up and craved the bigger waves. Family favorites are Hanalei (Lifeguard) and Kalihiwai on the north shore; and Kalapaki and Kealia (Lifeguard) on the east. Safety varies with surf conditions, and it's best to have a lifeguard (*Ocean Safety* p 80).

At Brennecke's Beach next to Poipu Beach Park, the famous wave pattern is forming again (after Hurricane Iniki washed the sand away in 1992). You can see dozens of kids ride the first break, then younger ones catch the wave as it re-forms closer in. Be careful of rocks by the seawall.

Skimboards: When surf is too flat (or too rough) for body boards, kids can catch long, exciting rides across the shallows at Kalihiwai and Hanalei (where the rivers flow into the ocean) and Kalapaki.

Surfing: Kite Surfing

Brando Wattson *Aloha Surf & Kiteboard School* offers private lessons: 808.639-WAVE; *www.surf.kauaistyle.com* as does *Akamai Kiteboarding School*, taught by Jeremy Fry: 808.821.1000 *www.trykauai.com*, and *Keith's Kiteboarding*: 808.635.4341. Best spots are off Tunnels Beach and Anini.

Surfing: Stand Up Paddle Surfing (SUP)

Beginner lessons in smooth river water are great for kids and families. Lessons: *Nephi Kalani Quereto:* 808.826.7612; *Charlie Smith:* 808.634.6979; *Andra Smith:* 808.635.0269; *Mitchell Alapa:* 808.337.9509. Rentals: Kauai Marriott, Lihue at *Kalapakai Beach Boys:* 808.246.9661; *Kayak Kauai,* Hanalei: 808.826.9844.

Sweets & Treats

Frosties. You'll love these tasty frozen fruits whipped smooth like soft ice cream in combinations of mango, banana, papaya, pineapple – whatever is in season – at the *Moloa'a Sunrise Fruit Stand* on Rt 56 north of Anahola and *Banana Joe's* in Kilauea. Stock up on local fruits. Tropical fruit 'smoothies' are made at fruit stands like *Moloa'a Sunrise, Banana Joe's* and *Mango Mama's* (Kilauea), *Killer Juice Bar* (Kapa'a).

Lilikoi chiffon pie is a Kauai tradition – a light confection of passion fruit. A local legend, *Omoide Bakery* at 13543 Kaumualii Hwy, Hanapepe, has baked great pies by secret family recipe since 1956. Buy frozen (order in advance: 808.335.5291) to keep for several hours in the car (best in a cooler). Sample pies at *Auntie Lilikoi* at 9875 Waimea Rd, Waimea: 808.338.1296. Try a slice at *Hamura's Saimin* at 2956 Kress Street, Lihue: 808.245.3271. On your way to the airport, pick up a frozen pie at Hamura's to bring onboard in a carry-on plastic insulator pack ($10 at Wal-Mart).

Chocolate. In the Port Allen Marina, try *Kauai Chocolate Company*'s homemade ice cream – macadamia nut, dark chocolate, coconut, and island fruit flavors – or chocolates hand made while you watch by Don and Marlene Greer and family – great after a long boat ride. Open 12pm - 5pm daily at 4341 Waialo Rd, Hanapepe: 808.335.0448 *www.kauaichocolate.us.* Tour and taste at island chocolate farms (p 95).

EASTSIDE: IN WAILUA, Don't miss bakery treats at *Sweet Marie's* (p 184) or *Icing on the Cake* (p 170). In Waipouli Complex, *Po Po's* macadamia nut cookies can be mixed with chocolate chips or coconut. At *Pono Market* in Kapaʻa, sample coconut manju or Shagnasty's natural rawhide honey. In Lihue try sweet pretzel cookies at *Hamura's Saimin.*

In grocery stores, look for *Kauai Tropical Fudge* in island flavors (banana, macadamia nut, Kona coffee, even pina colada) also *papaya seed dressing* which gives salad a whole new dimension. Look for *Huli Huli Sauce,* our favorite marinade for fish or chicken, and *Kauai Breadsticks Company*'s flavored sticks for great car snacks.

WESTSIDE: In Hanapepe, taro chips are made in the *Taro Ka* factory. When taro is scarce, they make potato chips flavored with special Chinese spices, as well as sweet potato chips. Island favorite *Kauai Kookie Kompany* factory store in Hanapepe (Rt 50) gives free samples. Try lilikoi granola or pina colada granola, as well as pastries, cookies, biscotti, trail mixes, macaroons at *Kauai Granola* in Waimea: 808.338.0121 *www.kauaigranola. com.* In Waimea, try *Aunty Lilikoi*'s mustard, with bite and sweetness, at the outlet store at 9875 Waimea Rd: 808.338.1296 *www.auntylilikoi.com.*

NORTHSHORE: Try *Hanalei Poi:* 808.826.4764 *www.hanaleipoi.com.* Local folks like it for dipping ahi poke or vegetables. Check out the T-shirts. *Healthy Hut* market in Kilauea has many locally made treats.

Tubing

As the island's economy shifts from sugar cultivation to tourism, the vast sugar lands are finding new uses. Tubing along Kauai's sugar plantation irrigation system doesn't require washboard abs and can include the whole family. You meet in Hanamaʻulu, drive upcountry to a launch dock where, encircled by your big innertube, you wade into the canal, then float with the gentle current towards the sea along the route carved out of dirt and rock by Chinese immigrant workers in the 1870's to bring water to the cane fields.

Make it a bumper car ride if you like, kicking off rocks or the sides of the canal, or even off each other, spin the tubes, or just relax and float through hidden Kauai. You'll pass through amazing tunnels, wearing your headlamp through the first four, trying the last one in the dark. The tour goes over a mini waterfall, supervised by staff and ends with a picnic ($99) 808.245.2506; 888.270.0555 *www.kauaibackcountry.com.* Map 1

Waimea Canyon Drive to Kokeʻe State Park

Drive to the top of Waimea Canyon, the 'Grand Canyon of the Pacific,' along the winding Kokeʻe Rd (Rt 550) from Rt 50 (about 45 minutes). As you travel along the canyon's rim, 10 miles long and 3,600 feet deep, pull over at spectacular scenic overlooks. Stop for lunch at *Kokeʻe Lodge* — excellent soups and sandwiches – and visit the *Kokeʻe Museum* (donation) for exhibits and trail maps. Plan a hike and sign up for an e-newsletter at *www. kokee.org.* Even a short hike in this wilderness preserve has great views (see Hiking, 115). Bring a jacket; at nearly 4,000 feet, temperatures can be cool.

Jeffrey Courson

At the end of the Waimea Canyon Road, a spectacular lookout.

Some hikes take only a couple of hours, like the trail to Waipo'o Falls which descends through wild ginger and orchids to a beautiful two-tiered waterfall. Mosquito spray, sun screen, canteen, camera (wildflowers are beautiful), and a hat are musts. Even if you don't hike, the drive takes you to a spectacular spot, the *Kalalau Lookout*, a vista of the island's west side. (Be careful: the railing won't keep small children safe.) Rental car companies will advise you to go easy on the brakes and use low gear on the curving road, especially on the way down. The road is hard on cars, as we learned when our 1984 red Suburban made it to the top, then coughed and sputtered to a halt in front of Koke'e Lodge. Your rental car will probably do just fine, but we'll never forget the trip back down, with 'Red Rover' – the family suburban – riding in style atop the gleaming flatbed, whimsically named 'A Tow in Paradise.' Only on Kauai would the driver park his enormous rig a half dozen times to share his favorite photo-stops!

Although commercial tours of Koke'e are no longer allowed, you can see some of the ecosystem, as well as Waimea Canyon, with *Aloha Kauai Tours* in 4x4 vans: 808.245.1113; 800.452.1113 *www.alohakauaitours.com*. *Kauai Nature Tours* offers unique naturalist guided tours with an emphasis on Kauai's natural and cultural history: 808.742.8305; 888.233.8365 *www.teok.com*.

Water Skiing

The Wailua River on the eastern shore is a great spot for water skiing, wake boarding, kneeboarding, slalom, and other water sports. With *Kauai Water Ski & Surf Co*, you get a driver, equipment, lessons, and boat for an hour for $140 ($75/half hour). Put up to five people onboard: 808.822.3574.

Weddings on Kauai

There are no residency, citizenship, blood test, or waiting period requirements. Bride and groom must both be 18 years or older to marry without parental consent, and both must apply in person for a license, valid for 30 days (pay in cash: $60). For a free 'Getting Married' pamphlet, contact State Department of Health, Marriage License Office, 1250 Punchbowl St, Honolulu HI 96813. Honolulu: 808.586.4545; Kauai: 808.241.3498 *www.hawaii.gov*.

Kauai Aloha Weddings, operated by Huanani Rossi, a native Hawaiian, emphasizes Hawaiian traditions: 808.822.1477 *www.kauaialohawed.com*. Marcia Sacco has a supportive manner and excellent connections, e.g. she arranged a beach wedding for cruise travelers (photo below) 800.776.4813 *www.kauai-wedding.com*. Musician/composer/vocalist Norman Ka'awa Solomon (p 127) plays unforgettable Hawaiian music and also does wedding planning: 808.651.8386 *kaawa_music@hotmail.com*. Gregg Winston of *Watersports Adventures* has even arranged weddings underwater.

You can make some important arrangements yourself. First stops: *www. hawaii.gov/dlnr* and *www.kauai.gov.* Contact the *Division of State Parks* for a list of scenic wedding sites: 808.274.3444. *Na 'Aina Kai Gardens* in Kilauea has a great beachfront site, unique garden areas, including a maze: 808.828.0525 *www.naainakai.com.* For a reception, reserve a private tea room at *Hanama'ulu Tea House* (call Sally or Arlene: 808.245.2511).

Order your cake from Andrea at *www.icingonthecake.com* (voted *The Knot's* Best of Weddings 2010 Pick) 808.823.1210, or Marie at *Sweet Marie's*: *www.sweetmarieskauai.com* 808.823.0227. Or choose superb pies from Sandy at *The Right Slice,* like chocolate/coconut/macadamia nut: 808.212.8320 *www.rightslice.com.* Order traditional leis (p 184).

In addition to hotels (the ultimate splurge: spectacular Makana Terrace, St Regis), restaurants with elegant private dining rooms include *Plantation Gardens:* 808.742.2216, *Gaylord's*: 808.245.9593 *www.gaylordskauai.com* and *Hukilau Lanai* which also has a dance floor: 808.822.0600 *www. hukilaukauai.com. Kintaro* has a small private room: 808.822.3341.

Wine (& Mead)

Chat with personable, Kauai-raised Daniel Braun, formerly Resort Sommelier for the Four Seasons Maui at Wailea. You'll enjoy his boutique collection of wines in Princeville Center. In Lihue (Puhi) at 4495 Puhi Rd, visit *The Wine Garden:* 808.245.5766. In Koloa, try *The Wine Shop:* 808.742.7305 *www.thewineshopkauai.com.*

In a tiny strip mall behind Kauai Pasta in Wailua, try tropical honey wine fragrant with unique combinations of flowers and fruits. At *Nani Moon*'s tasting room/brewery (small fee) at 4-939 D Kuhio Hwy, we tasted 'Pineapple Guava Sunset' and came to appreciate its dry and floral taste Owner/meadmaker Stephanie Krieger plans a 'Limahuli Mead' with mountain apple, and a 'Winter Sun Mead' with sun ripened starfruit and lilikoi. Closed Sundays, Mondays. 808.823.0483 *www.nanimoonmead.com.*

Windsurfing

Sheltered Anini Beach's offshore reef creates a peaceful lagoon in most winds, and on most days, you can see brightly colored sails and students from two windsurf companies. At *Windsurf Kauai,* Celeste Harvel can teach the basics as well as a complete certification course ($100/3 hr session), 9am or 1pm M-F; 808.828.6838 www.*windsurf-kauai.com.* A gifted teacher, she has special sized boards for kids, and a special dog, Kahili. *Anini Beach Windsurfing* also uses the latest in equipment and teaches surfers at all levels 808.826.9463. Both welcome small group lessons, drop-ins and rentals.

Kahili onboard at Anini Beach

Yoga

EASTSIDE: Studio programs: Lihue: *Kauai Athletic Club*: 808.245.5381 *www.kauaiathleticlub.com*. Kapaʻa: *Bikram Yoga Studio*: 808.822.5053 also Tai Chi. *Bodhi Tree Yoga*: 808.822.5053 *www.bodhitreeyogakauai.com*

NORTH SHORE: *Prince Clubhouse* classes and private sessions: 808.826.4093. *Yoga Hanalei* ashtanga classes and private sessions: 808.826. YOGA *www.yogakauai.com*. *Pineapple Yoga*, ashtanga yoga, Christ Church Parish House, Kilauea: 808.652.9009 *www.pineappleyoga.com*. For something special, try *Michaelle Edwards* personalized yoga in classes/private sessions, retreats in a serene rural setting. Her 'yogalign' method emphasizes breathing, natural alignment, painless yoga from the core, injury and back pain recovery: 808.826.9230 *www.manayoga.com*.

SOUTH SHORE: *Anara Spa* at the Hyatt: 808.742.1234 *www.anaraspa.com*. *Joy's Oceanfront Yoga* hatha yoga classes, private lessons, guided hikes, and yoga/wellness vacation planning: 808.639.9294 *www.aloha-yoga.com*.

RETREATS: *Encounter Kauai* retreats combine yoga with cultural, spiritual, and health-minded awareness in beautiful locations: 808.634.6812 *www. encounterkauai.com*. *Kahuna Valley* offers yoga and Qigong classes and workshops, as well as massage, bodywork, watsu (solar-heated salt water pool) in a serene 6 acre mountain retreat: 808.822.4268 *www.kahunavalley.org*

Zipline

For a bird's eye view of Kauai's beautiful terrain, try a zipline tour. It's empowering – even the most timid will come to love leaping off a platform (sometimes you are told to get a running start), sailing over trees, and surveying beautiful streams and waterfalls below before touching down hundreds of feet later. With up to 11 people on the tour, however, you can wait around a bit to be hooked up. Four tour operators take you to Kipu on the south shore and Hanamaʻulu on the eastside to explore rainforest and rolling ranch land you would not otherwise see. Most specify age (12 and over), weight (100-280 pounds), and require long pants and closed-toe shoes.

Kauai Backcountry offers a 3 1/2 hour tour through 7 ziplines, ranging to 950 feet. Guides describe tour and safety measures, then each adventurer zips off down the cable while a second guide waits at the other end, either to reel in those who don't quite make it or to act as a brake. Starting with a slow 'bunny slope,' the tour advances to increasingly exciting rides. $130 includes sandwiches, cookies: 808.245.2506; 888.270.0555 *www.kauaibackcountry.com*.

Just Live combines zipline with a treetop/canopy tour; once your feet leave the ground, you stay up in 200-foot-tall Norfolk Pines, zipping from treetop to treetop, crossing sky bridges (height 60 – 85 feet), exploring mango, pine, eucalyptus, and bamboo trees from the top, listening to bird song (3.5 hrs/ages 9 and up: $129). Other tours, including ropes course, from $79. Revenue helps fund youth adventure education: 808.482.1295 *www.justlive.org.*

Princeville Ranch Adventures offers a 4.5 hour tour with 8 ziplines and a suspension bridge ($145) or a 3-hour zip express tour ($125). Adventurers zip across the first 7 ziplines and cross a wooden plank suspension bridge before stopping for lunch (make your own pita sand-wiches, fruit, Kauai cookies) and a swim at a small waterfall. Guides describe local flora and fauna. A 'Ride N'Glide' tour takes you to the falls on horseback, then zipping afterwards ($145). 12 and older. 808.826.7669; 888.955.7669 *www.adventureskauai.com.*

Outfitters Kauai's unique tour ($178) ends at beautiful – and otherwise off limits as private property – *Kipu Falls*, and features a 'zippell' (a fairly vertical line in which the braking concepts of repelling slow your progress) and a tandem zip (2 people zoom across a stream on side-by-side ziplines). Outfitters provides a shoulder harness so that you can turn upside down – easier said than done! At beautiful Kipu Falls, you can try a 10 foot cliff jump and a 10 foot rope swing. The tour includes snacks (cheese and crackers, salami, grapes), juice, and water, and was recently expanded to start with a paddle down the Hule'ia River and end with a motorized canoe ride back home. Outfitters' Zipline Treck Nui Loa brings you to Kipu Ranch without a paddling component and features an 18,000 foot zipline ($148) 808.742.9667; 888.742.9887 *www.outfitterskauai.com.*

Restaurants

Eastside: Lihue, Hanama'ulu, Wailua, Kapa'a, 155

Lihue

Barbecue Inn	808.245.2921	Oriental	156	$$	BLD
Café Portofino	808.245.2121	Italian	160	$$$$	LD
Dani's	808.245.4991	Island-style	161	$	BL
Duke's Canoe Club	808.246.9599	Seafood/steak	162	$$$	D
Duke's Barefoot Bar	808.246.9599	Burgers/sand	163	$$	LD
Garden Island BBQ	808.245.8868	Chinese/BBQ	164	$$	LD
Gaylord's	808.245.9593	Continental	164	$$$$	LD
Gingbua	808.245.9350	Thai	166	*$$*	*D*
Hamura's Saimin	808.245.3271	Saimin	166	$	D
JJ's Broiler	808.246.4422	Steak/seafood	170	$$$	D
Kalapaki Beach Hut	808.246.6330	Burgers/sand	171	$	BLD
Kauai Pasta	808.245.2227	Italian	171	$$	D
La Bamba	808.245.5972	Mexican	175	$	LD
Naupaka Terrace	808.245.1995	American	176	$$$$	BD
Oki Diner	808.245.5899	Island-style	178	$	21 hrs
Sushi Bushido	808.632.0664	Japanese	184	$$$	LD
Tip Top Café	808.245.2333	Amer/Asian	185	$	BL

Hanama'ulu

Hanama'ulu Tea House	808.245.2511	Chinese/Japanese	167	$$	D

Wailua

Bobby V's	808.821.8080	Italian	157	$$	LD
Brick Oven Pizza	808.823.8561	Italian	157	$$	LD
Bull Shed	808.822.3791	Steak/PRib	158	$$$	D
Caffé Coco	808.822.7990	Vegetarian	159	$$	BLD
Eggbert's	808.822.3787	American	164	$$	BL
Hong Kong Café	808.822.3288	Chinese	168	$	LD
Hukilau Lanai	808.822.3441	Pacific Rim	171	$$$	D
Kauai Pasta	808.822.7447	Italian	172	$$	D
Kintaro	808.822.3341	Sushi/Japanese	172	$$$	D
Lemongrass	808.821.2888	Pacific Rim	174	$$$	D
Mema Thai Cuisine	808.823.0899	Thai/Chinese	175	$$	LD
Monico's	808.822.4300	Mexican	176	$	LD
Papaya's	808.823.0190	Vegetarian	180	$	BLD

$ under $20/pp $$ under $30/pp $$$ under $40/pp $$$$ under $50/pp $$$$$ over $50/pp

Pho Vy	808.823.6060	Vietnamese	181	$$	LD
The Oasis	808.822.9332	Pacific Rim	177	$$$	LD
Shivalek	808.821.2333	Indian	182	$$$	LD
Tutu's Soup Hale	808.639.6312	Organic	186	$	BL
Wahooo Seafood	808.822.7833	Seafood	187	$$$$	LD
Wailua Marina	808.822.4311	Island-style	188	$$	LD
Waipouli Deli	808.822.9311	Island-style	189	$	BLD
Kapaʻa					
The Eastside	808.823.9500	Pacific Rim	163	$$$$	D
Kountry Kitchen	808.822.3511	American	173	$$	BL
Mermaids Café	808.821.2026	Veg/vegan	175	$	LD
Norberto's El Café	808.822.3362	Mexican	177	$$	BD
Olympic Café	808.822.2825	American	179	$$	BLD
Ono Family	808.822.1710	American	189	$$	BL
TNT Steakburgers	808.651.4922	Hamburgers	185	$	L
Sukothai	808.821.1224	Thai/etc.	182	$$	D
Sushi Bushido	808.822.0664	Sushi	184	$$$	D
Verde	808.821.1400	Mexican	186	$$$	LD

North Shore: Kilauea, Princeville & Hanalei, 194

Kilauea					
Kilauea Fish Market	808.828.6244	Seafood	201	$	LD
Lighthouse Bistro	808.828.0480	Italian	203	$$$	LD
Pau Hana Pizza	808.828.2020	Pizza	201	$	LD
Princeville					
C J's Steakhouse	808.826.6211	Steak/seafood	196	$$$	LD
Kauai Grill	808.826.9644	Pacific Rim	199	$$$$$	D
Makana Terrace	808.826.9644	Pacific Rim	203	$$$$$	BLD
Nanea	808.827.8808	American	205	$$$	LD
Tamarind	808.825.9999	Thai/Chinese	209	$	BL
Hanalei					
Bar Acuda	808.826.7081	Pacific Rim	195	$$$	LD
Bouchon's	808.826.9701	Sushi/American	196	$$$	LD
Bubba Burgers	808.826.7839	Hamburgers	196	$	LD
Hanalei Dolphin	808.826.6113	Seafood/steak	197	$$$	LD

$ under $20/pp $$ under $30/pp $$$ under $40/pp $$$$ under $50/pp $$$$$ over $50/pp

Hanalei Gourmet	808.826.2524	Sandwiches	198	$$	BLD
Mediterranean Gourmet	808.826.9875	Mediterranean	205	$$$	LD
Neidie's	808.826.1851	Brazilian	206	$$	LD
Kalypso's	808.826.9700	American	198	$$	LD
Postcards Café	808.826.1191	Seafood/veget	206	$$$	BD
Red Hot Mama's	808.826.7266	Mexican	208	$	L

South Shore: Poipu, Koloa & Kalaheo, 210

Koloa

Koloa Fish Market	808.742.6199	Fish/local eats	221	$	L
Tomkats Grill	808.742.8887	American	227	$$	LD

Poipu

Beach House	808.742.1424	Pacific Rim	210	$$$$	D
Brennecke's	808.742.7588	Seafood/steak	212	$$$	LD
Casablanca	808.742.2929.	Italian	214	$$$	LD
Casa di Amici	808.742.1555	Italian	215	$$$	D
Dondero's	808.742.6260	Italian	216	$$$$$	D
Joe's on the Green	808.742.9696	American	217	$$	BLD
Josselin's	808.742.7117	Pacific Rim	218	$$$$	D
Keoki's Paradise	808.742.7534	Steak/seafood	220	$$$	D
Merriman's	808.742.8385	Pacific Region	221	$$$$	LD
Plantation Gardens	808.742.2216	Steak/seafood	222	$$$	D
Red Salt	808.828.8888	Pacific Rim	224	$$$$	D
Roy's Poipu Grill	808.742.5000	Asian Fusion	225	$$$$	D
Shells	808.742.1661	American	226	$$$$	BLD
Tidepools	808.742.6260	Seafood/steak	226	$$$$$	D

Kalaheo

Brick Oven Pizza	808.332.8561	Pizza	213	$$	LD
Kalaheo Café & Coffee	808.332.5858	Deli/coffee	218	$	BL
Kalaheo Steak & Ribs	808.332.9780	Steak/PRibs	218	$$$	D
Pomodoro	808.332.5945	Italian	222	$$$	D
Shrimp Station	808.338.1242	Shrimp/Sandw	229	$$	BLD

Westside: Hanapepe, Ele'ele & Waimea, 228

Hanapepe Café	808.335.5011	Vegetarian	229	$$	LD
Toi's Thai Kitchen	808.335.3111	Thai	230	$$	LD
Grove Café	808.338.9773	American	230	$$	LD
Wrangler's Steakhouse	808.338.1218	Steaks/sandw	231	$$	LD

$ under $20/pp $$ under $30/pp $$$ under $40/pp $$$$ under $50/pp $$$$$ over $50/pp

Island Favor...eats

Ocean view
Eastside
Bull Shed, 158
Duke's Canoe Club, 162
Café Portofino, 160
North Shore
Kauai Grill, 199
Makana Terrace, 203
South Shore
Beach House, 210

Creative Fusion
Eastside
The Eastside, 163
North Shore
Kauai Grill, 199
Makana Terrace, 203
South Shore
Josselin's, 218
Red Salt, 224

Steaks & prime rib
Eastside
Bull Shed, 158
South Shore
Keoki's, 220
Tidepools, 226
Kalaheo Steak & Ribs, 219

Sushi
Eastside
Kintaro, 172
Sushi Bushido, 184
North Shore
Hanalei Dolphin, 197

Fresh island fish
Eastside
Bull Shed, 158
The Eastside, 163
Duke's Canoe Club, 162
Hukilau Lanai, 171
North Shore
Kauai Grill, 199
Hanalei Dolphin, 197
Kilauea Fish Market, 201
Postcards Café, 206
South Shore
Beach House, 210
Brennecke's Beach Broiler, 212
Josselin's, 218
Red Salt, 224
Tidepools, 226

Best Mex
Eastside
Monico's, 177
North Shore
Neidie's Salsa & Samba, 206
Red Hot Mama's, 208

Family friendly
Eastside
Barbecue Inn, 156
Hanama'ulu Tea House , 167
Kountry Kitchen, 173
Ono Family Restaurant, 179
South & Westside
Brick Oven Pizza, 213
Tomkats, 227
Joe's on the Green, 217
Wranglers's, 231

Budget friendly
Eastside
Monico's, 152
Barbecue Inn, 156

Eastside Restaurants
'favor...eats'

The eastern shore's potpourri of dining reflects Kauai's rich multicultural heritage. In LIHUE, *Barbecue Inn's* bargain-priced lunches and dinners include soup, a beverage, fresh-baked bread, entrée, even dessert. In this family-friendly restaurant, you'll find one of the best values on the island. Looking for local saimin? Try *Hamura's Saimin* for great noodles; in nearby Hanama'ulu, *Hanama'ulu Restaurant and Tea House* combines reasonable prices and friendly service with excellent Japanese and Chinese cuisine.

Gaylord's at Kilohana provides a romantic garden setting for lunch and dinner in an elegantly restored sugar plantation estate house. At the Kauai Marriott, *Duke's Canoe Club* offers a beautiful beachfront setting, as well as excellent food, reasonable prices, and an extensive salad bar. *Duke's Barefoot Bar* downstairs has well-priced burgers and sandwiches. Nearby, at *Kalapaki Beach Hut*, try a first-rate hamburger or fish sandwich.

WAILUA: Ten minutes north of Lihue, Wailua has a range of cuisines and prices. *Kintaro* prepares about the best Japanese dinners, sushi, and sashimi on Kauai, though you'll probably have to wait for a table along with the local folks who like it too. *Hukilau Lanai* serves wonderful fresh fish and local vegetables. *Oasis* serves inventive fish and local products along with entertainment. Don't miss the *Bull Shed* for the biggest, tastiest prime rib on the island as well as steaks, chicken, and fresh fish – with an ocean view – at excellent prices. Go early to avoid the rush.

Vegetarian, or even vegan cravings? Try lunch or dinner at *Caffé Coco* (*Papaya's* or *Mermaid's* for take-out); breakfast and lunch at *Tutu's Soup Hale*, and gluten-free bakery delights at *Sweet Marie's* (opens at 6am).

On a budget? One of the island's best values is tasty Mexican food at *Monico's* in Wailua's Kinipopo Center. Local folks love it for generous portions and tasty ingredients. Try *Tutu's Soup Hale* around the corner for tasty, healthful lunch and breakfast choices. Just across the street is *Brick Oven Pizza*, a local favorite now expanded from Kalaheo. This intersection has become the go-to place for inexpensive eastside dining.

Just a bit north, *Pho Vy* near Safeway is a hidden noodle treasure. At the Coconut Marketplace, try *Aloha Kauai Pizza*. *Kilauea Fish Market* has located a second branch here with great fish wraps and sandwiches. Also try *Fish Hut*. In Kapa'a it's *Ono Family Restaurant* or *Kountry Kitchen for* hearty breakfasts in a family friendly environment. For coffee and muffins (and free wireless) try *Small Town Coffee* next door. For fresh fish wraps, curries and salads, *Mermaids* in Kapa'a is an absolute must stop. *Casa Bianca* across the street has great pizza.

Please note: we will designate each restaurant by it town, even though as far as zip codes go, Wailua and Kapa'a are the same (96746).

Barbecue Inn. 808.245.2921

Where do local folks go for a lunch which includes soup, a beverage, fresh bread, an entrée like a teriyaki chicken sandwich, and dessert for less than $15, as well as less expensive salads and sandwiches? Barbecue Inn has one of the best food values on the island. At dinner, nearly 30 choices – fresh fish, seafood, steak, salads, prime rib (Friday only) – include soup or fresh fruit, a salad, bread, vegetable, dessert, even a beverage ($14-$26).

A local favorite since 1940, family-owned Barbecue Inn is a place with something for everyone. Kids will love the cheeseburger for lunch, or the fried chicken, hamburger, spaghetti, or chow mein dinners, including a beverage, or a grilled cheese sandwich made on home-baked bread toasted crisp and golden. Grown-ups will love teriyaki steak ($19), a rib-eye with homemade sauce, or teriyaki beef kabob and light, crispy shrimp tempura ($16). Vegetarians can choose from several salads.

You will be surprised at the quality of the extras which many restaurants pay scant attention to. Miso soup is excellent. The fruit cup appetizer has fresh fruits in summertime– pineapple, papaya, watermelon, honeydew. The green salad would win no awards for imagination, but you'd be surprised at how much fun the kids have picking out the shredded cabbage and homemade croutons. And everyone will enjoy homemade pies – coconut, choco-late, or chocolate cream –$2 a slice. Buy a bag of home-made cookies or crispy 'cinnamon toast' to keep in the car.

You will see a lot of working people coming off the job, and the portions are so enormous you can understand why. Waitresses are unfail-ingly cheerful, even when small children decorate the floor with crumbs and ice cubes. All this makes Barbecue Inn a great choice for hearty eaters and hungry families.

Lihue, 2982 Kress St off Rice St. Closed Sundays. Breakfast 7:30am - 10:30am; Lunch 10:30am - 1:30pm; Dinner 5pm - 8:30pm (4:30 - 8:45pm Friday and Saturday). Air-conditioned. Credit cards. Maps 1, 2

Bobby V's Italian Restaurant. .808.821.8080

In the historic Awapuhi Building (built in 1895) opposite McDonald's on Kuhio Hwy in Wailua, Bobby V's serves an Italian menu including salads ($7-$9), sandwiches ($8-$9), calzones ($14-$15), inexpensive pastas, Italian entrées ($11-$15), and even kids' meals ($5-$6). But the real stars on the menu are the pizzas. Bobby's crust is thin, crisp, and light, made with homemade, hand tossed dough. 'Margherita' with fresh tomatoes, a gener-ous layer of real mozzarella, and Kauai grown basil was delicious, but might have been better with extra tomatoes instead of tomato sauce which was a bit sharp ($21.99). Plain cheese pizza starts at $14/12-inches, with toppings at about $2. While the pizza was first rate, eggplant parmigiana ($14) was on the small side, and the accompanying penne was overdone.

Eat inside the small dining room (short on atmosphere) or on the tiny porch where you can catch breezes and watch what's going down Rt 56. Soda comes by the pitcher as well as the glass, and everything is served with a smile. For anyone craving late night munchies, Bobby V's is one of the few places to eat on a Friday or Saturday after 9pm.

Wailua, 4-788 Kuhio Hwy. M - Thurs: 11am - 9pm. Fri - Sat 11am - 2:30am. Sun 12 - 9pm. Credit Cards. *www.bobbyvpizzeria.com* Map 1

Brick Oven Pizza 808.823.8561

For years our family has enjoyed Brick Oven pizza, making the long drive to Kalaheo from the eastside, anticipating the extraordinary pizza made with whole wheat or white crust, covered with generous amounts of cheese and toppings and

Island's best pizza

slathered with signature garlic butter. Now Brick Oven has opened a new branch in Kapa'a, and the magic is still there. Whether you want to enjoy a Hawaiian pizza with shaved ham and local pineapple (small for $15.50) or design your own (like fresh garlic and mushrooms), it's a definite must stop. Be sure to ask for a ball of dough for your actual or inner child to play with while waiting for the pizza to arrive. Green salads are not very expensive and make a nice addition.

Wailua, 4-4361 Kuhio Hwy. Tues - Sun 11am - 10pm. Credit Cards. 808.823.8561 for take-out. Map 3

The Bull Shed 808.822.3791

Since 1973, The Bull Shed has been famous on Kauai for high quality meals at unbeatable prices. Bull Shed's prime rib is truly special – a thick slice of tender beef, perfectly cooked with a tasty bone (if you ask for it), delicious au jus, and fresh horseradish sauce – at $28 (with rice and unlimited salad bar) the best deal for the best portion on Kauai. Fresh island fish is another winner, a huge portion filleted by manager Tom Liu himself and then perfectly grilled. At Bull Shed, 'surf and turf' sets the island standard.

A glance at the menu will tell you why the Bull Shed is so popular. Prices are reasonable; entrées come with rice and the salad bar; and several cost $16 or less. Combination dinners are served with a 7.5 oz tenderloin filet instead of the usual small sirloin. The wine list is also fairly priced, with half the primarily California selections around $20-$25.

It's great for families. Kids meals include the salad bar, and they can choose teriyaki chicken breast ($8 or $16/adult) perfectly soft and juicy, or fresh fish ($10). For adults, teriyaki sirloin ($17) is delicious. Fresh island ahi, a huge portion is juicy and fresh; rack of lamb, tender and tasty is served with a delicious teriyaki marinade. Even the salad bar can make a meal, ($7 by itself), or two can share a meal of prime rib and salad bar.

The Bull Shed offers one of the best food values on Kauai in a pleasant dining room with friendly, efficient service. It's popular, so try to arrive before 7pm to avoid the traffic jam. Or invite some friends because 6 or more can have a reservation. If it's warm, request a table by a window that opens (not all do). Bull Shed has not only great food and prices, but an ocean view. In fact, it's built as close to the ocean as technology allows, and our favorite table, in a tiny room by itself just a few feet from the edge of a seawall, offers a spectacular view of

Island's best prime rib

the waves rolling towards the wall and crashing in torrents of spray. During a storm, the waves splash right against the glass, an awesome sight. Come on a night when the moon is full, and watch the waves send gleaming ripples through the darkness.

Wailpouli, in Mokihana Resort, 4-796 Kuhio Hwy. Dinner 5:30pm - 10pm nightly. Credit Cards. Children's menu (under 13). Look for the sign (it's small) opposite McDonald's. Turn towards the water. Maps 1, 3

Caffé Coco 808.822.7990

In almost any season, something is blooming or bearing fruit at Caffé Coco. The dining room is actually a tropical grove of mango, avocado, pomolo (a grapefruit cousin), and papaya, with 'walls' of thick, tall sugar cane. The decor is bougainvillea, ferns, and orchids. Garden chairs surround a collection of tables, none quite matching, and plastic garden chairs, beneath a honeysuckle-covered arbor.

The cuisine emphasizes the natural – local vegetables, fruits, and herbs – and everything is fresh and organic. Some dishes are outstanding, like local mahi mahi crusted with black sesame seeds and accompanied with rice and a tasty wasabi cream sauce ($18). Or try fresh ono with cilantro pesto, served with 'silver noodle salad' of bean threads with a delicious homemade peanut ginger dressing ($5). Green salads arrive with unusual dressings

– creamy feta, for example – and vegetables are imaginative, like fresh corn and green beans with eggplant, or a tasty sweet potato dumpling. Lighter choices include an ahi nori wrap, with soup and salad as well as omelets and vegetable salads. At lunch we enjoyed homemade soup ($4) and an ahi sandwich on focaccia bread ($9). An ahi nori wrap, a generous portion, is wrapped in a flour tortilla ($12.50).

Local entertainers perform each night. You'll have to bring your own wine or try non-alcoholic beverages served in blue or yellow goblets, like ginger lemonade or pomolo fizz, made when the enormous pomolo tree bears its fruit. Desserts like mango tart feature local fruits.

You place your order at the counter where a refrigerated case displays the day's fresh ingredients. The staff will describe their favorites, even identify what's on a plate headed for the dining room, and everything is reasonably priced. Dine in the garden, or inside, in what is called with a grin, the 'Black Light Art Gallery.' The paintings glow – you will too, if you are wearing anything white. If mosquitoes pick on you while ignoring your friends, bring some 'Off' and request a mosquito coil. Browse the adjacent antique shop, Bambuli. Just turn left under the mango tree.

Wailua, 4-369 Kuhio Hwy (across from Kintaro). 11am - 9pm (T - F). Closed Mondays. Live music info/take-out: 808.822.7990. Credit cards. Maps 1, 3

Café Portofino 808.245.2121

Café Portofino's oceanside location at the Marriott, and its well-earned reputation for more than 20 years, make it a favorite for Italian cuisine. From tables on the deck, you can watch the waves roll across Kalapaki Bay and enjoy the evening breezes. Giuseppe Avocadi, a one-man band of talent and energy, is committed to high food quality and professional service.

The dining room is spacious, with tables separated for privacy, covered in linen and set with shining crystal. The menu offers fresh fish, homemade pastas, chicken, veal, and fish. Portofino's Italian cuisine is light and healthful, with sauces based on vegetable flavors rather than heavy with cream. Flavorful minestrone is served in a generous portion for a modest price ($7), and kids will love mozzarella marinara ($9). Vegetable lasagne ($20) is as festive looking as a wrapped birthday present with wonderful marinara sauce and tasty chunks of tomatoes. Our fresh ono was tender and moist, if on the small side, served with a delicious mushroom sauce. Other good choices are 'scampi alla limone' ($28), zesty and attractive, served with perfectly cooked broccoli. A dinner salad ($9) is nicely presented; goat cheese salad with fresh mixed greens is excellent.

Everyone seems to care about your dinner, willing to fetch extra bread or answer questions. At Café Portofino, you'll find an attractive setting, nightly music, and friendly service.

Lihue, at Kauai Marriott. Dinner 5pm - 10pm nightly. For live music info: 808.245.2121. Credit cards. *www.cafeportofino.com* Maps 1, 2

Casa Bianca 808.822.5743

This small, street front restaurant is surprisingly spacious, clean, and offers pleasant music. Our waitperson suggested the house special sausage pizza, with the addition of pesto made with fresh local basil, and it was a great idea, very tasty, generous with cheese, and with a crisp, thin crust brushed with high quality olive oil. The large (14 inch) size is generous enough for two. Caprese salad is another standout, with lots of fresh mozzarella, tomatoes, olive oil & basil, almost a meal in itself. The chef prepares sauces and entrées according to family recipes handed down from Sicily and incorporated into restaurant fare by the founders of the first Casa Bianca (1955, Eagle Rock, California) Sam and Jennie Martorana. For friendly service, excellent food at a great price, you can't beat Casa Bianca.

4-1345 Kuhio Hwy, Kapa'a (across the street from the gift store, Hula Girl.) 11:00am - 9:00pm. Closed Sunday. 808.822.5743 Map 1

Dani's 808.245.4991

At Dani's, you won't find an orchid on your plate, but you will find hot, tasty, and filling meals, emphasizing local-style Hawaiian foods. Kona coffee comes free with breakfast, and you can choose from eggs, omelettes, pancakes, and tasty Hawaiian dishes from $5. The ham and cheese omelette is very cheesy and stuffed with ham, though the hotcakes are on the heavy side. The lunch menu offers a wide variety of Hawaiian, American, and Japanese dishes, as well as sandwiches and hamburgers. Prices start at $7 and include soup or salad, roll, rice, and coffee or tea. With prices this low, expect to sacrifice atmosphere. The color scheme is woodgrain formica accented by fluorescent lights, but on the other hand, the large dining room is bright, clean, and comfortably air-conditioned.

Lihue, 4201 Rice St. 5am - 1:30pm (1pm on Sat). Closed Sundays. Credit cards. Maps 1, 2

Duke's Canoe Club 808.246.9599

One of the most popular restaurants on Kauai, Duke's offers a sumptuous salad bar, which can truly be a meal in itself, as well as high quality, reasonably-priced steak and seafood dinners. Duke's also offers the Polynesian glitz which has made its sister restaurants, Keoki's on Kauai, and others throughout the islands and Southern California, so successful, plus it has a bonus: it's perched right on the edge of Kalapaki Bay, so you can be in the real Hawaii as well as the Hollywood version.

beachfront with salad bar

From the downstairs bar, a stone stairway carved into an indoor waterfall draped with trailing flowers takes you up to the dining room, a perfect spot to look out over Kalapaki bay. Duke's reasonable dinner prices (from $19 for chicken) include the wonderful salad bar, with freshly made Caesar salad as well as an array of fresh vegetables and lettuces, fruits, pasta salads, tofu, fresh-baked banana macadamia nut muffins– great for vegetarians ($15 alone).

Fresh fish entrées ($25-$28 for 8-10 oz) can be prepared 6 ways, including baked, sautéed, steamed in ti leaf, clean grilled with pineapple salsa, roasted 'firecracker' and 'seven-spice.' Since some sauces may seem too strongly flavored, you might ask for sauce served on the side.

The large portion of prime rib ($38 or $26/smaller cut) at nearly 22 ounces is almost like a family-size roast, tender as well as juicy, served underspiced rather than over-salted. Described on the menu as "while it lasts," you might reserve a portion as soon as you arrive. The wine list offers several good choices in the moderate range.

Everyone in the family will enjoy Duke's. Children's dinners include fries and the salad bar (about $6), and adults can order 'Lighter Fare' (pasta, pizza, or a cheeseburger) for around $10. Don't miss famous 'Hula pie.'

What comes to your table will be well-prepared and efficiently served in a setting where you can watch the ocean. Reservations help, though there's usually still a wait. Think twice about going in the rain, however, for you won't see the view when they close the shutters.

Duke's Barefoot Bar. 808.246.9599

Downstairs, right next to Kalapaki Beach, Duke's Barefoot Bar serves lunch, informal dinner, and munchies all day. Try excellent hamburgers and sandwiches ($8-$11), as well as salads and crisp, hot french fries. You'll love the fresh island fish daily dinner special – one fin each night, perhaps teriyaki ahi, or grilled moonfish. The vegetable plate is fresh and colorful, and, if you are lucky, you can visit the salad bar upstairs.

Many evenings, you can listen to live music, a favorite with local folks on 'Tropical Fridays' (4pm-6pm) when drinks are discounted.

Lihue, Kalapaki Beach, access through the Kauai Marriott. Free valet parking. Dinner 5pm - 10pm nightly. Reservations at least a day in advance but be prepared to wait. *Duke's Barefoot Bar* downstairs: 11am - 11pm. Call for entertainment schedule. Credit Cards. *www.dukeskauai.com* Maps 1, 2

The Eastside 808.823.9500

Kapa'a's most exciting new eastside eatery, with delicious food and friendly staff, opened in a down economy and has succeeded in developing a loyal local following for a fresh, inventive menu blending many cultures. One of two brother/owners, chef Jonathan Pflueger tries to blend what he calls 'European refinement, American ingenuity, Japanese minimalism and poetic elegance' in his culinary creations, and he demonstrates a deft, imaginative touch in all the offerings on his small menu. Island favorites are interpreted in novel and exciting ways. Appetizers are intriguing, even playful, like shrimp and scallop dumplings in coconut sauce ($11) or kalua pig spring rolls ($12). You may find sensational shrimp tempura and avocado served maki style, rolled with ahi, or a flat bread pizza with goat cheese. Or try a unique lobster soup with tropical fruit and coconut milk ($13).

Entrées are also exceptional. Local mahi mahi is served in a light miso broth over oriental noodles ($24). Fish and chips are made with just-caught mahi mahi lightly battered, served crisp and hot, and garnished with home made taro chips ($22). Braised beef short ribs are extremely tender ($25).

Even with its recent expansion, the dining room is small, yet seems intimate rather than crowded; tables are well separated and comfortable. Live music makes the evening pleasant, and the staff could not be more friendly and efficient. The menu is always changing, so you can dine more than once during your stay; what remains consistent is beautiful presentation and high quality ingredients.

Desserts are excellent, the wine list well-selected and reasonably priced. Local musicians make an attractive accompaniment to dining.

Kapaʻa, 4-1380 Kuhio Highway. M - Sat 5:30 - 9pm; closed Sundays.
Reservations helpful: 808.823.9500. *www.theeastsidekauai.com* Map 1.

Eggbert's at Hula Girl. 808.822.4422

Once upon a time, when eggs were king, many an enormous omelette was whipped up at Eggbert's in Lihue. After Hurricane Iniki in 1992, Eggbert's closed, and the world synched with a different diet. Now Eggbert's has re-opened at a time of low cholesterol chic. When you've got 'egg' all over your name these days, you take a hearty risk!

For 23 years, Eggbert's has been known for breakfast, particularly omelettes (even eggbeater options), and eggs benedict in 5 styles and 2 sizes (from $8). Now located inside Hula Girl Restaurant, Eggbert's tasty banana pancakes with coconut syrup or french toast delight everyone ($6).

Wailua. Coconut Plantation Marketplace, Kuhio Hwy (Rt 56). Open daily 7am - 3pm. Credit cards. Keiki breakfasts. Maps 1, 3

Garden Island Barbecue. . . 808.245.8868

Garden Island Barbecue in downtown Lihue serves large portions for small prices. At lunch or dinner, the rather spartan dining room will probably be full of local folks, and a glance around will show you why. Platters are mounded with colorful heaps of noodles and vegetables, and the four page menu has prices around $8. Food quality won't win any awards for inventiveness, but what the chef cooks is tasty and hot. Saimin steams in the bowl; wontons feature shrimp as well as ground meat, and vegetables are still crunchy. Lunch or dinner entrées include scoops of rice and macaroni salad. Barbecue plate ($7) with rice includes a generous teriyaki chicken breast and beef thinly sliced and delicious. Shrimp with locally grown choi sum, a green vegetable similar to broccoli leaves and flowers, is very tasty.

The dining room is clean, cooled by fans, and seems friendly from the moment you walk in. Garden Island may not be fancy, but if you're on a budget, you'll appreciate the generous portions of inexpensive, tasty food.

Lihue, 4252A Rice St. 10am - 9pm. Closed Sundays. Cash only. Maps 1, 2

Gaylord's 808.245.9593

Once the heart of a 1,700 acre sugar plantation, Kilohana is a special place. Rooms have the spacious beauty of large proportions and wide verandas, and you can easily imagine the gracious pace of life before airplanes and traffic lights. Named for Gaylord Wilcox who built Kilohana, the restaurant's dining room and veranda look out over the mountains, a manicured lawn, and garden lush with leafy ferns and brilliant tropical flowers. In the evening, the flagstone terrace is lit with lanterns, and rattan chairs surround comfortable tables decked with white linen. Gaylord's is one of the most romantic restaurants on Kauai, with the kind of setting you'd want to star in if your life were a black and white movie.

At Gaylord's you'll do best if you order simply, with sauces served on the side. Sautéed fresh island onaga and grilled ahi were both perfectly cooked, moist and flavorful, much better without their strongly flavored sauces. The special steamed vegetable entrée made to order for our vegetarian was fresh, attractive, and tasty. Prime rib is a good bet ($27/10 oz or $29/13 oz), served with lots of au jus. Entrées arrive with rice, potato, or pasta, as well as a vegetable, like crunchy sugar peas in the pod and sliced red peppers. Most cost more than $24 (fettuccine with chicken) unless you come for 'light supper' (5pm - 6:30pm), and soup or salad increases the cost quickly. Gaylord's wine list is expensive but has some reasonable choices.

The dining experience at Gaylord's can be wonderful. Waitpersons are polite, attentive, and professional, and in the quiet courtyard, you escape the usual noisy distractions of clattering trays and dishes. Small details get lots of attention: water is served in elegant iced glasses with tangy lemon slices, and coffee cups are watched carefully. If you like to linger after dinner, bring a sweater, for winter temperatures can be chilly.

With such an elegant setting, Gaylord's is one of the island's special dining experiences, an image to haunt you when temperatures plunge back

home. The food never quite seems to match the setting – possibly because of the setting. We have had better luck at lunch, with excellent sandwiches, salads, vegetable platters, burgers, and fresh seafood ($11-$13), like fresh mahi mahi salad ($13) with 3 large pieces (though we were glad we ordered the rather spicy sauce on the side). You can enjoy the garden in the full splendor of sunshine. Children's menu, weddings, luaus.

Lihue, on 3-2087 Kaumualii Hwy (Rt 50) just west of Kukui Grove Center. Lunch 11am - 3pm; Dinner 5:30 - 9pm daily. Sunday brunch: 9:30am - 3pm. Weekly luaus. Credit cards. *www.gaylordskauai.com* Maps 1, 2

Gingbua 808.245.9350

On the back corner of Harbor Mall in Lihue, opposite JJ's Broiler, this tiny Thai restaurant on a breezy corner veranda offers reasonable food at reasonable prices. Best is Tom Ka Gai, a traditional coconut soup with chicken fragrant with spices ($10). Vegetable summer roll ($9) is generously stuffed with crunchy, colorful vegetables including fresh mint and served with delicious plum dipping sauce. We had less luck with pineapple fried rice with tofu ($11) which was a bit dry; chicken with eggplant was bland. Tamarind duck with black mushrooms ($17) arrived with delicious sauce. Service was friendly if slow, but the dining veranda was so pleasant in the evening breezes that no one really minded. These growing pains will fade, for the new owner shows a real determination to do well.

Lihue, 3501 Rice St. Open 11am - 9pm; Sun 3 - 9pm. Maps 1,2

Hamura's Saimin Stand 808.245.3271

For more than half a century, Hamura's has served some of the finest saimin around, and you come to want to believe the local legend that Oahu businessmen have flown to Kauai just for lunch. The newly painted (bright blue) small building encloses – just barely – three horse-shoe shaped counters with stools. Although a recent face-lift has made the room look cleaner and more like a luncheonette, you can still watch the cook stir and chop and make things sizzle. The inevitability of change, yes, though some traditions die hard. A sign still warns: "No Gum Under the Counter."

Airfare from Oahu could certainly be offset with bargain food prices: $7 buys the saimin special – tasty and fragrant soup with

hidden

saimin

noodles, chock full of vegetables and meats. Perfectly flavored won ton soup or won ton min is only $5. To take the saimin out costs 25 cents for the container, but you can escape the cramped little room and head for Kalapaki beach. Perfectly spiced barbecued beef or chicken sticks ($1.25) are another find. Kids love homemade *manapu*, a sweet cousin of the pretzel ($2/bag). Don't miss lilikoi chiffon pie ($2) or one of the best buys on Kauai, $14 for the whole pie. (We take a pie home on the plane, frozen, in a soft plastic picnic cooler from Wal-Mart.)

When the waitress takes your order, she passes a bowl of the appropriate size and color over the counter to the cook, who inserts the proper mix of ingredients, then covers all with ladles of steaming broth. Experienced diners mix hot mustard and soy sauce in their spoons, dipping the mixture into the soup as necessary, and using chopsticks to pull the noodles through.

There's not much variety, but what the cook cooks is very good indeed, and the visit is like a trip into the island's past – about seventy years – a time before tourism brought butcherblock tables and bentwood chairs, air-conditioning and gourmet teas – a time when sticking gum under the counter, though frowned upon, was still possible. So throw away your Bubble Yum before going inside, and try this taste of authentic Kauai!

Lihue, 2956 Kress St. M - Sat 10am - 9pm. Open (and less crowded) Sundays for lunch. Cash only. Maps 1, 2

Hanama'ulu Café & Tea House. 808.245.2511

You could not select a better place to share a really special evening with friends than the Tea House. This restaurant combines delicious food with the friendliest service on the island, and, as if that weren't enough, a Japanese garden setting to make everything seem just a bit magical. Here you can dine on soft mats at low tables next to the goldfish and water lilies. Children can wander around and count the carp (tell them to be careful; one of our two-year-olds tumbled in). Local families have been coming here for more than seventy years. Today they still appreciate excellent cooking at reasonable prices, and it's a rare wedding, anniversary, welcome, or farewell party that does not take place in one of the tea rooms by the garden.

The menu offers 35 Chinese and Japanese entrées at reasonable prices from $4.75-$14.75. We recommend the won ton soup ($6) garnished with scallions, pork, and slices of egg foo young. Outstanding! Children will love crispy fried chicken with its delicate touch of ginger ($6); the boneless pieces are just right for little hands.

When our party is large enough, we ask the owner to order a several course dinner, and we are always delighted with the new dishes we discover. Tempura with fresh island fish or shrimp is spectacular, served on an enormous platter, and taste just as wonderful ($9.75). Vegetarians will love the vegetable

Island style & family friendly

tempura ($6.50) or crispy tofu tempura served with teriyaki sauce and green onions. Sashimi of ahi and ono is fresh, elegantly arranged, and of the best quality. A specialty, mushrooms stuffed with crab is lighter than many versions of the dish, and very tasty. Chinese chicken salad has lots of chicken, lettuce, crispy noodles, and wonderful dressing. The sushi bar features excellent salmon skin handrolls with crispy grilled salmon.

Reserve several days in advance to choose where you dine. Avoid the rather nondescript front dining room, and try the teppan yaki room and sushi bar. Our favorite, however, is the tea house by the gardens, where we can listen to crickets sing the songs of evening while stars light up the sky. If mosquitoes like to pick on you while ignoring your friends, ask for a mosquito coil. The incense smell is pleasant and keeps the bugs away.

In more than twenty years of dining, this special restaurant has never let us down. The service is exceptionally friendly, and children are treated with more than usual tolerance by waitresses like Sally and Arlene who genuinely love them. This is a restaurant where you should sample as many dishes as possible, and because it is such a special place, we save the Tea House for our last night, asking any *kapunas* who might be listening to speed our return. You shouldn't miss the Tea House either.

Hanama'ulu, 3-4291 Kuhio Hwy (Rt 56). Reserve a tea room in advance. Lunch 10am - 1pm; Dinner 5pm - 8:30pm. Take-out from 3:30pm. Sunday night buffet ($22/adult). Closed Mondays. Full bar. Banquet facilities. Ask Sally and Arlene about special wedding menus. Credit cards. Map 1

Hong Kong Café 808.822.3288

Wailua's Hong Kong Café offers an excellent alternative to generic fast food. The nine green and black formica tables in an air-conditioned dining room are often full because the menu offers many choices – roast duck, crispy chicken, lo mein and chow mein, sweet and sour dishes, or vegetarian creations – and almost everything is inexpensive ($7-$14). Choose plate lunches ($7-$9), bentos ($7-$8) or a la carte dishes, including a delicious eggplant with tofu. We like saimin, of which there are 9 varieties, served in huge, steaming bowls ($4-$8). Bring your wine or beer. It's not pretentious, and you can enjoy reasonable food at reasonable prices. Fax your order (808.822.3298). They will deliver nearby.

Wailua Shopping Plaza, 4-361 Kuhio Hwy (Rt 56). 11am - 9pm weekdays; 1pm - 9pm weekends. Credit cards. Maps 1, 3

Hukilau Lanai 808.822.3441

The restaurant in the Kauai Coast 'Beachboy' Resort combines excellent dinners with a wonderful location looking out over the landscape to the sea. As darkness falls and evening breezes cool the open air patio and dining room, you can enjoy the night sky, spectacular in moonlight.

In the comfortable two-tiered dining room and dining lanai, every table has a garden view, enhanced by soft lighting, soft music, and performances by local musicians several nights a week. Dinner begins with homemade foccacia, which you can enjoy with a first-rate pineapple martini.

The menu features flavors of the Pacific Rim – fresh island fish, as well as poultry and meat. Entrées come with rice, potatoes, even risotto, and the kitchen will even prepare pasta you bring in yourself. Start with ahi nachos or sweet potato ravioli. If you are a seafood lover, try Hukilau mixed seafood grill ($24), a family favorite, with two good-sized pieces of fresh fish, like ahi and ono, and a shrimp skewer; be sure to ask for delicious homemade teriyaki sauce. Other fish choices include grilled ono, shiitake mushroom and panko crusted opah ($19), and opakapaka dusted with herbs baked in a ti leaf with lop cheong, cilantro, and green onion ($24). Or try a generous seafood linguini. Meat lovers can try the grilled rib-eye steak with garlic mashed potatoes ($22). Beach Boy Burger is less expensive ($11). Don't miss desserts – tropical shortcake with lemon curd is a standout, as is chocolate macadamia nut cheesecake.

Hukilau can satisfy the most exacting tastes and diets. Switch what comes with the entrées? No problem. Bring your own pasta? A snap. Steam fish or vegetables in their own juices? Easy. And no extra charge for this personalized service. The chef once created a fresh vegetable plate for our vegetarian – a spectacular array of grilled eggplant, tomato, mushrooms, vegetable ragout ($13).

Children are welcomed with a special menu. An interesting idea, the wine list announces 20 wines costing around $20.

Wailua, 520 Akela Loop behind Coconut Plantation Marketplace in Kauai Coast Resort. Dinner from 5pm. Closed Mondays. Credit cards. Banquet room. Weddings. *www.hukilaukauai.com* Map 1

Icing on the Cake 808.823.1210

A successful island baker for nearly for fifteen years (including a stint as pastry chef at Roy's in Poipu), baker/owner Andrea Quinn is best known for her wedding cakes (*Knot Magazine* 2010 award). Follow your nose to her small shop in the Kinipopo Center and sample a delicious bran muffin (sweetened with raisin puree), scone, or sinfully delicious green tea shortbread.

One of only two places outside the San Francisco Bay Area serving *Blue Bottle* coffee, her shop also offers teas by sustainable growers.

Wailua, 4-356C Kuhio Hwy in Kinipopo Center. 8am - 5pm T - Th; until 8pm F and S but call 808.823.1210. *www.icingonthecakekauai.com* Map 1

JJ's Broiler 808.246.4422

More than thirty years ago, Kauai's first steak house opened in an old plantation house on the main street of Lihue, then a sleepy town with a single traffic light. JJ's achieved local fame for its specialty, 'Slavonic steak,' a sliced London broil marinated in garlic sauce.

Today, JJ's offers a reasonable meal at a reasonable price (dinners $20-$30) when you consider the salad bar which arrives at your table in a huge bowl of greens surrounded by vegetables and condiments in a lazy susan (by itself, one of the best inexpensive meals on Kauai). On one visit, the New York steak was tasteless and tough, while fresh opakapaka was well prepared, though served with a sauce so heavy that we were glad to have ordered it served on the side. Macadamia nut rack of lamb was both tender and moist, if a bit heavy on the mustard sauce. Bread is undistinguished, served without a plate to hold the crumbs.

JJ's multi–level design affords each table privacy as well as an ocean view. Above the polished wood tables, in the enormous space of the open beam ceiling, hang actual sailboats. JJ's costs the same or more than other steak houses like Bull Shed in Wailua, or Duke's Canoe Club right down the beach, where, in our opinion, portions are larger and the food tastier.

Lihue, 3416 Rice St in Anchor Cove Center. Lunch 11am - 5pm. Dinner 5pm - 10pm daily. Full bar. Credit cards. *www.jjsbroiler.com* Maps 1, 2

Kalapaki Beach Hut 808.246.6330

In the green building right behind Kalapaki Beach, you will find one of our favorite sandwiches on Kauai – a fish sandwich with ono (usually) flash frozen, (always) cleanly grilled, (always) moist and tender, and wrapped in a soft roll with lettuce and juicy tomatoes. You will also find some of the best hamburgers on Kauai – no surprise since the owner, Steve Gerald, originated 'Ono Burger' in Anahola more than twenty years ago. Since then, the term 'Ono Burger' has achieved near legendary status, a name spoken with reverence whenever fine hamburgers are discussed on Kauai.

Steve Gerald has flame-broiled many a burger, either beef or turkey, or even buffalo. Beef burgers are extra juicy, extra tasty, and delicious. The entry level burger comes with lettuce, tomato, and mayonnaise on a sesame bun. Buffalo burgers are about $2 more (though just think of the savings for your arteries). Teriyaki or barbecue style, or bacon and cheddar or mushroom melt can be had for $1-$2 more. Kids' burgers include fries and soft drink. French fries are hot and tasty, with vinegar as well as catsup available. Vegetarians can try a veggie sandwich or a salad. Everything is cooked to order, so be patient, or phone the order in ahead.

Lihue, on Kalapaki Bay, 3464 Rice St. BLD: 7am - 8pm daily. Cash only. Order ahead: 808.246.6330. Maps 1, 2

Kauai Pasta 808.822.7447

Popular with local folks who appreciate good food in generous portions, Kauai Pasta delivers on both price and value with traditional Italian food. Lasagna ($13, or $15 with meat sauce) fills the plate; fettuccine alfredo is lightly executed; pasta with meat sauce is chunky with meat and Italian sausage. You can also choose a tasty pesto grilled chicken breast ($14.95), or whiskey marinated tri tip ($26). Pasta entrées start at $10, and for a few dollars more you can add chicken ($4), shrimp ($7) or grilled steak ($10). Caprese salad features local mozzarella and a delicious balsamic reduction ($8). Pasta sampler (3 pastas) is a tasty bargain ($13), as is vine-ripened tomato bruschetta ($8). For dessert, try coffee with ladyfingers ($2.50).

Don't expect fancy dining. You won't find tablecloths, crystal, or even fresh fish on the menu. On the other hand, the recently expanded dining

Wailua sunrise

room in Kapa'a is comfortable and strives to create a more sophisticated ambiance with low lighting and a black-clad staff. A new lounge towards the back of the restaurant features booths and its own menu, including non-Italian items such as duck spring rolls ($8) and edamame ($3) also available in the main dining rooms. Watch out for the early bird crunch around 6:30pm. Local folks love it so much that a second branch is now open in Lihue. Kids have a great menu with prices starting around $5.

Wailua, 4-939B Kuhio Hwy. 808.822.7447. Dinner: 5pm - 9pm. Closed Mondays. Lihue location: 3-3142 Kuhio Hwy. Call about music. 808.245. 2227. Credit cards. *www.kauaipastarestaurants.com* Map 1

Restaurant Kintaro. 808.822.3341

There's almost always a line out the door of Kintaro, and with good reason. For nearly 20 years, Kintaro has remained Kauai's most popular Japanese restaurant, a must if you are looking for delicious food in an attractive setting. A fountain and a sushi bar take up one long wall. Nut-colored wood tables are set with chopsticks, blue napkins, and blue and tan tea bowls. Ceiling fans and air conditioning make Kintaro comfortably cool.

Island's favorite sushi

Even with a reservation, you'll probably have to wait, which is a bit more pleasant in the new cocktail lounge than in the old days, when there wasn't much room between the front door and Kuhio Hwy.

In the main dining room, you can sit at the teppan yaki tables and watch talented chefs chop and flip and make things sizzle. They will be happy to show you the fresh, high quality ingredients. Teriyaki NY steak ($20) or island chicken teriyaki ($15) are tender, tasty and juicy. If you prefer the reasonably-priced dinners on the regular menu, you might be seated in the smaller dining room next to the sushi bar.

Dinner begins with delicious miso soup, followed by entrées presented on traditional sectioned wooden platforms with rice, zaru soba (chilled buckwheat noodles with a seasoned soy-based sauce) and pickled vegetables, along with tea served in a blue and tan pottery teapot. Crispy shrimp tempura with vegetables ($14) is light and delicious, particularly the green beans. Teriyaki beef with slices of NY steak is exceptionally tender ($17). Beef sukiyaki in a cast iron pot ($16) is dark and dusky with translucent noodles, meat, vegetables. Teriyaki chicken is a family favorite.

Take a seat at the sushi bar and watch the chef prepare rolls at lightning speed. Local people consider the sashimi (high volume usually means everything should be very fresh) the island's best: thin slices of ahi, translucent slivers of ono, dark strips of pungent smoked salmon, shrimps cooked so perfectly that they seemed to melt as you taste them. Spicy tuna rolls are great; California rolls are made with fresh crab; scallop rolls, hamachi rolls, soft shell crab hand rolls, salmon skin hand rolls are all favorites. Don't miss the Kilauea Roll or 'Bali Hai Bomb.'

Children are welcome, as is appropriate for a restaurant named in honor of a Japanese boy hero, and service is polite and usually unrushed.

Wailua, 4-370 Kuhio Hwy (Rt 56). Dinner 5:30pm - 9:30pm. Closed Sun. Reservations: 808.822.3341. Say 'Hi' to Evelyn when you check in at the desk. Credit Cards. Maps 1, 3

Kountry Kitchen 808.822.3511

For years, and despite changes in ownership, a great spot for breakfast on the island's eastside has been the Kountry Kitchen, with terrific food at equally terrific prices. The large menu offers delicious eggs, expertly cooked

Family breakfast favorite

bacon and sausage, as well as omelette creations, including sour cream, bacon and tomato, or 'vegetable garden.' You can also design an omelette with separately priced fillings. Kountry Kitchen's omelettes are unique – thin pancakes of egg rolled around fillings like a crepe – tender, moist, delicious. Or try Eggs Margo – Eggs Benedict with turkey instead of ham. Our children have all loved 'Cheesy Eggs' – toasted English muffin with bacon and poached eggs, covered with golden cheese sauce. Our babies have loved honey and wheat pancakes. All come with perfectly golden, crisp pancakes of shredded potatoes. For home style breakfasts, it's the best.

Kapaʻa, 1485 Kuhio Hwy (Rt 56). Breakfast 6am - 9am; Lunch 11am - 2:30pm. Credit cards. Maps 1, 4

La Bamba 808.245.5972

In Kukui Grove Shopping Center, La Bamba's hardworking owners try to combine the best ingredients at the best price into their family's favorite dishes. The dining room is roomy and cheerful, with Southwest scenes on walls, Mexican hats above the booths. The chef hails from El Salvador, and you will be delighted with the fresh ingredients in generous portions. Mexican salad ($8) fills the plate, stuffed with beans and chunks of chicken ($8). Entrées range from $8-$14, including rice and beans, as well as and à la carte choices, like a delicious chicken enchilada ($5) with lots of tasty sauce. La Bamba has the somewhat slow service that goes with an informal, friendly family atmosphere. Try Mexican beer, wine, margaritas.

Lihue, 3-2600 Kaumualii Hwy in Kukui Grove Shopping Center. Open 11am - 9pm daily. Credit cards. Map 1

Lemongrass Grill 808.821.2888

An offshoot of the popular Mema's, the two-story Lemongrass has an upstairs pine-paneled dining room open to the rafters and cool with breezes, while an outdoor dining terrace lit with tiki torches and rimmed with wagon wheels is more visible from the street.

Pacific Rim entrées range from $16-$25 and are colorful with vegetables and deft Thai seasoning. Salads are attractive with fresh local greens and tasty dressings like guava pineapple or lemongrass vinaigrette. Pork with tangy Thai barbecue sauce is a generous, tasty appetizer. Grilled fresh island fish is perfectly cooked, flaky and very tasty ($24), and, since we ordered sauce served on the side, we could experiment with combinations.

The fish tasted even better with light Thai salad dressing, and our server cheerfully brought us seconds. At Lemongrass, service is polite and efficient, and everyone works hard to make dining enjoyable.

Wailua, 4-885 Kuhio Hwy (Rt 56). 4pm– 10pm daily. Full bar. Credit cards. Maps 1, 3

Mema Thai & Chinese 808.823.0899

Mema features Chinese and Thai dishes, and what comes to the table is both tasty and attractive. Spring rolls are crisp, served with fresh leafy lettuce and peanut sauce, and can be ordered vegetarian style ($7). On the Chinese menu, cashew chicken ($10) is chock full of nuts, and lemon chicken ($10) is excellent, crispy and golden with a light lemon sauce.

Dishes can be very spicy, so ask your server for advice if you have a sensitive palate. Each dish can be prepared with vegetables or tofu ($9), with chicken, beef, or pork ($10) or with shrimp, fish, or calamari ($12). Green curry with coconut milk, lemon grass, kaffir lime leaves, eggplant, and fresh basil is not overly spicy. On the other hand, red curry looks deceptively placid, garnished with fresh basil and chopped cabbage, but it's a scorcher ($10). Mahi mahi sa-teh is delicious ($11). Vegetarians have many choices, and the chef will also tailor dishes to specific tastes.

While experts may grumble that no authentic Thai peppers blister the dishes, Mema offers tasty food at reasonable prices.

Wailua, 4-369 Kuhio Hwy (Rt 56). 808.823.0899. Lunch 11am – 2pm M - F; Dinner nightly 5pm - 9:30pm. Credit cards. Maps 1, 3

Mermaids Café 808.821.2026

At the tiny, walk-up window, you can order some of the tastiest, most inventive dishes on Kauai – and organic for good measure. Portions are generous bordering on enormous, seasoning judicious, and prices amazingly reasonable. Choose wraps and burritos made with tofu, chicken, or fresh fish ($8-$10), tempeh burgers, bakery treats, tea and espresso.

Don't miss the ahi wrap ($9), one of the best taste treats on Kauai: fresh grilled ahi and nori are stuffed into a giant, delicious spinach tortilla. Or try an excellent coconut chicken curry heaped with vegetables and rice ($10), or local organic salad ($9). Foccacia is crisp and fluffy, a treat all by itself, or as a sandwich with chicken, tofu or fish ($9). Have hibiscus iced tea ($2).

It's not fancy, and the only seating is outside: a couple of chairs in the sun or some stools. So pack up and head for the beach – as lots of folks do.

Kapa'a, 1134 Kuhio Hwy (Rt 56). 808.821.2026. 11am - 9pm daily. Credit cards. *www.mermaidscafe.com* Maps 1, 4

Monico's Taqueria 808.822.4300

Monico's in Kinipopo Shopping Center has attracted loyal local followers for excellent Mexican food at unbeatable prices. Fresh ahi burrito is packed with tender fish, cleanly grilled perfectly medium rare, and delicious rice ($11). Shrimp quesadilla and pulled pork burritos are enormous. Vegetarian burrito has sautéed fresh vegetables (can be grilled without oil upon request) with beans and rice and can be made vegan as well ($9). Or try a tasty garden salad ($6). Kids have a great menu (quesadilla, bean and cheese burrito, or nachos).

> *Great Mexican take-out*

Dine indoors, or in the small, quiet courtyard, or carry out. Take-out orders are packaged with chips and salsa. While you wait, visit Goldsmiths Kauai next door for beautiful jewelry designs at reasonable prices. At Monico's, prices are reasonable, portions generous, and the service swift and polite. A great combination, and first-rate value.

Wailua. 4-356 Kuhio Hwy in Kinipopo Ctr (next to Kintaro). Lunch 11am - 3pm; Dinner 5 - 9pm. Closed Tues. Credit cards. Take-out. Maps 1, 4

Naupaka Terrace Kauai Hilton . 808.245.1955

Tucked inside the Kauai Beach Hotel, Naupaka Terrace has a bright, clean dining room with a lanai winding around a lagoon where the occasional carp leaps into the air. Seasoned chef Mark Sasson has designed a menu to please a variety of diners, so that each fish or meat selection can be prepared in different ways.

Prices are on the high side, as expected in a hotel dining room. Entrées range from pasta ($21) to NY Steak ($34). Appetizers include adequate sashimi ($12.50) to a meaty portion of barbecue ribs spiced with lihimoi ($14). Best was Caprese salad with balsamic reduction. Among the entrées, Thai Tofu in coconut curry sauce was most successful ($22). Service can be inefficient, e.g. an inexplicable wait to be seated on our last visit despite a reservation and a half empty dining room. If mosquitoes like to pick on you, request a coil. The incense smell is great, and it keeps the bugs away.

Lihue, 4331 Kauai Beach Drive off Kuhio Hwy, near Hanama'ulu. Breakfast 6:30 - 11am; Dinner 6 - 9:30pm daily. Credit cards. Map 1

Norberto's El Café 808.822.3362

In the heart of Kapa'a, Norberto's has served Mexican food on Kauai since 1977. White stucco walls, hanging plants and sombreros, and woodgrain tables create a setting like a cantina. Over the years, prices have not changed much (dinners from $13-$20), and almost everything is reasonable, including margaritas by the pitcher and à la carte entrées, as well as complete Mexican dinners with soup, vegetable, beans, chips and salsa for about $18. Ask for flour tortillas chips. Nachos are generously covered with cheese. After finishing our bean soup, we were even offered seconds.

The Burrito El Café deserves to be called a house specialty – a tortilla generously stuffed with flavorful beef, beans and cheese, baked enchilada style and topped with guacamole and fresh red tomatoes and lettuce. Tostada is huge and colorful, mounded over a crisp tortilla, and the chili relleno is dipped (not drowned) in egg and gently cooked. An El Café specialty, taro enchiladas are first rate, the taro leaves tasting a bit like spinach. Almost all dishes can be ordered vegetarian style.

A banana flower bearing fruit

Service is friendly, prices are reasonable, and children are treated with tolerance, even when cranky. When the salsa proved too hot for the short people, our fast-thinking waitress brought over a bowl of bean soup. Once kids started dipping chips, all you could hear was happy crunching.

Kapa'a, 4-1373 Kuhio Hwy (Rt 56). Dinner 5 - 9pm. Closed Sundays. Credit cards. Maps 1, 4

Oasis 808.822.9332

The oceanfront restaurant in the Waipouli Resort has a young, imaginative chef (Zack Sato) with a philosophy promoting local growers. From a tiny kitchen that looks suspiciously as if converted from the poolside hamburger grill, some really inventive presentations emerge: crispy shrimp

Island sunsets are especially lovely when reflected on eastern shores.

cake with fresh goat cheese and local greens, served with a delicious papaya pineapple salsa. Small touches make big differences: beet salad arrives with a superb dressing using macadamia nut oil.

Vegetarians will love ulu (breadfruit) curry, just spicy enough so you can still taste the flavors of local vegetables. If you love fresh fish, try the catch of "the minute" prepared either sautéed or glazed with miso. Ask for sauce on the side so you can appreciate the flavors of the ono or papio and then savor creative sauces. Bread is by local bakery Country Moon Rising.

Dine outside on the lanai and watch the waves as you savor desserts, including a trio of creme brulé (coffee, ginger, lilikoi) or a wonderful macadamia nut cookie with apple banana.

Wailua. 4-820 Kuhio Hwy, in Waipouli Resort. Tues-Sun: 11:30am - 2:30pm 5:30 - 9. Call about music. Accessible. 808.822.9332

Oki Diner 808.245.5899

Your body's still on east coast time and you're hungry in the middle of the night. Well, Oki Diner is open 21 hours a day, 7 days a week, with local style food. For breakfast, a full range of eggs and pancakes (from $7) including banana with strawberry syrup; for other times, there are sandwiches, burgers, noodle dishes of all kinds, and 25 'local favorites' like stir fry or beef stew, Hawaiian style ribs and pork, complete with rice and salad, and saimin. Service varies with the staff. Pumpkin crunch pie is a local icon, available by the square for $3.40.

For large portions of straightforward meals at honest prices, and at any hour, it may just be what you need until you get on Hawaiian time.

Lihue, 4491 Rice St. 6am - 3am daily. Credit cards. Map 1

Olympic Café 808.822.2825

On the upper floor of the Hee Fat building, Olympic has a view of the mountains above main street Kapa'a, and it's a great spot for people-watching while you eat one of your 3 squares, or down a beer or cocktail. Lunch and dinner choices include burgers, salads (including a tasty tofu salad), sandwiches, wraps, burritos, and fresh fish tacos (from $10). Coffees and cappuccino, as well teas and herbal blends, fill out the full bar menu.

The main attraction here is portion, as in huge. Presentation lags behind; your food may be heaped on the plate rather than arranged. At dinner, stir fry chicken, for example, arrived more or less inverted over a pile of rice ($16). Ahi burrito was smothered with so much guacamole you could hardly find the fish ($13). Calamari closely resembled onion rings ($10). Fresh island fish (grilled or blackened $20) was adequate, though best was the quesadilla ($10).

The lunch menu, available all day, offers sandwiches (from $8), salads (from $6), wraps (from $8), and burritos. Tofu may be substituted for chicken, or ordered on a giant bed of lettuce and tomatoes. Chicken salad, a moist chicken breast, arrived with mixed greens and delicious dressing ($9.50). Sandwiches come with either chips or a half papaya – a healthful option. Olympic is a good choice for lean pocketbooks and hefty appetites.

Kapa'a, 1387 Kuhio Hwy. BLD: 7am - 9pm daily. Credit cards. Maps 1, 4

Ono Family Restaurant 808.822.1710

Ono Family Restaurant is a long-time local favorite for delicious, wholesome, and inexpensive family meals. Breakfasts and lunches (inquire about dinners) are served in a cozy dining room, with polished wooden booths, some with a removable partition to accommodate large groups. Breakfasts are a favorite among local and tourist families; more than 30 egg creations are priced

Family favorite

from $6, including 17 omelettes. Banana and macadamia nut pancakes with coconut syrup are a local legend, as are eggs benedict. Lunches are filling and tasty, with sandwiches, salads as well as steaks and fresh fish choices, ($6-$10).

Service can be slow, as each dish is cooked to order, but everyone is friendly and cooperative. Wait persons are helpful with things like crackers, straws, extra napkins, and extra cups for tastes of grown-up coffee – those etceteras of family dining that don't seem essential until they're missing. On one occasion, when we could not find our waitress to get a glass of water that had suddenly become a necessity, an adjacent Daddy passed over an extra. Just outside the door, two old timers shared their donuts with a wandering seven-year-old, patted his head as he chewed, and listened politely to his latest fish story.

4-1292 Kuhio Hwy (Rt 56), Kapa'a. Open 7am - 1:30pm daily. Credit cards. Look for the line at Ono's new shave ice stand just outside. Maps 1, 4

Ono Char Burger 808.822.9181

For years, the shack at Anahola was famous among local people for delicious hamburgers and fresh fruit smoothies. As tourists heard about the hamburgers, the shack, along with its reputation, expanded. Picnic tables grew up under the tree, and the menu lengthened. Despite ownership changes, the burgers are still delicious, if somewhat smaller than before (from $5). Quarter-pounders can be made with various cheeses (even blue cheese) or teriyaki style.

Our favorites remain the 'local girl' with teriyaki, swiss cheese, and fresh pineapple, and the vegetarian sandwich. Children can order 2.5 oz hamburgers or deep fried chicken strips that will make the rest of the party want to order the adult portion. Add sizzling crisp french fries, and wash it down with smoothies and ice cream shakes, floats, and freezes. Service can be slow, particularly at peak lunchtime. Be patient, pack up your sandwiches (each half will be separately wrapped) and head for beautiful Anahola Beach just a mile down Aliomanu Road.

Anahola, 4-4350 Kuhio Hwy. Open 10am - 6pm daily; Sunday from 11am. Save time and phone in your order: 808.822.9181. Credit cards. Map 1

Papaya's 808.823.0190

Papaya's is actually a full-service natural foods store. The deli offers a wide range of organic vegetarian and vegan foods, including sandwiches and casseroles flavored in Mexican, Cuban, Indian, Szechwan, Thai, Greek and

Wailua sunrise

Italian styles, as well as tempeh, fish, or chicken burgers, 'garden lasagne,' or spanakopita ($4 to $10). Grilled tofu is excellent, as is the fresh ahi sandwich. We also love the tofu 'egg-less' salad and tempeh 'tuna' salad. You'll also find espresso, cappuccino, lattés, mochas, fruit smoothies, and teas. Dine outside at tables on the patio.

The Papaya's branch in Hanalei village has a wonderful fresh soup and salad bar, as well as great smoothies, and sandwiches.

Wailua, 4-1387 Kuhio Hwy. Kauai Village Center (near Safeway). 9am - 8pm daily. Credit cards. *www.papayasnaturalfoods.com* Map 1

Pho Vy 808.823.6060

Step inside Pho Vy's tiny dining room opposite Safeway in Wailua, and you are instantly soothed—soft music plays, air conditioning cools your skin, and pleasant green walls help you relax. Everything is clean, and the tables, with crisp white paper coverings, greet you with a friendly arrangement of chopsticks and sauces, one hot (chili), one savory (hoisin). The menu features hot and cold noodle dishes, as well as spring rolls, rice plates with meat, chicken, tofu, or shrimp.

We chose one hot noodle dish (pho) and one cold one (vermicelli) and were delighted with both. Pho

A cooler noodle

made with beef stock was delicate and at the same time distinctively flavored. Noodles were perfectly cooked and garnished with traditional condiments—lime, bean sprouts, fresh Thai basil, and jalapenos. Chicken Pho is fresh and subtle, the meat soft, cleanly cut with no fat. Cold noodles with beef was another tasty choice, served with lettuce, bean sprouts and flavored sauce we could add as we chose.

Service is quick and pleasant, with soft spoken owner Jaclynn Pham ready to answer questions and help with choices. Try a flavored 'pearl' drink ($3.50), a frozen blended drink served with oversized straws to snag tapioca balls, chewy almost like gum, hidden at the bottom.

Prices are reasonable (actually the same) at both at lunch and dinner, priced in 'regular' and 'large' portions ($9 or $10 for most choices). At dinner, you can bring your own wine or beer. Don't miss Pho Vy for a delicious meal in comfortable surroundings.

Wailua, 4-831 Kuhio Highway, Kauai Village Shopping Center. Open 11am - 2pm; 5 - 8:30pm. Closed Sundays. Credit cards.

Shivalik Indian Cuisine 808.821.2333

First there were none. Now in one year, two restaurants featuring Indian cuisine have opened on the eastside. Shivalik specializes in tandoori and Indian curries, upgrading the space where Lizard Lounge once served up drinks and bar food next to Foodland in Wailua. The dining room is bright and inviting, impressing you with its clean looking saffron walls and teal ceiling. Paintings of Indian life and a flat screen TV playing Indian films at inaudible volume help create a mood. Linen napkins and cloths protected by paper covers make the room quiet and yet informal.

The hardworking staff greets you with a friendly welcome. On the extensive menu you'll finds lamb, chicken, seafood specialties in addition to a large roster of vegetarian options, both small and large plates. We recommend the small plates, particularly at least one order of naan, wonderful crisp Indian bread. It's wise to take the temperature of the seasoning with a small serving. The some who don't like it hot may find it difficult to discover dishes that are truly mild. The owner cheerfully created a new dish for us that was more to our definition of mild, but even so we ordered some yoghurt with diced cucumber, roasted cumin seeds and cilantro ('raita') to dilute it even more.

Murgh tikki masala arrives with large chunks of white meat chicken, very tender and soft, in a tomato based sauce ($18.95). It is a perfect foil for the Indian unleavened bread which we ordered in three ways: the soft naan heated in the tandoori oven ($2.50), paratha (whole wheat), and

Sandy beaches rim the Eastside near Lydgate Park in Wailua

tandoori roti ($2.50). Chana masala made of chick peas is simmered in onion sauce with cumin and fenugreek ($14.25). Order delicious mango chutney.

For dessert, rasmalai (cheese patties soaked with milk flavored with cardamom and saffron) was a gentle way to complete the meal. If you like things hot, Shivalik is the place for you! Otherwise ask for lots of water and be prepared to negotiate.

Wailua, 4771 Kuhio Hwy, in Foodland Shopping Center. Lunch: 11:30 - 3 and Dinner: 5 - 9:30 daily. Credit cards. *www.shivalikindiancuisine.com*

Sukothai 808.821.1224

Sukothai offers a larger menu than Mema – Thai-Chinese Vietnamese, and, as if that weren't enough of a challenge for the kitchen, barbecue. The small dining room welcomes you with flowered tablecloths and flowers, and air conditioning makes dining comfortable. Most dishes cost about $8. 'Tom Kar,' or coconut and lemon grass soup, is presented in a lovely earthenware serving bowl ($8). Deep fried rice pancakes filled with minced chicken are also delicious ($8). Vegetable fried rice is colorful with vegetables ($7), and pad Thai, made with rice noodles, is excellent ($8). Don't ask to alter a dish or to modify the spicyness, as sauces are prepared in advance. Lunch specials are a bargain.

Kapa'a, 4-1105 Kuhio Hwy, in Kapa'a Shopping Center (near Big Save).
10:30am - 9:30pm daily. Take-out: 808.821.1224. Credit cards. Map 1

Sushi Bushido 808.822.0664

Sushi Bushido originated on Kalapaki Beach in a spartan dining room with plastic picnic tables. Local popularity has led to a larger, more attractive new home in the former location of Blossoming Lotus in downtown Kapa'a. The dining room blends Japanese and Hawaiian motifs into a hip yet comfortable atmosphere, but, as in the original restaurant, the sushi is what really shines. Here you'll find specialty rolls that are really special, like 'Lava Roll' in which scallops, crab, and shrimp are rolled with yellowtail, cucumber, gobo, and avocado, then wrapped with fresh salmon, topped with saki aoli, and baked – a unique taste combination ($14). Prices are high but so is quality.

Consider 'Sunrise Roll' filled with yellowfin tuna, yellowtail, flying fish eggs, cucumber and papaya ($12), or a favorite, 'Lollipop Roll' of salmon, yellowtail and naguro wrapped up in cucumber instead of rice and seaweed and drizzled with a sweet sauce ($14). Some rolls are deep fried; some are even seared dramatically with a blowtorch. Sashimi is first rate, the yellowtail like butter and the salmon fresh. Edamame is served cold ($5 for a very small bowl), and cold tofu is spicy. Japanese beer, sake ($8-$22), inventive tropical drinks.

Kapa'a: 4504 Kukui St. Open11am - 10pm daily. Call about local musical performers: 808.632.0664. Credit cards. *www.sushibushido.com* Maps 1, 2

Sweet Marie's 808.823.0227

At Kauai's only gluten-free bakery, you will find all kinds of delicious and even decadent rice-flower based treats, including chocolate coconut macaroons, snickerdoodles, double chocolate fudge brownies, chocolate lilikoi cake, sour cream coffee cake, and unique wedding cakes.

Hours are limited in this tiny bakery, and your taste buds will go on alert as soon as you park; just follow your nose. Baker/owner Chef Marie Cassel once made the special desserts for A Pacific Café.

Wailua, 4-788 Kuhio Highway. T - Sat 6am - 2pm or call 808.823.0227.
Closed Sunday and Monday. *www.sweetmarieskauai.com* Map 1

Tip Top & Sushi Katsu. 808.245.2333

With a name that conjures up 1950's expectations (a clean room, a square meal), Tip Top still delivers after nearly 80 years. If you manage to find it on a side street in Lihue, you'll find more local people than tourists in the spartan dining room, and you'll enjoy roomy booths, comfortable air-conditioning, reasonable prices, and great breakfasts – delicious macadamia nut pancakes (also banana, pineapple or raisin), french toast, omelettes, or bacon and eggs, accompanied by a scoop of hash browns. Meals are well-prepared if unexciting, but homemade pineapple and guava jam is special. Have it on toast, but that's à la carte. The specialty is oxtail soup, available even at breakfast. For take-out treats, check out the bakery.

At lunch, try burgers, plate lunches ($6), or visit Sushi Katsu, a small sushi bar (there are only 8 seats) inside Tip Top, and sample a California roll, or a spicy ahi roll, or an enormous bowl of saimin. You can enjoy Sushi Katsu's complete Japanese dinners at modest prices.

Tip Top is a Kauai tradition. Breakfasts are hot, fast, and filling – perfect for mornings when you're going to the airport and need every ounce of strength to get through security without misplacing anything – or anybody!

Lihue, 3173 Akahi St. Tip Top is open 6:30am - 2pm. Sushi Katsu is open 11am - 2pm and 5:30 - 9:30pm: 808.246.0176. Both are closed Mondays. Credit cards. Map 1

TNT Steakburgers 808.651.4922

Drive into Kojima's parking lot in northern Kapa'a and you will find a little trailer with solar panels and an awning. While TNT Steakburgers does not look like much from the street, here you'll find sandwiches and the main attraction, remarkable hamburgers. Choose the size of your hand-formed patty (up to 16 oz) ranging from 'small' ($6.75) to 'average' ($9.75) to 'double' ($13.60) (or, really, large

to larger to extremely large) and pick your fixins. Or you can choose house specialty burgers like the Belly Bomb or the amazingly hot Volcano Burger. The owners, husband and wife, use only high quality locally grown meat and then add spice combinations.

Local people love the steak fries made from whole, unpeeled fresh potatoes, deep fried on the spot and served piping hot and crunchy. Hawaiian sun plus parking lot can add up to hot picnic tables, but right across the street you can find a nice shady spot on the beach. Also on the menu are some vegetarian options and a fish sandwich.

Kapa'a, 4-1543 Kuhio Hwy by Kojima's. Open T - Sun 11am - 8pm; F/S until 9pm. 808.651.4922 Map 1

Tutu's Soup Hale 808.639.6312

Chef-owners Sage and Bert create terrific breakfasts as well as lunchtime soups and sandwiches in a tiny building once a shop in the old Coco Palms Hotel and relocated to Kinipopo Center. The dining room is pleasant and informal, with surf memorabilia and comfy seats. Despite their low rent prices (you can eat for less than $10), Sage and Bert believe food is 'comfort,' as close to the heart as the stomach; so they serve on china, not paper.

Try splendid soups (about $7/bowl), for example a Portobello mushroom vegetable soup with a touch of rosemary, or a vegetable lentil brown rice soup with a peppery punch. 'Baked potato soup' is just what the name suggests, made from baked potatoes and lots of cream, and sinfully savory. Soups come with home made corn muffins instead of crackers, and you can request a taste of Bert's wares before you choose. Panini sandwiches on homemade focaccia are so light they seem to melt away as you chew; you can really taste the special fillings, like portobello mushroom grilled with mozzarella ($7).

Tutu's Soup Hale is a great choice for carefully crafted soups, sandwiches, and homemade breakfasts with eggs, quiche, or great french toast ($6-$8), and a welcoming new spot for vegetarians and vegans.

Wailua, 4-356 Kuhio Hwy (next to Kinipopo Center). Open M - Sat 7:30am - 9pm; Sunday 10am - 6pm. Credit cards. Order ahead: 808.639.6312 Map 1

Verde 808.821.1400

Tucked in the Big Save Shopping Center by the Shell Station, Verde's menu reflects the Albuquerque roots of its chef-owner. The menu is not south of the border Mexican, or Cali-Mex or Tex-Mex but 'New Mexican,' where chilis are the heart of the cooking. Your order can be as mild or spicy as you want, and even, vegan, or gluten-free. Local folks love Verde's wonderfully spiced seared ahi tacos ($12 or $14.49/plate) or stacked enchiladas

Fishing net floats wash ashore from as far away as Japan

served with red, green or "Christmas" salsa ($13-$15). Fresh fish burrito is cooked slightly breaded on the griddle, rather than cleanly grilled ($13). Many regulars love sopaipillas, a New Mexican pastry 'puffs which puffs like a blowfish,' in both vegetable style or as a treat sweetened with honey.

The owner cooks, and his wife serves and works the register. You place your order at the counter, where you receive a basket of home baked chili dusted chips. There is a salsa bar and also a margarita bar. Children's menu.

Kapa'a, 4-1101 Kuhio Hwy, next to Foodland. Open 11am – 8:30 pm. Closed Mon. and Tues. Credit cards. ***www.verdehawaii.com*** Map 1

Wahooo Seafood Grill & Bar. . 808.822.7833

People either love Wahooo or are puzzled by its contradictions. The seafood menu offers fresh local fish not found in other island restaurants, but prepares them in complicated preparations that conceal their unique flavors. Entrées are elaborate (plain grilling is hard to find unless you strenuously request it) and expensive. Fish entrées are prepared with at least 4 flavors in the sauce and garnish, sometimes in combat rather than cooperation ($27). At the suggestion of our server, a local fisherman, we tried shutome (broadbill). It was excellent, though with a lilikoi sauce so strong we were grateful to have confined to a side dish. However, you can choose an ahi sandwich (a bargain at $11) and pair it with a bay shrimp salad, a small, colorful mountain of really fresh greens, shredded carrots and tasty dressing ($9) for a reasonably priced dinner.

Appetizers (like crab cocktail $14) dramatically increase your dinner price, so instead of a high priced appetizer, you can request the smaller portion (not the full bowl) of delicious Maui onion soup ($6) or a small salad ($7), choices tucked away on the back page. Meat eaters can choose baby back ribs ($19), prime rib ($23/9oz), and vegetarians have several pasta options ($18-$21).

Wahooo's pleasant dining room has a breezy feel, next to a coconut grove. It can be chilly, but if you sit inside the more sheltered interior section, you don't get to see the goats or the donkey, Rosie, in the pasture.

At Wahooo's, you'll find sometimes spectacular entrée presentations, some (but not all) at high prices. Choose carefully and consider having all sauces served on the side for testing. Enjoy local musical entertainers.

Wailua. 733 Kuhio Hwy (Rt 56). Lunch 11:30am – 3pm; Dinner from 5:30 daily. Call 808.822.7833 for entertainment info, reservations. Credit cards. ***www.wahooogrill.com*** Map 1

Wailua Marina Restaurant . . .808.822.4311

For more than 30 years, the Wailua Marina has been a local favorite for family dining, so an evening here is a glimpse of authentic Kauai. The large dining room features an enormous mural of an underwater vista complete with stuffed fish and a turtle shell. Weather permitting, ask to sit outside on the large covered porch overlooking the Wailua River. Local ahi stuffed with crab is well seasoned and flavorful, and local ono is also tasty. Fried

Political fish – blends in with current conditions!

chicken ($14) may be more moist than teriyaki chicken, but kids love the teriyaki sauce for dipping, so order some on the side. Most entrées cost less than $18 and include rolls, rice or potato, a vegetable and salad bar. We prefer crispy french fries to fried rice, although even that's not too bad when

the kitchen's justly famous teriyaki sauce can jazz it up.

To keep prices down, the Marina cuts a few corners, but they're the kind no one really misses if you catch the spirit of the place. Paper napkins and placemats are a small price to pay for the salad bar, which may lack imagination, but you can fill your plate with vegetables. Children can chose from ten dinners for about $3 less than adult prices. The dozen wines are not very exciting, but most cost less than $25, and you'll love the homemade pies.

Wailua, 5971 Kuhio Hwy (Rt 56) in Wailua River State Park, just south of Wailua Bridge. Lunch 10:30am - 2pm; Dinner 5pm - 9pm. Early Bird Special 5 - 6pm. Closed Mondays. Credit cards. Maps 1, 3

Waipouli Deli & Restaurant . . 808.822.9311

Does this sound familiar? Your body clock is off. You're fully awake – and starving – 3 hours early. You'll never make it until lunch, but you want to spend the morning on the beach and not in some dark, air-conditioned restaurant with poky service. Well, the Waipouli Deli is for you. Generous portions of tasty food coupled with speedy delivery and unbeatable prices have made the Waipouli Deli a favorite spot on the eastside for local families and increasing numbers of tourists. It looks like formica city, so don't go expecting orchids on the table. But though short on atmosphere, it's got a 'breakfast special' ($7) deserving of the name – an egg, two slices of bacon, and two pancakes – perfect for hungry children, not to mention adults. Eggs are expertly cooked, side meats not overly fatty, and pancakes light. Service is fast, efficient, and friendly.

Wailua, 4-771 Kuhio Hwy (Rt 56) in Waipouli Town Center (behind McDonald's. Breakfast & Lunch 7am - 2pm (Tues - Sun). Dinner 5 - 8:30pm (Wed - Sat). Credit cards. Maps 1,3

Vegetarian & Vegan Adventures

Once upon a time, the best you could do on Kauai for vegetarian food was a salad bar, or in a pinch, some meatless pizza or vegetable chow mein. Today vegetarian, vegan, and natural food eateries are sprouting everywhere.

EASTSIDE: In Wailua, *Monico's* makes a sensational vegetable burrito, vegan if desired, and nearby *Tutu's Soup Hale* creates terrific soups and panini sandwiches. Take-out *Caffé Coco*'s special vegetarian/vegan dishes or enjoy its informal garden setting. For pizza, try *Aloha Kauai Pizza* in Coconut Plantation Marketplace and *Bobby V's* across from McDonald's.

Near Safeway, *Papaya's* (another branch is in Hanalei) offers organic groceries, fresh fruits and vegetables, and fresh prepared choices for breakfast, lunch, and dinner, including garden burgers, tempeh burgers, vegetarian sandwiches, pasta, salads, and stir-fries. Or try *Hoku Natural Foods* in Kapa'a (behind Sushi Bushido) for groceries and supplies.

In downtown Kapa'a, *Mermaids Café* has unbeatable tofu (or fish) wraps, curries, foccacia sandwiches, and organic salads for take-out. *Casa Bianca* has great pizza. *The Eastside* has first-class fish and vegetable dishes, and *Olympic Café* offers a variety of salads. In Lihue, try *Kalapaki Beach Hut's* vegetarian sandwich or salads. Sample outstanding soups and sandwiches on fresh baked bread (sweet bread is legendary) at *Deli & Bread Connection*, Kukui Grove Shopping Center (call ahead to avoid the line-up at lunch: 808.245.7115). *Duke's* salad bar is famous.

WESTSIDE: *Kalaheo Café & Coffee Company* in Kalaheo serves salads and vegetarian entrées, and *Brick Oven Pizza* across the street is an island legend for vegetarian pizza. In Hanapepe, *Hanapepe Café* serves vegetarian salads, sandwiches, and (occasionally) dinners. At *Wrangler's* in Waimea, try vegetarian sandwiches, pizzas, veggie wraps, salad bar. *Grinds* has vegetable sandwiches on fresh baked bread, and salads.

SOUTHSHORE: *Josselin's, Red Salt,* and *Merriman's* devise remarkable, imaginative vegetarian dishes. *Pizzetta* serves cheeseless vegetable pizza.

NORTHSHORE: PRINCEVILLE: Pom at *Tamarind* will make wonderful Thai tofu and vegetable dishes. HANALEI: *Postcards Café, Kauai Grill* and *Makana Terrace* at the St Regis serve inventive entrées and appetizers. *Pizza Hanalei* will make pizza with 'tofurella' cheese upon request. Across the street *Papaya's Market* makes soups, salads, and tofu treats, and *Neidie's* serves wonderful Brazilian vegetarian dishes. Near the end of the road, *Red Hot Mama's* has tasty Mexican creations. In Kilauea, try *Pau Hana Pizza's* vegetable pizzas with excellent crust, and vegan baked goods. *Kilauea Fish Market* has vegetarian wraps, and next door, *Healthy Hut* is a full market with organic island produce, gluten-free baked goods, and other treats.

Kauai in the Movies: Golden Sand, Silver Screen

2010	Soul Surfer
	The Descendents
	Just Go With It
	Whose Wedding Is It Anyway
	Priates of the Carribean: On Stranger Tides
2009	Run's House
	High School Reunion
2008	High School Reunion
2007	Avatar
	Tropic Thunder
	Wedding in Hawaii
	A Perfect Getaway
2006	Supergator
2005	Band of Pirates
	Komodo vs Cobra
2003	Tears of the Sun
	Hilary Duff Birthday Bash
2002	The Amazing Race 3
	The Bachelor
	The Time Machine
	Dragonfly
2001	Jurassic Park III
	Manhunt
	Moolah Beach
	The Time Machine
2000	War To End All Wars
	Dinosaur
	The Testaments
1998	Fantasy Island
1997	Mighty Joe Young
	Six Days, Seven Nights
	The Lost World
1995	Outbreak
1994	North
1993	Jurassic Park
1992	Honeymoon in Vegas
1991	Hook
1990	Flight of the Intruder
	Lord of the Flies
1989	Millennium
1988	Lady in White
1987	Throw Momma from the Train

1986	Islands of the Alive
1983	The Thorn Birds
	Uncommon Valor
	Body Heat
1981	Behold Hawaii
	Raiders of the Lost Ark
1980	Seven
1979	Last Flight of Noah's Ark
1978	Deathmoon
	Acapulco Gold
1977	Fantasy Island
	Islands in the Stream
1976	King Kong
1974	Castaway Cowboy
1970	The Hawaiians
1969	Lost Flight
1968	Yoake No Futare
	Lovers at Dawn
1966	Lt. Robin Crusoe, U.S.N.
1965	Operation Attack
	None but the Brave
	Paradise Hawaiian Style
1964	Gilligan's Island
1963	Donovan's Reef
1962	Diamond Head *
	Sanga Ari
1961	Blue Hawaii
	Seven Women from Hell
1960	Wackiest Ship in the Army
1959	Forbidden Island
1958	South Pacific
	She Gods of Shark Reef
1957	Jungle Heat
	Voodoo Island
	Thunder Over Hawaii
1956	Between Heaven and Hell
1954	Beachhead
	Hawaii Chindochu
1953	Miss Sadie Thompson
1951	Bird of Paradise
1950	Pagan Love Song
1934	White Heat

Want to be a vegan chef? Chef Mark Reinfeld of Blossoming Lotus, Kauai's award-winning vegan restaurant now closed, offers classes, workshops, and private chef services. With partner Jennifer Murray, Mark has also authored cookbooks *www.veganfusion.com.*

Cheap Eats & 'Local Grinds'

EASTSIDE: LIHUE. *Barbecue Inn* has one of the largest, most reasonably-priced lunch and dinner menus on Kauai. Try wonderful saimin at *Hamura's,* 2956 Kress St. *Tip Top* is a Kauai tradition for fast, hot, and filling breakfasts, and also lunches and sushi from *Sushi Katsu* (inside Tip Top).

At Kukui Grove, *Deli & Bread Connection* makes delicious take-out sandwiches and tasty soups: 808.245.7115, or try *La Bamba* for inexpensive Mexican plates, or *Quizno's.*

Near Kalapaki Beach, *Kalapaki Beach Hut* makes burgers, fresh fish sandwiches, and salads: 808.246.6330. Across from Wal-Mart, *Fish Express* is a favorite for bentos, plate lunches, poke: 3343 Kuhio Hwy 808.245.9918.

WAILUA: In Coconut Marketplace, *Aloha Kauai Pizza* is a family favorite, and north shore favorite *Kilauea Fish Market's* new branch makes great fresh fish sandwiches, tacos, wraps. Also try the old favorite, *Fish Hut.*

In Kinipopo Shopping Village *Monico's* has about the best take-out/eat in Mexican food on Kauai: 808.822.4300. *Tutu's Soup Hale* makes delicious soups, sandwiches and breakfasts: 808.639.6312. Across the street. *Brick Oven Pizza* has great pizza: 808.823.8561; *Mema Thai Cuisine* has excellent food, and *Caffé Coco* is a good choice for soups, salads, and fresh fish in a quaint garden setting. Also try *Hong Kong Café* for Chinese food.

In Safeway Center, *Pho Vy* is terrific for cleanly cooked chicken and delicate noodles. Nearby *Papaya's* is a market as well as organic food deli.

KAPA'A now has a cluster of small eateries with real personality. *Mermaids Café* makes outstanding vegetarian/vegan dishes, and one of the best ahi wraps on Kauai (spinach tortilla, ginger infused rice and wasabi cream sauce) as well as burritos, stir fry, salads with tofu, chicken, or ahi: 808.821.2026. *Java Kai* brews great coffee, with mango cinnamon muffins, chai tea, bagels, smoothies, breakfast waffles and eggs. *Ono Family Restaurant* offers bargain-priced breakfast and lunches. *Casa Bianca* has great pizza at a great price. Down the street, *Bubba's* serves up hamburgers, fries, rings, but don't miss *TNT Burgers* (next to Kojima's) and try the 'Volcano Burger' if you like things spicy. Burgers are generous and tasty.

Further north in ANAHOLA is *Ono Char Burger.* While service can be pokey, the burgers, french fries, onion rings, and fried chicken are often worth the wait: 808.822.9181. Have a beach picnic at Anahola Beach.

NORTH SHORE: KILAUEA: Near the Kong Lung Store, *Kilauea Bakery & Pau Hana Pizza* features breads, rolls, cookies and pizza with local vegetables: 808.828.2020. Try deli sandwiches, fresh local fruits, vegetables, and salads at *Kilauea Market* next door.

Don't miss *Kilauea Fish Market* across the street for outstanding fresh fish sandwiches, wraps, plate lunches and dinners, vegetarian specials. The owner has contacts with local fishermen: 808.828.MAHI. Also in Wailua.

In PRINCEVLLE CENTER, try deli treats at *Foodland* (great caprese salad panini sandwich $6), and tasty Thai food at a great price at *Tamarind*. In HANALEI, *Tropical Taco* makes fresh fish burritos and other treats: 808.827.8226 *www.tropicaltaco.com.* Try *Hanalei Wake Up Café*'s home-cooked, inexpensive breakfasts and lunches daily: 808.826.5551. In Ching Young Village, try *Subways* inside Big Save. *Polynesia Café* has tasty Chinese/Polynesian lunch plates and wonderful ice cream. *Pizza Hanalei* makes crisp homemade crust with generous toppings: 808.826.9494.

Across the street, *Hanalei Gourmet* serves sandwiches on fresh-baked breads and rolls, *Bubba Burgers* fries up burgers, and *Neidie's* makes exceptional Mexican/Brazilian lunches and dinners. *Java Kai* serves hot and cold drinks, fresh bagels, muffins, snacks, and (pay) wireless. On your drive to the end of the road, stop at *Red Hot Mama's* walk-up window in Wainiha for tasty Mexican treats made with vegetables, tofu, pork, chicken, beef: 808.826.7266.

SOUTH SHORE: In KOLOA, don't miss *Koloa Fish Market* for local-style plate lunches, ahi sesame, sashimi, and other treats: 808.742.6199. Newcomer *Koloa Deli* by the post office is gaining a local following for excellent sandwiches and treats, as well as pie from *The Right Slice*. *Pizzetta* serves excellent pizza, inexpensive pastas and calzones: 808.742.8881. *Tomkats* has a family-friendly menu. *Sueoka's* has local style plate lunches.

In POIPU, Kuku'iula Village, you can find *Bubba's Burgers* and *Dude Dogs*. In Kiahuna Shopping Center try *Tropical Burgers* for burgers and *Papalani Gelato* for outstanding gelato made with local fruits. *Puka Dog's* 'Hawaiian style' hot dogs start with a hole (*puka*) in the bun which is filled with condiments, including relishes of star fruit, mango, banana, or papaya, then stuffed with choice of sausage: *www.pukadog.com.*

A few miles down Rt 50 in KALAHEO the island's best pizza (also sandwiches) is served at *Brick Oven Pizza:* 808.335.8561. *Kalaheo Café & Coffee Company* serves deli treats and gourmet coffees: 808.322.5868.

WESTSIDE: Check out *Grinds* in Ele'ele for coffees, breakfast, fresh-baked treats, and sandwiches on wonderful fresh bread: 808.335.6027, or try *Toi's Thai Kitchen* for saimin and hamburgers. In WAIMEA, it's *Ishihara's Market* for plate lunches and poke (local marinated fresh fish).

Hanalei Bay at Sunset

North Shore Restaurants
'favor...eats'

Perched on the ocean bluff, some restaurants in PRINCEVILLE have unforgettable ocean views. From the restaurants at the St Regis Hotel, *Makana Terrace* and *Kauai Grill*, you can watch the sun set over Hanalei Bay, a simply breathtaking view. Try a breakfast buffet, lunch, sunset dinner, or come for tea or cocktails at the hotel lounge overlooking the bay and perhaps listen to Kauai's talented musicians play. Bring your camera.

In nearby HANALEI, *Postcards Café* takes healthful, organic foods into a whole new dimension, with wonderful pastas and delicious fresh island fish. At *Neidie's Salsa & Samba*, tasty Mexican lunches and dinners have a Brazilian flair and unbelievable prices. A long-time favorite lunch and dinner spot for fresh island fish is the *Hanalei Dolphin,* and the newer *Bar Acuda* has become a popular tapas and wine bar destination as well.

Red Hot Mama's in Wainiha is a must stop for Mexican carry out on your trip to the end of the road. In Hanalei's Ching Young Village, try *Pizza Hanalei's* homemade whole wheat crust pizzas, or *Polynesia Café's* sandwiches. Across the street, *Bubba Burgers* offers hamburgers, and *Hanalei*

Gourmet next door makes deli sandwiches. Down the street, *Tropical Taco* creates wonderful Mexican treats. After lunch, try shave ice at *Wishing Well* in the white trailer near Kayak Kauai. In Princeville Center, try *Tamarind* for inexpensive, expertly prepared Thai food; dine in the patio or take out.

In KILAUEA, *Pau Hana Pizza* serves imaginative, home-baked pizza, soups, and bakery treats. Just around the corner, *Kilauea Market* makes deli sandwiches, soups, and vegetarian delights. For some of the best local fresh fish (and vegetarian) wraps, sandwiches, burritos, as well as salads with home made dressings, you can't beat *Kilauea Fish Market* for price and portion. Worth a postcard home! Map 5

Bali Hai Restaurant 808.826.6522

The view of sunset all gold and orange above the magnificent angles of the dark and mysterious mountains have made Bali Hai Restaurant one of our favorite Kauai dining spots. We hope both it and Happy Talk Lounge re-open by the time you visit. For an update, call Hanalei Bay Resort: 808.826.6522.

Bar Acuda 808.826.7081

While it has always been difficult to cover the cost of delivering fine ingredients to the north shore, and to deal with a labor force which might just decide to head out when the next swell moves in, it looks as though Bar Acuda has done it with its combination wine-bar and tapas dining. The menu offers a workable compromise between high-end tasty food and the small portions which can be priced reasonably enough to attract visitors looking for an informal nite spot at the end of a hard day of vacationing. Sit on the outer porch lit with lanterns, or inside the small dining room, and enjoy mellow music or jazz. If the mosquitoes start to view you as another small plate, ask for bug repellent.

The menu has a Mediterranean flavor, the creation of chef-owner Jim Moffatt. Try a small, tasty pizzetta ($11), tomato bruschetta with leeks and balsamic vinegar ($8). Consider Humbolt fog goat cheese served with Marshall Farm honeycomb and pear ($12), or a tasty beet salad with Kanuna Farms goat cheese ($9), more interesting than a rather bland Spanish tortilla ($8). A side of polenta ($6) which our vegetarian spotted accompanying braised beef short ribs, was also delicious. Hungrier diners can order larger portion plates at about $16 (fresh ono or pork shoulder).

Bar Acuda is a interesting and fun, a good choice for informal dining on those nights when your appetite is too tired to face a long or heavy meal.

Hanalei, 5-5161 Kuhio Hwy. Dinner nitely 6:pm. Credit cards. Map 5

Bouchon's Restaurant & Sushi . . . 808-26-9701

On the second floor of Ching Young Village, Bouchon's is the new moniker for Sushi and Blues. Signature elements are music (local musicians perform here) and camaraderie. For decor, the aim is industrial chic, with a silver ventilation system on the black ceiling setting the scene. You can see Hanalei's main street and even the mountains from tables on the open side. The menu features sushi and pu pus, as well as entrées from $17 (pasta pomodoro) to $31 (surf and turf). The sushi bar offers a wide range of specialty rolls (not open for lunch). Prices are at the upper end of the island sushi scale, though hand rolls are generously thick. Live music Thurs-Sun.

Hanalei, 5-5190 Kuhio Hwy in Ching Young Village. Dinner from 5:30pm daily. Full bar. Call about entertainment: 808.826.9701. Credit cards. *www. bouchonshanalei.com* Map 5

Bubba Burgers 808.826.7839

There are now three Bubba's on Kauai, with the laid-back, reasonable menu that has made Bubba's so popular. Kids will like the "frings" (fries topped off with a couple of onion rings). Kauai beef burgers range from single to a triple patty (a half pound), to the 'Slopper' (with chili), or choose Budweiser chili or hot dogs. Looking for a healthy lunch? There are now tempeh burgers for vegetarians, who can also visit Papaya's soup and salad bar next door. Picnic tables available for all. See the Hanalei's Bubba Burgers in Colbie Caillat's music video for her hit "Little Things."

Hanalei, 5-5183 Kuhio Hwy.10:30am - 8pm daily in Hanalei, Kapa'a on Rt 56, and Poipu in Kuku'iula Village. *www.bubbaburger.com* Maps 4 & 5

C J's Steak House 808.826.6211

C J's Steak House replaces the popular Chuck's Steak House, giving it a fresher look while retaining the steak and salad bar menu that has made the Chuck's chain popular. Dinners range from $23 (chicken breasts) to $30 (14oz prime rib), including rice, warm bread, and the salad bar. Request pacing the dinner, or your entrée may arrive when you've barely finished your salad. Dinners are reliably well-prepared. New York steak ($30/12 oz) has great flavor and is very tender (ask for teriyaki sauce). Fresh fish is moist and cleanly sautéed ($27). Wines are fairly priced. Children's menu.

Dinners at C J's will be reasonably priced and reasonably good. On the other hand, you don't get anything special either, in food or ambiance. C J's offers no views of Hanalei's magnificent mountains or valleys to paint a memory for dark winter evenings back home.

Princeville, 5-4280 Kuhio Hwy in Princeville Center. Lunch 11:30am - 2:30pm (M-F); Dinner 6 - 9:30pm daily. Credit cards. Map 5

Hanalei Dolphin. 808.826.6113

For years, the Dolphin has had the reputation of serving wonderful fresh fish in a comfortable, informal setting. The menu hasn't changed much, and neither has the no-reservations policy, which can start your meal off with an irritating wait. Service, though often friendly, can at times be harried, as the small restaurant is almost always crowded. Choose a weeknight and arrive before 7pm for your best shot at a quick seating. If there's a line, you can order wine and appetizers on the porch.

In the softly lit dining room, shutters are raised to let in evening breezes, and lanterns glow pleasantly on polished table tops. The menu features locally caught fresh fish with rice or hot, crispy steak fries. Depending on the season, you may find opah or moonfish, a sensationally light monchong, as well the familiar ahi and ono.

New owners have made some good changes: a new sushi bar is fast becoming a destination in itself for high quality, inventive rolls like 'Rainbow poke martini' ($12) with tuna, salmon, and whitefish, all fresh and spicy. Two and sometimes three chefs alternate during the week, both in the kitchen and sushi bar, and so the preparation inevitably varies – sometimes excellent, sometimes needing more (or less) doneness. Fresh fish (on our last visit we tried monchong) is cleanly broiled, with no taste of the grill (about $29 for an 8 oz filet). Ahi teriyaki is one of the most delicious fish dinners on Kauai – juicy, tender, and full of spark. Non-fishy eaters can try 'Hawaiian' chicken ($22) or NY steak ($29). Not so hungry? Some entrées are available in 'menehune' portion ($18 instead of $22 for chicken). Dinners include bread and rice, baked potato, fries, or vegetable brochette.

Dolphin's signature 'family style salad,' a huge bowl of lettuce, cherry tomatoes, bean sprouts, and choice of oil and vinegar, or creamy garlic or Russian dressing is

Heliconia Parrot's Beak

now a paid option ($14/2 persons; $24/4 persons or $7/single), but it comes with organic greens from Kailani Farms instead of Romaine. The wine list offers good choices in the $25-$40 range, like Kendall Jackson chardonnay.

At lunch, you can try Dolphin's sandwiches – with terrific ono or ahi ($12), as well as steak burgers, chicken and vegetable sandwiches, and wonderful fish & chips made with swordfish – light, crisp, and flaky. Dine at picnic tables next to the Hanalei River, or stop at the Dolphin's well stocked fish market tucked behind the restaurant and cook your filet at home.

The Dolphin has been a local favorite for years with its pleasant riverside setting. If mosquitoes tend to pick on you, bring Off and ask for a mosquito coil, for there are no screens. The fish is usually delicious, though warn the waiter that any overcooked fish will be thrown back, if not into the ocean, at least onto his tray!

Hanalei, 5-5016 Kuhio Hwy (RT 560). No reservations. 11am - 10pm daily. Credit cards. *www.hanaleidolphin.com* Map 5

The Hanalei Gourmet 808-26-2524

On your way to the beach at Hanalei? Pick up picnic sandwiches at Hanalei Gourmet where you'll find cheeses, soups, even wines. Order a sandwich ($7- $9) at the deli counter, phone ahead, or take a table in the 'classroom' next door, converted into an attractive café cum bar for those who would prefer to skip the sand altogether. A surprisingly large assort-ment of entrées range from $11 to $23, including pastas, salads, as well as chicken, fish, and steak. We love the spinach and artichoke dip. Try Big Tim's hamburger (1/3 pound for $9) or fresh ahi sandwich ($10). Early bird dinners are from 5:30pm - 6:30pm.

Hanalei, 5-5161 Kuhio Hwy 96714 in Hanalei Center. 8am – 10:30pm daily. Call about music: 808.826.2524 or check *www.northshorekauai.com.* Picnic Baskets. Credit cards. *www.hanaleigourmet.net* Map 5

Kalypso's 808.826.9700

Kalypso's is the new face of Zelo's, but offers pretty much the same menu of well-prepared meals at reasonable prices, with most sandwiches, burgers, and salads around $12 and most full sized entrées $17 - $25. A favorite from the Zelo's menu, specialty fish chowder ($8) is thick, creamy and tasty. Hamburgers (from $9) are excellent, served on a sesame seed bun with fries. Other choices include wraps, salads, fish tacos and sandwiches. Fish & chips are made with fresh island catch, and fish tacos are made with ahi ($14). Dinner entrées range from pasta ($15) to NY steak ($24) and

A world class view, St Regis Hotel

include only a small vegetable. To add a salad, like a 'lite' Caesar, will cost $6 more; a tasty waldorf salad with apples, blue cheese, and nuts adds $14. Macadamia crusted fresh mahi mahi is moist, tender, and flavorful with a lilikoi sauce and rice, reasonably priced at $20. With a full bar and espresso machine, Kalypso's can provide you with almost any beverage you desire.

The dining room is clean, cheerful, and comfortable, with the ceiling open to the rafters and doors open to the outside. Service is sometimes friendly and efficient, sometimes not. Given the reasonable prices and main street location, it's often crowded. Expect to wait on line if you come at peak mealtimes, so go early if you plan to take the kids.

Hanalei. 5-5156 Kuhio Hwy. 11am - 9pm daily. Weekend Brunch 8am - 2:30pm. Credit cards. Call for evening entertainment: 808.826.9700. *www.kalpysokauai.com* Map 5

Kauai Grill, St Regis Hotel 808.826.9644

Once upon a time a very fancy Italian restaurant nestled into the corner of the beautiful Princeville Hotel. If you were lucky enough to get a seat next to one of the beautiful windows that opened onto a spectacular view of Hanalei Bay, you were in for the night of your life. If you weren't so lucky, however, you had a view of the backs of the lucky people's heads. In the St Regis Hotel remodel, all windows have been enlarged, so that everyone has equal access to the panoramic view of Hanalei Bay.

Before the night sky turns dark, diners can watch the sun set into the glistening waters of Hanalei Bay through a long, curved wall of giant windows. Once the sun sinks into the sea, the restaurant's subdued lighting gives the feel of a big city lounge with dark walls, large circular booths, and a center chandelier whose long strings of lights change colors every few minutes. Waiters dressed in black glide from table to table ensuring that water glasses are never empty and bread plates are always full. But you could easily be in New York City.

Kauai Grill, under the direction of executive chef Jean-Georges Vongerichten, creates first-rate food in this exceptional space. The menu varies seasonally. Appetizers may include Japanese hamachi with sugarloaf pineapple, incredibly fresh, the tang of pineapple a perfect complement to the flavor of the fish ($15). Grilled black pepper octopus is another standout ($16). Or try roasted foie gras with mango and ginger ($20), or spiced chicken samosas crunchy on the outside and steamy on the inside ($9). Salad of local watermelon pairs the sweet fruit with a perfect foil, Kanuna Farms goat cheese from Kilauea.

A signature entrée, moi is delicately prepared butterfish with a nut and seed crust ($32). Onaga too is perfectly moist and tasty, although in this case we found the sauce very strongly flavored for this light-textured fish ($34). Salmon (flown in from New Zealand) is prepared as well as you can find anywhere, served with steamed sugar snap peas and shaved fresh wasabi.

Vegetarians can request a special plate, such as a spetzel entrée or tofu with a nut and seed crust. Entrée portions run a bit small, so consider delicious vegetable side dishes ($6-$9) like roasted mushrooms. Sommelier Nicolas has excellent recommendations on the small, well-selected list.

Stunning sunset views (in summer), distinguished food, and unique décor combine to make Kauai Grill a truly memorable experience. You have two first rate dining choices at the St Regis, each with a different chef, menu and price range. Makana Terrace is both more costly and more romantic, with its option of outdoor tables right perched at the edge of Hanalei Bay's lovely colors and wave sounds. Kauai Grill's windows do not open, and after dark, particularly at the earlier dinner hour in winter, reflections from interior lights keep you from hearing the waves or watching the lights flicker around the bay. Nonetheless, the dining experience will make a wonderful memory.

Princeville, St. Regis Hotel, 5520 Ka Haku Rd. 6 - 10pm. Closed Sun & Mon. Reservations: 808.826.9644. Credit cards. ***www.kauaigrill.com*** Map 5

Kilauea Bakery & Pau Hana Pizza . . 828-2020

The small bakery behind Kong Lung has tasty soups, delicious sand-wiches, and inspired pizzas, as well as crusty breads (Hanalei poi sour-dough, sun dried tomato, molasses loaf, gluten-free), cookies (including wonderful macaroons), and macadamia nut sticky buns. Soups change daily. Mulligatawny is a tasty soup flavored with mango, coconut, and curry, bright without being sharp. Try cheeseless vegetable calzones or wheat bread rolled with spinach and tomato. Order pizza whole or by the slice; all are amazingly light and tasty. Pizza may combine goat cheese, sun dried tomatoes, and eggplant, or perhaps be made with feta cheese (or even tofurella), olives, zucchini, fresh mushrooms, and tomato slices. Sometimes available, smoked fresh fish makes for a great combo with vegetables on the Billie Holiday pizza. By the slice: $3.75; 10 inch: $16.53; 16 inch: $31.28.

Try organic coffee, chai lattes, and fruit smoothies. Eat at a half-dozen tables inside, or outside at patio tables with umbrellas to protect from the sun as well as the sudden showers that can threaten to dampen your lunch.

Kilauea, 2484 Keneke, in Kong Lung Center. 6:30am- 9pm; pizza from 11am. Credit cards. Call ahead to order: 808.828.2020. Map 5

Kilauea Fish Market 808-828-MAHI

On the back corner of the old plantation stone building, the Kilauea Fish Market is just large enough to fit a counter, a shining refrigerated case,

Hanalei Valley's fields of taro

and a lively cooking area behind it which houses the grill and stove, where four sauté pans may be sizzling merrily with fresh ahi, or mahi, or even opakapaka for the signature fat, juicy wraps. Local fishermen keep the chef-owner supplied with fresh snappers and tuna (even when most restaurants have to make do with ahi). She uses the freshest organic greens, bright red tomatoes and peppers, and orange sun dried tomato burritos for her wraps. Fresh fish wrap ($11) is a bargain for the size, stuffed with fish, choice of brown or white rice, lots of vegetables, and one of her special sauces. Tip: Ask for sauce packaged in a separate container to keep the wrap dry on the way to the beach, and to have the halves wrapped separately.

Grilled mahi mahi sandwich or teriyaki sandwich are served on a round toasted roll with Maui onions, tomatoes, cilantro, scallions, organic greens, and a home-made creamy oriental dressing. The spicier fajita burrito blends pinto beans, brown rice, fresh tomato salsa, cheddar, sour cream, and organic greens with ahi or tofu. Vegetarians can choose a delicious wrap with tofu and vegetables, or organic greens salad ($7 each).

best in local fish!

Looking for an inexpensive, tasty dinner? Try chicken and beef barbecue or teriyaki plates, kalbi beef ribs plate ($9) or the fresh fish filets, ahi poke, or even the corn-fed beefsteaks displayed temptingly in the case. Bring wine or beer. Kids' menu starts at $6. Eat outside at patio tables (kids can play and run around), or take your meal home.

Everything is cooked to order, so be patient because Kilauea fish market is a must stop on the north shore. Popular demand is so good that there is a new eastside branch in Coconut Marketplace, Wailua. Try it out.

Kilauea, 4270 Lighthouse Rd on the left almost opposite Kong Lung. 808.828.6244. 11am - 8pm. Closed Sundays. Credit cards. Map 5

Lighthouse Bistro 808.828.0480

Italian cuisine with local ingredients is the specialty here, served in an informal, open air setting. The attractive grey and white dining room has sliding glass doors that open to evening breezes, and a spare decor that, in candlelight, has its own charm. The menu features fresh fish ($26), steaks ($24-$35), chicken, and pasta (from $13) accompanied by rice, vegetable, and a small bread loaf. To add a green salad boosts your dinner cost ($7). In the past, we have found sauces to be on the strong side, and so we ordered our onaga plainly sautéed rather than ginger crusted. It arrived overcooked, a problem cheerfully remedied by the kitchen. The vegetarian dish, polenta tower, was also over-cooked. Really hungry? Try the all-you-can-eat pasta bar ($14); one visit (plus dinner salad) is only $16.

The 30 or so wines are mostly reasonably priced, though you might try a delicious flavored martini ($7) like 'pineapple upside down cake' (vanilla and pineapple vodkas with fresh fruit juice). Service is friendly and mostly efficient. Children's menu. At lunch try excellent sandwiches ($7-$12).

Kilauea, 2484 Keneke St in Kong Lung Center. Lunch 12 - 2:30pm; Dinner 5:30 - 9pm. Credit cards. *www.lighthousebistro.com* Map 5

Makana Terrace, St Regis Hotel .808.826.9644

The St. Regis Hotel (formerly the Sheraton Princeville) is blessed with one of the most spectacular views in the world: a panorama of Hanalei Bay with shimmering waters, angular mountains and golden beaches. Even in the rain, you can watch mountains peek out through veils of mist. Or watch as the sun's sorcery transforms the landscape from smoky greys into blazing colors – vivid greens and golds, brilliant blues, and on the mountains above the bay, shining silver ribbons of waterfalls.

At sunset, as the sky turns orange and turquoise behind the darkening cliffs, enjoy a cocktail on one of the plush couches in the elegant room. But who can stay inside at sunset? Outside, the terrace is enclosed by waist-high glass, so that you can enjoy the spectacular panorama of Hanalei Bay without a railing to obstruct your view. Boats glide silently; the only sound is the soft music of the waves. Mountains are shrouded in clouds, and the

An outrigger canoe glides across Hanalei Bay

sky turns to gold as the sun slips slowly into the sea, while colors deepen the reflections in tall glass windowpanes.

As Hanalei Bay recedes into the velvet darkness and the first stars appear, walk downstairs to *Makana Terrace* and be seated at one of the tables laid with elegant china and sparkling crystal. You may think nothing could make that moment any better. And then you take your first bite.

An *amuse-bouche* arrives from the chef, in our case, a tiny but delicious savory pear salad with a bite of brie. The menu changes seasonally. Appetizers are excellent: you may find a perfectly textured ahi poke ($20); tender 'lamb lollipops' served with minted yoghurt ($16); a sensational tomato gazpacho with grilled tiger prawn ($14); or a generous and crisp green salad topped with a tangy carrot miso vinaigrette ($12).

Understatement is the secret to preparing fresh fish. The chef's lemongrass crusted ahi is among the island's finest presentations of a fish that can be delicate when treated deftly ($39). Tender pieces of perfectly textured fish surround a sweet and spicy glass noodle salad – almost too beautiful to eat but impossible to resist. Crispy onaga is another winner, perfectly cooked, light and tasty ($32). Hamachi made a spectacular appearance – and then quickly disappeared, a wonderful array of fish and flavors.

Some menu choices are surprisingly inexpensive, like pasta ($16) or risotto ($22). Vegetarians can select from nearly a dozen vegetable side dishes ($7 each) or a tofu entrée, in our case a black tea smoked tofu with a somewhat spicy tomato sauce ($20). The wine list contains some reasonable options by the glass, and some good choices by the bottle, like a Byron pinot noir ($55). An appropriate finale to an exceptional dinner is 'chocolate trio,' a delicious blend of three creamy layers of chocolate.

As the name suggests, most tables are on the terrace to afford a full experience of the sights and sounds of Hanalei Bay, though you can also dine inside. The view of Hanalei is spectacular, so if you only have one night on the north shore, and if you can splurge for unforgettable dining,

Makana Terrace is for you. Take the elevator down to the beach after dinner and listen to the music of the waves and melodies in the evening breezes.

Princeville, St. Regis Hotel, 5520 Ka Haku Rd. Breakfast: 6:30 - 11am; Lunch: 11:30 - 2:30pm; Dinner: 5:30 - 9:30pm. Reservations: 808.826.9644. Credit cards. *www.stregisprinceville.com/dining.* Map 5

Mediterranean Gourmet. 808.826.9875

Mediterranean Gourmet serves a limited menu in a pleasant beachfront location in Ha'ena. Wood tables and comfortable rattan chairs face the ocean; fly fans encourage breezes and windows open to views of kite surfing on the breezy point. In this kitchen, garlic is a favorite. Hummus has a sharp bite, and we ended up sending ours back in exchange for an excellent tabbouleh ($13). Greek salad has lots of olives, feta, and tasty dressing; we ordered fresh ahi as an add-on; and the generous piece was perfectly cooked medium rare (or seared) adding $10 to the salad price ($12). Service is pleasant and the setting relaxing. You can also order a take-out picnic.

Ha'ena, 5-7132 Kuhio Hwy, in Hanalei Colony Resort. Dinner 4 - 8pm M - Sat; Lunch 11am - 4pm daily. Credit cards. Pat Durkin plays jazz guitar some evenings. *www.kauaimedgourmet.com* Map 5

Nanea 808.827.8700

Nanea in the Westin Princeville has a dining veranda next to the pool and waterfall to serve hotel and timeshare guests. The veranda is more pleasant than the dining room inside, where music can be a distraction. The menu offers entrées from $18 (pasta) to $29 (fresh fish). Seafood chowder was thick rather than creamy, heavier on potatoes than fish, and strongly flavored with thyme ($8). A better appetizer was a beautiful salad of fresh local greens with papaya, tomato and cucumber ($9). We tried two local fish entrées recommended by our server as fresh that day. Monchong arrived overcooked, both dry and tough. Sesame crusted seared ahi, on the other hand, arrived still cold in the center. We sent it back, and when heated through, the fish was much more satisfactory, although the ponzo sauce which accompanied it was far to strong and we were happy to have ordered it confined to a side dish. Service is cheerful and efficient in the garden patio next to the pool, where candles light the tables and the sounds of waterfall make the evening pleasant. The St Regis dining room at Makana Terrace offers pasta entrées for the about the same price, and fresh fish for a few dollars more, with the added benefit of a much more elegant dining room and a spectacular oceanfront setting.

Princeville, 3838 Wylie Rd. Lunch, dinner, daily. Credit Cards. Map 5

Neidie's Salsa & Samba. 808.826.1851

On a back porch in Hanalei, with only a tiny sign out front, you will find a slight woman cooking in a tiny kitchen just across a counter from a half dozen tables. Don't be fooled by appearances. Neidie makes magic in there, deftly blending Brazilian spices with Kauai's fresh vegetables and fruits. You may have to wait for one of these tables inside or on the porch outside. There are only ten, and they are usually full.

The reason is a combination of great food and great prices. Home-made chips and delicious fresh salsa start the meal, but save room for Neidie's wonderful Brazilian cooking. She weaves Kauai's fresh fruits, vegetables, and fish into recipes from her homeland. Local fish is cleanly grilled and tasty, with a delicious coconut milk sauce, served on a large platter with Brazilian rice and vegetable – at only $15, one of the best bargains on Kauai. Or try a vegetarian pancake with fresh pumpkin, tropical squash and whatever vegetables have tempted Neidie at the market ($9). Demand for Neidie's pumpkin pancake has shifted a neighboring farmer into hyperdrive to keep her supplied. Service may be on the slow side but for the right reason – Neidie cooks everything to order. Spicing is subtle rather than flashy, so if it's not hot enough for your taste, you can add as many chilis as you want. Prices are amazing considering the size of the portions. You can take-out some of her magic and enjoy a picnic at the beach.

For delicious, carefully spiced and imaginative Brazilian dishes served with a pleasant, personal touch, don't miss Neidie's!

Hanalei, 5-5161 Kuhio Hwy in Hanalei Center. For take-out, reservations: 808.826.1851. 11am - 3pm; 5pm - 9pm daily. Credit cards. Map 5

Postcards Café 808.826.1192

As you round the bend in the winding road into Hanalei, you'll see Postcards Café in the historic green Hanalei Museum building. Despite its modest exterior, Postcards surprises you with a carefully crafted dining experience — an interesting, thoughtful cuisine served in a comfortably informal atmosphere. You enter Postcards from a small porch. Inside, you'll find an intimate dining room with open beamed ceilings and soft lighting that makes everything look at once clean and relaxing. Vintage Hawaiian postcards appear under glass table tops and in collages on the walls, along with black and white photographs of old Hanalei, even old-time ukuleles.

deliciously healthful

Dinner is café-style informal. Tables in this charming plantation cottage are set without linens, and windows, with the modern addition of screens, slide open for evening breezes, or close for occasional showers. The cuisine is exceptional, both in concept and execution, and everything is generous and fresh, prepared without meat, poultry, or chemicals. Taro fritters ($9) make a wonderful appetizer, the small patties deep-fried and served with a tangy homemade mango chutney. In salmon rockets, tender slices of salmon are rolled in layers of lumpia and nori and quick fried ($10). Summer rolls ($9) are delicious, as is homemade soup.

The dinner menu is small, only seven entrées featuring locally grown vegetables and fresh island fish. Least expensive are pasta primavera or a Chinese vegetable dish with roasted tofu and a tamari ginger sauce ($15). Fresh ono was cleanly cooked, moist, flavorful and flaky, and although we sampled all four sauces on the menu and enjoyed each unique flavor – particularly the coconut – we preferred the fish cleanly grilled. Of the three pasta choices, two vegetarian, we liked 'Seafood Sorrento,' a delicious combination of shrimp with medallions of all four fresh fish on the menu, gently seasoned in a sauce of mushrooms, tomatoes, bell peppers, and as requested, only light on garlic ($22). The portion was so generous that our son raved about the leftovers the next day. Children can choose pasta or quesadilla ($8). If you can't decide, the kitchen is ready to prepare your request, or you can opt for a beautiful local salad ($8).

On Kauai, poinsettia bloom along the road, and glisten in rain showers.

Desserts, made without refined sugar, are elegant and delicious. Lilikoi mousse arrives in a lovely colored tumbler, and vegan chocolate silk is amazingly light for its dense chocolate flavor, or try coconut sorbet (all $8). The wine list is small, though well-selected, and includes some delicious organic wines, or try organic smoothies and juices, or organic Kona coffee.

Waitpersons are friendly, like the owners who stop to chat and give sound vacation advice to diners whom they treat as guests.

Postcards Café is a must stop on the north shore for an imaginative cuisine served in an attractive, comfortably informal dining room. If you aren't a vegetarian, Postcards might change your mind.

Hanalei, 5-5075 Kuhio Hwy. 6pm - 9pm daily. Reserve at least a day in advance: 808.826.1191. Credit cards. *www.postcardscafe.com* Map 5

Princeville Golf Course 808.826.5050

With a spectacular panoramic setting amid mountains, rolling fairways, and ocean, the clubhouse restaurant at the Prince Course is a great spot for a surprisingly inexpensive lunch or breakfast. The entry is all glass, and through enormous windows you can see all the way to the horizon as you walk downstairs, past the glass enclosed health club, to the dining room.

The restaurant has never seemed equal to the setting, and now, while the Prince Course is renovated, the popular island restaurant chain, Roy's, is helping to develop a new concept. When your visit rolls around, we hope you'll let us know what you find out.

Princeville, 5-3900 Kuhio Hwy (east of Princeville's main entry). Map 5

Red Hot Mama's 808.826.7266

Tucked up next to the Wainiha General Store is a tiny take-out window which advertises the best Mex on the north shore (since Neidie's is Brazilian, we agree!). You can have beef, chicken, fresh island fish, pulled pork, or vegetarian tacos or burritos in a small ($9) or 'fat mama' size. 'The fat mama' is truly stuffed — brown or white rice, sour cream, beans, chicken or tofu, fresh fish, or sliced steak, all wrapped in a generous sun dried tomato burrito. Kids can have a PBJ burrito.

Hard-working owner Melissa wants to support local organic farmers, so greens and herbs are always fresh. She uses brown rice and grass-fed beef;

fish tacos ($6 each or 3/$16) use only a fresh local tasty catch. Breakfast is in the works. Each burrito and taco is made to order, so be prepared to be patient if someone is ahead of you on line. It's well worth the wait.

Wainiha, 5-6607 Kuhio Hwy. Call in your order: 808.826.7266. 11am - 5pm. Cash only. Map 5

Tamarind 808.826.9999

The open air food court in the Princeville Center is an unlikely place to find a first rate Thai restaurant. However, Tamarind creates real magic in a meticulously clean kitchen with almost no turn-around room buzzing with sizzle and pop. The menu features a wide range of vegetarian dishes (to which chicken, pork, or tofu can be added) as well as appetizers, Chinese dishes, curries, fresh island fish (from $14) and noodle soups. Pom, the hardworking owner, takes orders with a smile, and will customize the extensive menu choices to fit the most complex parameters, then deliver your choices to outdoor tables on china platters. Even take out packaging shows her detail oriented approach: each styrofoam box is lined with aluminum foil to preserve the heat, and soup containers are triple taped then tied carefully in a plastic bag.

Try Tom Kar with chicken, delicately seasoned and chock full of cleanly sliced white meat, fragrant with lemongrass, coconut, and ganagal. We also enjoyed piquant eggplant with large chunks of tofu. Tamarind can cook for a party with a 2 day notice. If you want a great take out meal for your hotel room or condo lanai, Tamarind is an excellent choice for reasonable prices and friendly service.

Princeville, Princeville Shopping Center. 808.826.9999 for take-out. 10:30am - 9pm daily.

Jeffrey Courson

South Shore Restaurants

'favor..eats'

For a spectacular oceanfront setting, particularly at sunset, try the *Beach House Restaurant* near Spouting Horn. In Poipu, *Roy's Poipu Bar & Grill* features the Euro/Asian cuisine of Roy Yamaguchi in a bistro setting. Next door at *Keoki's*, families and hearty eaters can enjoy generous steak and seafood dinners at reasonable prices. For pasta and fresh local fish in one of Kauai's most romantic garden settings, try *Plantation Gardens*. Or visit *Casablanca's* garden setting at the Kiahuna Tennis Club for Mediterranean style cuisine and local entertainment.

The new Kukuʻiula Center features Kauai new-comer *Merriman's,* and Kauai old-timer Jean-Marie Josselin in his new tapas venture *Josselin's* with inventive dishes you will find nowhere else on the island. Nearby in the new Poipu Koa Kea Hotel, *Red Salt* offers a carefully designed and delicious cuisine in a small and elegant bar/dining setting. Wherever you dine, stroll through the beautiful *Grand Hyatt Resort* afterwards, a treat which can be yours for the modest cost of the tip for the valet who parks your car. Enjoy Hawaiian melodies at the Seaview Lounge overlooking the ocean (W and Sat between 6 and 8pm), or stop in at Stevenson's Library for an after dinner drink or game of billiards, or simply stroll the hotel's lovely grounds. Dinner at *Tidepools*, while expensive, offers excellent steak and fresh island fish.

On a budget? Try generous breakfasts and lunches at *Joe's on the Green* in the Kiahuna Golf Course clubhouse. Don't miss the *Koloa Fish Market* for tasty plate lunches and some of the best seared ahi you will find – at bargain prices. But don't stay in Poipu. Take a short drive to Kalaheo for wonderful, reasonably priced restaurants – *Kalaheo Steak & Rib* (new owners), *Kalaheo Café & Coffee Company* for deli treats, or *Brick Oven Pizza*, a favorite for the island's best pizza. *Pomodoro* offers carefully prepared meals and professional service you'd expect at higher prices.

Beach House Restaurant 808.742.1424

A longtime favorite of both residents and visitors, the Beach House once perched on a sea wall only inches from the waves, a great spot to watch the sun set into the ocean. In fact, tables were so close to the waves that when Hurricane 'Iwa struck in 1982, the restaurant was swept out to sea – leaving only the concrete slab to mark the spot where so many evenings had passed so pleasantly. Rebuilt at a more respectful distance from the waves, Beach House was again destroyed by Hurricane Iniki, and then re-opened once more in the same location, clearly hoping the third time is the charm.

The menu is Pacific Rim, with steak, salmon, and rack of lamb ($36), as well as chicken ($26) and seafood. Entrées average $20-$40, although two could make a light meal of several appetizers ($9-$18).

Appetizers arrive with delicious bread. Salad with fresh local asparagus, tomatoes, and goat cheese ($9) is tasty (though no longer made with Kauai's special white asparagus), as is wild mushroom gnocchi served with organic greens and smoked salmon ($9). A small dinner salad of greens from nearby

Poipu Beach

Kauai's cardinals can have red heads

Omao is fresh and colorful with a light sesame and orange vinaigrette ($7). Entrées, particularly fresh local fish, are delicious, like fire roasted fresh ahi, both flaky and tender ($33), or macadamia nut mahi mahi served with a delicious citrus miso sauce.

The setting is truly lovely. Tables are well-separated, and sliding glass doors open to the evening air and spectacular views of surfers catching waves as the sun sets into the shimmering sea. It's beautiful even after dark, as the last light of sunset fades, and you can linger over coffee and watch the waves begin to glisten with moonlight. It's such a special spot that you might emphasize to your server to *slow* the dinner pace, so you have time to enjoy nature's splendor. Servers have been known to try to hasten the departure of diners, so sit firm and hint at a large tip.

Poipu, 5022 Lawai Rd. Dinner nightly 5:30 - 10pm (September 15-March 31); 6 - 10pm (April 1-Sept 14). Reserve at least a day in advance: 808.742.1424. Request a window table, but be prepared to wait up to a half hour for it. Credit cards. ***www.the-beach-house.com*** Map 6

Brennecke's Beach Broiler. . . 808.742.1424

For almost twenty years, Brennecke's has served tasty, reasonably-priced dinners for the whole family, with a varied menu, a first-rate salad bar and friendly, efficient service. It's second-storey perch gives you a bird's eye view of Poipu Beach Park across the street, and in its informal open air dining room, you'll feel comfortable no matter what you're wearing. The decor looks very plain – a porch in soft grey and white tones – but everything is clean, the paint fresh looking, the chairs and grey formica tables immaculate, even the flowers in the window boxes bright and cheerful.

The food receives equal attention to detail. Dinner entrées include fresh island fish (Brennecke's specialty), as well as beef, pasta, poultry, even prime rib in three sizes ($21-$29).

Returning Brennecke's diners may notice that the signature kiawe wood grill has been replaced by a conventional gas stove, and that chef Ligea has retired after decades of kitchen magic, but we know that time does pass by. What doesn't change in owner Bob French's commitment to excellence.

A new chef and a new dining manager have revamped the menu to include a wonderful new combination option – 2 different fresh fish filets of your choice on one plate – for only a dollar or so more than the regular portion ($28). Dinners include rice, sautéed fresh vegetables, and a visit to a first-rate salad bar – fresh, colorful, ripe, and appetizing. Instead of rice, try a huge baked potato ($2 extra). Not hungry enough for a full dinner? Brennecke's offers reasonably-priced burgers ($9 including a vegetarian variant) sandwiches, and small plates. Clam chowder ($4/cup) is creamy rather than thick, generous with clams, and well seasoned. Tiger eye sushi, fresh ahi wrapped in rice and nori and quick fried, keeps the fish cool while the wrapper is hot ($13.50). Fresh fish sandwich is cleanly grilled and served on a soft bun. Vegetarians will enjoy vegetable stir fry or pasta dinners ($22) or the attractive salad bar ($9 by itself or $4 with a sandwich).

Though small, the wine list is fairly priced, with a Kendall Jackson chardonnay at about $25, or try an exotic drink from the full bar. The 'under-12's' have a great menu, including pizza ($8), fish sandwich ($9), or spaghetti, burger with fries, or soup & salad ($5). The sandwich menu is served all day, and at lunch you can enjoy the view in full sunshine.

Poipu, 2100 Ho'one Rd. 11am - 10pm daily; happy hour 2 - 5pm. Reservations 808.742.7588. For menu, surf report, or to order tee-shirts, Nukomoi surf wear: 808.742.8019; *www.brenneckes.com* Maps 6, 7

Brick Oven Pizza 808.332.8561

Ask just about any Kauai resident where to find the best pizza, and you'll probably hear, 'Brick Oven.' We agree. And we're not alone, for tourists, as well as local families, have made Brick Oven a favorite for years. The cheerful dining room has red–checked tablecloths and murals of pizza serendipity – a pizza shaped like the island of Kauai, for example, with a 'Garlic Grotto,' 'Mushroom Valley,' 'Grand Pizza Canyon,' and 'Port Anchovy.' Friendliness is in the air.

Kauai's best family pizza

Good as all this is, the pizza is even better. The homemade dough – either white or whole wheat – is delicious, crunchy without being dry and with a fluted crust like a pie, shiny with garlic butter. The sauce, in the words of the teenage judges, has "awesome spice, cooked just right." There is lots of cheese, the Italian sausage is made right in the kitchen, and tomatoes are red, juicy and fresh. Portions are generous and quality unbeatable. You may also be tempted to try one of the outrageous special creations, like the 'super.' Or consider a delicious sandwich on fresh baked roll, or a salad. Wash it all down with a pitcher of ice cold beer or soda (ice comes in the glasses, not in the pitcher). Kids love to watch the dough spin into pizza during that hard, hungry time of waiting, especially at peak hours when it's jammed.

At Brick Oven, you'll find a smile and pleasant word for short persons no matter how cranky. When one child spilled coke, our waitress not only wiped her dry but brought a new glass filled to the brim.

Each child can ask for a ball of pizza dough, which feels so good in the hands that it (usually) manages to stay out of the hair – all the way home.

Kalaheo, 2-2555 Kaumualii Hwy (Rt 50) Also in Kapa'a: 808.332.8561. 11am-10pm. Closed Mondays. Credit cards. Map 6.

Casablanca 808.742.2929

Walk down a torch-lit path through the Kiahuna Golf and Tennis Club and you will find a little slice of the Mediterranean. Open air setting, with wicker furniture and green plants, creates a comfortable, romantic atmosphere for lunch, dinner, tapas or cocktails. Local musicians play.

Casablanca incorporates local Kauai produce and seafood, and Big Island beef, into an interesting menu which varies seasonally. Dinner begins with fragrant, crusty bread still warm from the oven. 'Mozzarella Fresca' ($11) is served with a tasty port sauce over poached figs. 'Insalata Caprese' with roasted cherry tomatoes is a better choice than 'Panzella Salad,' a rather ordinary green salad with garlic dressing and croutons. Small plates are also tempting, featuring prawns, lamb, a house specialty lobster 'ceviche,' and crepes – plenty of choices to make an interesting meal.

There's also a surprising variety of dinner entrées. Duck is seared, served with a balsamic sauce ($21), and roast pork is also excellent. The kitchen prefers to use natural juices and vegetables to enhance entrée flavors rather than overpower them. Even vegetable couscous, a tasty combination of roasted root vegetables over couscous, has distinctive individual flavors, and vegetarians have other options. Desserts are outstanding. Panna cotta is very light with a delicate boysenberry sauce. Blueberry noisetta, chunky with blueberries, is lighter than the ricotta cheese cake, and chocolate mousse with orange is deliciously creamy. Prices are similar to Plantation Gardens or Casa di Amici, with entrées averaging more than $20 and appetizers about $10. Keiki menu includes PB&J and grilled cheese.

Nature's disposable container

Poipu, KiahunaTennis and Swim Club, 2290 Poipu Rd. Closed Mondays. Lunch/tapas: 11am - 3pm; dinner 5 - 9pm; Sunday Brunch 10am - 2pm. Local music W - Th 6 - 8pm; happy hour 2 - 6pm. Credit cards. Call about entertainment: 808.742.2929. *www.casablancakauai.com* Maps 6, 7

Casa di Amici 808.742.1555

Casa di Amici's new chef/owner, Rey Dikilato, the talented sous chef for many years, is giving the restaurant his personal stamp of quality and dedication, emphasizing old favorites as well as new ideas.

The dining room feels romantic yet comfortable, with well-separated tables lit with candle lamps and open to evening breezes. You feel island hospitality in the air. The menu welcomes those who don't want a huge and expensive meal: some entrées priced in either 'full' or 'light' portions include an impressive selection of veal and poultry, fresh fish, pastas, and vegetable entrées. Asian salad with goat cheese, macadamia nuts and a delicious sesame ginger vinaigrette ($9) is a stand-out. Prices range from $22/light or $27/full for chicken or eggplant casserole, to $28 for 'Tournedos Rossini,' medallions of beef, paté de foie gras and mushroom caps.

Dinner begins with a loaf of crusty bread served with butter or a rather strong hummus. Appetizers ranging from $9 (salads) to $15 include 4 risottos. Something you crave is not on the menu? The chef will individualize any dish, and our vegan loved the result: vegetable risotto made with vegetable stock and no oil, filled with still crunchy vegetables.

The menu's strength is the quality of the ingredients and the generosity of the portions. Ahi for example is light, flaky, delicately flavored, and so fresh it must have just come off the boat (the chef, born and raised on Kauai, has close contacts with fisherman). When ordering fish, we usually request sauce to be served on the side, so we can judge the quality and freshness, and it is a good policy here so you can taste fish so perfectly prepared that its flavor could not be enhanced. Braised lamb shank is another good choice, and here the tender rich cabernet sauce makes the entrée wonderful. We also liked crispy sautéed duck breast flavored with cherries.

Everyone is friendly, as is appropriate in a restaurant which calls itself Casa di Amici, from servers to the hostess who asks you how you enjoyed your dinner and reminds you to drive safely. The parking lot is small; you may have better luck parking on the street.

Poipu, 2301 Nalo Rd. Dinner nightly from 6pm. Credit cards. *www.casadiamici.com* Maps 6, 7

Dondero's, Grand Hyatt 808.742.1234

Decorated in vibrant green and white, Dondero's elegant dining room is designed to capture the leisurely pace of the 1920's, before jet-set timetables pushed life into permanent fast-forward. Arranged on two levels, tables are comfortably spaced for privacy. The room seems poised on the edge of a seaside garden, with large windows and french doors opening to the terrace. China and silver are softly lit by the golden glow of crystal lamps.

Dondero's new menu features entrées from $26 (chicken) to $36 (steak or fresh fish) as well as pastas ($14-$17) and several risotto creations ($10-$14). Fresh local sea bass ($36) was perfectly tender and moist, though we were glad to have ordered the very spicy tomato broth on the side. You can also create an inexpensive, interesting meal from several of the 20 or so inexpensive antipasti, including calamari (sautéed or fried $6); beef carpaccio ($5); a wonderful Caprese Salad with soft, tender fresh mozzarella ($9); two large pieces of rosemary skewered lamb ($5); a first rate grilled eggplant with burrata cheese and candied lemon ($5). Most wines cost more than $50, but many are available by the glass. You'll love the desserts – chocolate mousse, and an outstanding tiramisu.

At Dondero's, prices are expensive, though the new menu offers several reasonable options, and the hotel comes with the meal. Consider your dinner as a single course in your entire evening. For an aperitif, walk around the hotel and listen to Kauai's musicians perform in the Seaview Lounge. After dinner, stroll the beautifully lit gardens and enjoy the breezes of evening.

Poipu, Grand Hyatt Hotel. 1571 Poipu Rd. Reservations: conciergekauai@ hyatt.com or 808.742.1234. Free valet parking. Children's menu. Credit cards. *www.kauai.hyatt.com* Maps 6, 7

Joe's on the Green 808.742.9696

The restaurant at the Kiahuna Golf Clubhouse has long been a favorite of local families for large portions at reasonable prices. Breakfast includes wonderful macadamia nut pancakes ($7) or 'make your own omelettes' ($9), and there's even an early bird special before 9am ($5). At lunch, sandwiches include Joe's Mama Burger ($10); a quarter-pound 'Dog named Joe' with sauerkraut ($8); an excellent fresh fish sandwich ($12); and several salad options, including a 'build-your-own' (from $9.50). Soup with a half-sandwich or a salad is a tasty choice for $9. Vegetarian choices include sandwiches, veggie burgers, and salads.

The dining room is open on three sides, with welcome breezes and mountain views. Two nights a week you can enjoy dinner with music by local Hawaiian entertainers. Call to find out who's playing: 808.742.9696. For anyone looking for unpretentious food on large, rather than small plates, it's a great choice.

Poipu, Kiahuna Golf Course. Breakfast 7 - 11:30am; Lunch 11:30 - 2:30pm daily. Live Hawaiian music and pu pus Sun - Thurs 5 - 7pm. Happy hour: 3 - 7pm daily. Credit cards. *www.ygli.bluedomino.com* Maps 6, 7

Josselin's Tapas Bar & Grill . .808.742.7117

After an absence of several years, Jean Marie Josselin is back cooking on Kauai, this time in his new tapas restaurant in Kuku'iula Center. You'll find a large menu of small plates, which give the appearance of reasonable prices ($12 or less) and allows this imaginative chef to create a panorama of flavors and preparations to delight visitors to his small dining room cum open kitchen. Try scallops in cardamom coconut broth; tempura ahi in soy ginger beurre blanc; fire cracker salmon rolls; coffee flavored pork served with bao, a flaky banana flavored pastry. Vegetarians have many options: summer risotto, steamed vegetables in small dumplings, as well as soups, 'live greens,' and vegetables from local farms. Those who remember A

Pacific Café will recognize the wonderful specialty sesame-crusted wok-seared island mahi-mahi with lime ginger beurre blanc sauce ($20) and a spectacularly smooth butterfish ($23) on

J. Courson

the 'large plate' menu. It's a deal – a full sized portion at a tapas price.

In keeping with the trend to end stuffy dining by blurring the line between bar and dining room, sangria is served from a roving cart, either with red wine with pomegranate and tropical fruits or pinot grigio flavored with lychee. Sip with wonderful ginger muffins or sesame buns. For dessert, macadamia nut profiteroles filled with peppermint ice cream and served with a dense chocolate sauce are wonderful.

The restaurant is elegant, with well-spaced tables and big windows which fill the room with light. Keep in mind, though, that a menu based on 'small plates' encourages each person to order at least 2-3 dishes and may make your bill larger than you expect.

Koloa, 2829 Ala Kalanikaumaka St in Kukuʻiula Center. Dinner nightly. Reservations: 808.742.7117. Credit Cards. Map 7

Kalaheo Café & Coffee Co . . . 808.332.5858

Kalaheo Café & Coffee Co has spacious quarters across from Brick Oven Pizza in Kalaheo. Tall ceilings and fans keep the air moving inside, while outside, tables on the porch offer a view of what's going down Rt 50. You follow the 'House Rules': 'Grab a menu, Grab a table. Place your order.' You wait at the table for the food to be delivered by runners.

The menu offers a variety of breakfast and lunch options. Turkey burger is very fresh, tender, and moist ($8) served on fresh baked roll. Loyal customers rave about 'bagel benny,' toasted with ham, turkey or grilled veggies, topped with a poached egg and hollandaise sauce (with rice or potatoes), and served even at lunch. Try a croissant egg sandwich, or a delicious wrap filled with tuna, bacon and melted cheddar and avocado. Don't miss the grilled vegetable sandwich (eggplant, zucchini, and lettuce and tomato), memorable for its unique spices, or grilled tofu and eggplant. On the children's menu, you'll find grilled cheese or PB&J ($3.50). For breakfast try delicious eggs, waffles, pancakes, bagel creations, and fresh pastries. For a beach picnic, call ahead. You can also buy Kauai coffee to take home.

Kalaheo, 2-2560 Kaumualii Hwy (Rt 50) 6:30am - 2:30pm (M - S); 6:30am-2pm (Sun). Table service at dinner Wed-Sat from 5:30pm. Credit cards. *www.kalaheo.com* Map 6

Kalaheo Steak and Ribs 808.332.4444

Completely renovated by new owners, and just as much a local favorite, Kalaheo Steak and Ribs has opened in the old Kalaheo Steak House location. A meat lover's delight, entrées feature top 8% Kansas beef. Even mac and cheese for kids is homemade. The cozy, knotty-pine interior is freshly finished (owner Ernie Kanekoa spent five days sanding floors to bring back luster) and fitted with comfortable booths, roomy tables. Photographs show historic Kauai scenes.

Beef or pork rib entrées ($18-$20) are, to quote a local friend, 'ono.' Steaks (from $18/teriyaki flank steak to $26/NY) are tasty and generous; prime rib (10oz/$20; 14oz/$24; 16oz/$28) is juicy and tender with little waste. Entrées come with a small side salad and choice of potato or rice. Vegetarians can try vegetable brochettes ($12) and gluten-free pasta. You can make a small meal of an appetizer (e.g. a generous cut of calamari steak $12)

and an a la carte salad ($9). Desserts include a home-made, sinfully choco-late cheesecake, and delicious mango lilikoi fruit pie by Sandy at 'The Right Slice.'

With real island friendliness and fair prices, Kalaheo Steak House is an excellent alternative to high priced Poipu dining. No reservations.

Kalaheo, 4444 Papalina Rd. Dinner T - Sun 5 - 9:30pm; Early bird 5 - 6pm; 9:30 - 10:30pm. Credit cards. *www.kalaheosteakandribs.com* Map 6

Keoki's Paradise 808.742.7534

At Keoki's you may feel as if you've wandered onto the set of a Tommy Bahama commercial. Tables on several levels surround a wandering stream, where taro grows among lava rocks, and a frog or two rest among the lily pads. Wooden tables are roomy and rattan chairs comfortably upholstered. Ask to be seated outside, where dining is cooled by evening breezes and you can watch the sky turn luminous with stars. Should a passing shower threaten to douse the table, waiters will set the awnings.

Keoki's offers reasonable prices as well as an atmosphere of South Pacific chic. In busy times, a line of hungry diners begins to form at 7pm. To the right of the entrance is the bar, where you can eat pu pus, salads, hamburgers ($8), sandwiches ($9), and local style plates like grilled fresh fish ($13), or stir-fry chicken ($10). Come early and sit at one of the half dozen tables near the bar and you can put together an inexpensive dinner.

Keoki's main dining room features a reasonably priced, steak and seafood menu. Dinners include fresh baked rolls and bran muffins, white rice or rice pilaf, and Caesar salad (or romaine lettuce, oil and vinegar). Fresh fish ($23-$29) can be ordered in 5 styles, including 'simply healthy,' cleanly grilled with no butter or oil, and served with pineapple salsa. This is the preparation of choice, as we have found the sauces and marinades to be of varying quality, often too strong for the fish. Fresh-baked opakapaka was moist, generous, and cleanly grilled, a first-rate piece of fish. Prime rib is tender, and though a bit bland, its appearance at 24 oz was a show stopper ($32). The small wine list offers a nice selection of California wines mostly in the $35 range. Don't miss 'hula pie' (the drive guides may have coupons).

Keoki's reasonable prices and generous portions attract a large clientele. Service is friendly, and you can often enjoy local entertainers. Call to see who's playing.

Koloa. Poipu Shopping Village. 2360 Kiahuna Plantation Drive. Reserva-tions a must: 808.742.7534. Bar menu: 11am - 11:30pm; Dinner 5 - 10pm nightly. Credit cards. *www.keokisparadise.com* Maps 6, 7

Koloa Fish Market 808.742.6199

Do you want the best in plate lunches, the tastiest poke (3 styles), the freshest seared ahi? Look for this tiny store front on main street Koloa for deli deals and fresh fish filets. Seared ahi is buttery smooth. Plate lunches (including pork ribs, chicken lau lau, and stir fry) are heaped. Good bets: summer rolls ($3.50), edamame ($3.50), and seaweed salad.

Local folks love it, so be prepared for a line-up at lunch time. The staff is fast and efficient, more than up to dealing with the crowd, and you can't beat the prices – or the poke.

Koloa, 5482 Koloa Rd next to Big Save.10am - 6pm (M - F); 10am - 5pm (Sat); closed Sundays. Take-out: 808.742.6199. Cash only. Maps 6, 7

Merriman's 808.742.8385

Ever since ground broke at the new Kuku'iula Village Shopping Center next to Kauai's first and only roundabout, Poipu residents eagerly awaited the opening of Merriman's, one of Hawaii's most famous restaurant chains. Like its sister restaurants on the Big Island and Maui, Merriman's in Poipu prides itself on its regional offerings from both maki (sea) and mauka (land).

The restaurant is large, open, and bright— much like a plantation house, with tables seating 5 or 6 all along its rear deck. An extensive bar fills one part of the main dining room, but the restaurant's 25 tables are so well spaced, you hardly even notice it. Bread arrives steamy from the oven in a straw basket with a closing top to keep it warm. For an extra $6, you can order local goat cheese and organic papaya-strawberry jam.

Roasted south 'shoreganics' include a generous serving of Kunana Dairy feta and candied cashews ($11). We loved the ahi and local water-melon poke ($16), a surprising and delicious combination of flavors. Baked Kunana Dairy goat cheese phyllo ($15) is another good choice served with a beautiful side salad with Kula strawberries, although the shaved Maui onions were strong.

Merriman's 'original wok charred ahi' ($37) accompanied by a fruit filled pineapple fried rice is tasty, though we found the fresh fish special, sautéed opakapaka, on the dry side and overcooked. Local Hanalei taro cakes ($22) sautéed to a crispy golden brown, are a delicious alternative to the standard veggie burger, although the garden herb salsa verde was heavy on capers. With two days notice, the chef can prepare special plates for vegetarians or vegans. Merriman's also offers a unique duo plate for indecisive diners. For $47 ($58 if one of the dishes is lobster), you can choose two entrées for one plate.

Merriman's offers a large range of desserts, including a molten chocolate cake ($12) and a pineapple upside down cake ($11).

Merriman's Downstairs Café   808.742.8385

Below the main dining room is a smaller café serving soups, salads, pizzas, and pasta at reasonable prices in what is called 'fast casual' service. Order at the counter, and your food will be delivered to you either indoors or out on the patio. Choose from salads ($6-12), flatbread pizzas ($9-12), pasta ($10-15) or sandwiches including hamburgers ($9), fish tacos ($12) and hummus & pita ($9).

Koloa, in Kuku'iula Village Shopping Center. 2829 Ala Kalanikaumaka St. Open daily 5:30 - 10pm. Downstairs Café opens at 11am. Reservations: 808.742.8385. Credit Cards. *www.merrimanshawaii.com* Map 6

Plantation Gardens 808.742.2121

For more than 20 years, the lovely Moir Gardens have provided an especially romantic setting – a beautiful old plantation home, where you can dine outside on a veranda cooled by evening breezes fragrant with tropical flowers, and see water lilies glow in moonlit ponds like night-blooming stars. Plantation Gardens has been through several re-designs and name changes. On the menu, you'll find salads and pu pus from $9-$22, and less than a dozen entrées ranging from $19 (vegetables and udon noodles) to steak and fresh fish ($31). Roasted duck spring rolls ($10) explode with

flavor. Local pear salad with fresh Kailani Farms greens is crisp and fresh, and the Big Island Kamuela tomato salad ($11) is filled with ripe, plump tomatoes. Sashimi platter ($14) could have been more fresh.

Of the entrées, fresh mahi mahi was perfectly cooked and moist ($29). Island stir fry was filled with fresh fish, prawns and vegetables ($21). Our

Water lilies bloom at night in Moir Gardens.

vegetarian's plate of grilled mixed vegetables was delicious, and the steal of the night at only $4. A favorite is 'Seafood Lau Lau,' with fresh fish, shrimp, and scallops steamed in their own juices inside a ti leaf, a dramatic and tasty presentation ($25). Baked Hawaiian desert is terrific, so save room.

If you are looking for a romantic dinner with quiet conversation, Plantation Gardens is a good choice. The setting, almost more than the menu, is a gorgeous centerpiece to your meal. Dine on the veranda, or if you prefer a more informal experience, on the porch near the bar, and see the gardens by candle light.

In Kiahuna Resort, Poipu. Dinner 5:30pm - 10pm daily. Reservations: 808.742.2121. Request the veranda. Credit cards. *www.pgrestaurant.com* Maps 6, 7

Pomodoro 808.332.5945

Once upon a time, two hardworking brothers from Italy arrived on Kauai via New York City (where one found a wife) and opened the island's first Italian restaurant. Over the years, as Casa Italiana grew into a success-ful restaurant, they imported the island's first pasta machine from Italy. As time went by, other restaurants began to order their pasta, and so they sold Casa Italiana and became full-time purveyors of fine noodle creations. But long hours with eggs and flour were just not as interesting as working with people. A true New Yorker, Gerry missed all those midnight hours in the restaurant, the seven-day workweeks, the temperamental customers and frazzled servers. So the family sold the pasta company, opened Pomodoro Restaurant, and Gerry is once more in her element, bustling from table to table keeping her diners happy.

Pomodoro is attractive and small, only ten tables. The dining room, filled with leafy green plants, is clean, comfortable, and informal. Every-thing is prepared to order: pastas from $12 and the most expensive dishes, veal specialties, at $27. Add salad or soup, and the price goes up about $8. Children can eat spaghetti, ravioli, or small portions of some entrées.

What comes to the table is fresh, light, and tasty. Dinner begins with homemade foccacia served with extra virgin olive oil and balsamic vinegar instead of butter. Mixed greens ($8) look beautiful with purple and green spinach as well as various fresh organic lettuces. Minestrone arrives in a large bowl generous with noodles, beans, and still crunchy vegetables.

Pomodoro's sauces are light and flavorful without being overpowering, for example in pasta primavera, where the vegetable-based sauce perfectly complements fresh zucchini, carrots, tomatoes, green onions. Traditional pastas are more robust, like delicious manicotti, thin crepes generously stuffed with cheeses, or cannelloni stuffed with meat and spinach. Or try ravioli filled with ground beef or ricotta cheese, and even served with tasty meatballs, or a delicious lasagne.

There's no fresh fish on the regular menu, but you'll find meatless choices like chicken cacciatore or eggplant parmigiana. There's a full bar (try an excellent chi chi) as well as reasonably priced wines.

At Pomodoro, two can enjoy a first rate dinner for about $65. For excellent Italian cuisine and professional service at reasonable prices, Pomodoro is well worth the short drive from Poipu to Kalaheo.

Kalaheo, 2-2514 Kaumualii Hwy in Rainbow Shopping Center. Dinner nightly. 5:30 - 9:30pm. Closed Sundays. Credit cards. Map 6

Red Salt 808.828.8888

The last of the Poipu hotels to re-open following Hurricane Iniki, the Koa Kea, formerly the Poipu Beach Hotel, is worth the wait. The modern, bright lobby has a lounge and long, shiny bar with two flat screen TVs where you can enjoy a colorful cocktail ($13-$15), sushi two nights a week, and snacks like edamame. At the opposite end, Red Salt restaurant has stylish, comfortable high backed black wicker chairs around tables spread out in a square dining room and a large semi-circle alcove that looks like a huge bay window. Ceiling fans keep the dining room pleasant and breezy while the alcove is cooled by four giant ceiling fans moving side to side.

Red Salt takes its name from the unique red salt found on Kauai's Salt Pond Beach, and Chef Ronnie Sanchez creates a menu combining tastes and textures in appropriately special ways. You will even be served red salt (of a slightly different origin) with your bread and butter, with an explanation of just how much is enough to make your bread pleasantly piquant.

After a chef's taste of Tahitian ceviche for the meat eater and a baby

potato with garlic aoli for the vegetarian, our dinner began with warm hamakua mushroom bisque ($12), a light yet creamy blend of four types of mushrooms. Salad of mixed greens from JR Farms with hamakua tomatoes, macadamia nuts, hearts of palm and avocado vinaigrette ($10) is crisp and

J. Courson

refreshing. Seared sea scallop with pea sprouts is truly wonderful. The house special, red salt poke ($16), recommended by our server is served de constructed or layered rather than mixed like traditional poke.

lively Pacific Rim dining

The big island vanilla bean seared mahi mahi is a stand-out ($33), the perfectly cooked mahi mahi accented with a cool avocado ginger salsa on top, and a tangy 'forbidden' black rice to cushion the fish below. Fresh seared opah with crab mashed potatoes is a dish that would stand out on any menu ($33). Our vegetarian enjoyed three sides: marinated grilled tofu with a touch of ginger, served on Chinese bamboo rice, an excellent edamame-cilantro risotto (usually served with seared ahi), and cauliflower couscous (usually served with seared rack of lamb). For arresting preparation and outstanding execution, Red Salt is worth the drive to Poipu if you are staying elsewhere. Walk the grounds after dinner.

Poipu, Koa Kea Hotel, 2251 Poipu Road. Breakfast, lunch, dinner, bar. 6:30am - 10pm. 808.822.8888. Credit cards. *www.koakea.com* Map 6

Roy's Poipu Bar & Grill 808.742.5000

Roy's was the first to lead the way out of staid fresh fish and steak house dining and into chic new Asian fusion cuisine. The Poipu Roy's is one of a constellation following Roy's on Oahu (1998) with branches in Hawaii, Guam, Tokyo, and Pebble Beach, California, all with the same cuisine, the same dining style. But today, the Poipu Roy's faces stiff competition from new chefs who are forging ahead with an expanded dining approach to sustainable local ingredients and imaginative preparations. Red Salt in the new Koa Kea Hotel (a re-make of the old Poipu Beach Hotel) and Josselin's in Kuku'iula Village, in particular, have brought a new dining flair and experimentation to the densely visited tourist area of Poipu.

The first sign of trouble on our most recent visit was a dining room with empty tables. The second sign was a similarity in taste in every dish we ordered. Three dishes (one fish, one tofu, one grilled vegetable) tasted salty, and worse, two incorporated ingredients not stated on the menu. In fact, when we asked the manager to compare the stated menu ingredients with what was actually served on the plate, he was as confused as we were.

It may be that Roy's era of dominance in inventive cuisine has passed with newer restaurants arriving on the island, or it may be that the restaurant is simply in between managers, as we were told this time, and Roy's will once again be a leader in south shore dining when your visit rolls around.

Poipu, 2360 Kiahuna Plantation Dr. Dinner 5:30 - 9:30pm. Reservations: 808.742.5000. Credit cards. *www.roysrestaurants.com* Maps 6, 7

Shells, Sheraton Kauai 808.742.1661

The main restaurant of the Sheraton Kauai Resort Hotel, Shells offers sweeping views of Poipu Beach in a large, comfortable dining room with a relaxed ambiance. Tall ceilings keep temperatures cool. What were once three separate restaurants with different menus and chefs have shrunk to one large establishment, however, with a Japanese buffet one nite a week.

Shells offers à la carte entrées from $29 to $45. Appetizers quickly increase your dinner cost, with the least expensive a green salad ($9).

Poipu, Sheraton Kauai Resort. 2400 Hoonani Rd. 6:30 - 10:30am; 5:30 - 9:30pm. Sunday Brunch. Credit cards. *www.sheraton-kauai.com* Map 6

Tidepools, Grand Hyatt Resort

Nestled at the bottom of the cliff in the center of the lovely Hyatt Regency Hotel, Tidepools combines an elegant ambiance with expertly prepared dinners, particularly fresh island fish. To get to Tidepools, you walk down from the hotel lobby, a spectacular marble perch built into the cliff and overlooking the sea. At the bottom, clustered near the edge of the hotel's wandering waterways, is the restaurant, laid out like a 'village' of connected Polynesian style huts.

The dining room is comfortable, spacious, and attractive. Parquet tables with cloths of Hawaiian tapa design are well spaced for privacy (there's

Tidepools Restaurant, Hyatt Regency Resort Hotel

really not a bad table in this restaurant). Candle lamps glow golden in the evening light, reflected in dark blue glassware.

Tidepools features steak and seafood, some choices in contemporary versions of Hawaiian recipes flavored with local spices and ingredients. On the appetizer menu, mango lobster and crab cake is wonderful ($15), and you'll find several salads from $9. Entrée choices include prime rib ($38), chicken ($25), and fresh island fish, which can be steamed, sautéed, grilled, or even blackened. Try grilled ahi ($34), Hawaiian opah (moon fish) ($38), or onaga, our favorite snapper ($34). We like the unique flavor of the fish, and so usually order sauces served on the side. Or choose lamb, chicken, prime rib, steak, or vegetarian options. Beef tenderloin ($40) is excellent, crisp on the outside, moist and tender inside. Kids have a great menu: chicken nuggets, grilled cheese, fish, pasta, or hot dog.

At Tidepools, portions are reasonably generous, presentation attractive, service polite and unhurried. Prices are high, but the hotel comes with the meal. Explore the lovely grounds after dinner; walk along the ocean and find a hammock, lie back, listen to the waves, and look up into the bowl of stars.

Poipu, Grand Hyatt Hotel. 1571 Poipu Rd. Reservations: conciergekauai@ hyatt.com or 808.742.1234. Dinner nightly 5:30 - 10pm. Credit cards. Valet parking. *www.kauai.hyatt.com* Maps 6, 7

Tomkats Grill 808.742.8887

In a covered veranda at the rear of Koloa's historic Kawamoto Building, Tomkats offers informal, open-air dining at reasonable prices. About a dozen tables with cushioned rattan chairs cluster on the plank floor, and just beyond the railing is a small quiet garden, fringed with red ginger. Fly fans encourage breezes, and even in a sudden shower, this sheltered spot is peaceful, the rain beating a muffled tattoo on the tin roof. A full bar, adjacent but not intrusive, offers various tropical specials.

Tomkats courts families and features a special 'kittens' menu with hamburgers or grilled cheese. Adults can dine on a wide range of reasonably priced sandwiches, burgers, salads, and complete dinners. Sandwiches are carefully prepared and attractively served in baskets piled high with french fries. We loved the homemade kalua pig sandwich ($9.95) and the fish taco with mahi mahi ($8.95) served with chips and salsa. The honey ginger hot wings were a zesty blend of sweet and spicy ($10). Portions are generous, service friendly, and the hours make Tomkats a convenient after-beach stop, when some of your party may be hissing with hunger.

Central Koloa. 10:30am -10pm daily. Take-out. Credit cards. Maps 6, 7

Na Pali Coast

Westside Restaurants
'favor...eats'

In Hanapepe, *Hanapepe Café & Espresso* serves wonderful vegetarian dishes, as well as sandwiches and coffee drinks for lunch, and occasionally dinners. After lunch (or before) visit beautiful Salt Pond Beach Park, a great spot for family picnics. In nearby Ele'ele, try *Toi's Thai Kitchen* for inexpensive, delicious Thai food, and *Grinds* for tasty, generous sandwiches on home-baked bread.

Visiting Koke'e or the westside beaches? In Waimea, stop in at *Wrangler's Steakhouse* for excellent hamburgers and salad bar; next-door a smaller room serves pizza, calzones, and first-rate sandwiches. Stop at *Waimea Brewing Co* for fresh fish sandwiches and salads. Walk into *Ishihara's Market* and step back in time; sample delicious poke, deli salads.

Stop in at *Jo Jo's Shave Ice* in 'downtown' for an ice-cold treat, or *Yumi's Bakery* for early morning fruit turnovers.

Hanapepe Café 808.335.5011

The sign to Hanapepe announces 'Kauai's Biggest Little Town,' and Hanapepe Café is a major attraction for vegetarian cuisine with an island flair. You'll find scones flavored with passion fruit, as well as a changing menu reflecting what's up with the chef and what's fresh at the local farmers' market. A half-dozen tables, with fresh flowers and leafy green plants, surround the gleaming tiled counter, a remake of the 1940's curved lunch counter of the Igawa Drugstore. The bakery serves tasty delights (some gluten-free) including snickerdoodles, chocolate macaroons and cake.

The menu features healthful, reasonably sandwiches, salads, and Italian entrées. Garden burger (made from oats, carrots, cottage and mozzarella cheeses) is served on a cracked wheat roll with bright red local tomatoes, lettuce, a tasty spinach spread, and excellent potato salad. Vegetable frittata is stuffed with red and green peppers, zucchini, squash, mushrooms, mozzarella – and topped with fresh local tomatoes. 'Healthnut' sandwich is spread with homemade hummus and served open faced with tomatoes, lettuce, sunflower sprouts, cucumbers, and onions. Pasta can feature local vegetables with a light, delicious creamy tomato sauce. Afterwards, stroll the main street – it won't take you very long. You can try out the swinging bridge, visit Banana Patch Studio, and sample taro chips made at the Taro-Ka 'factory,' just around the corner.

Dinner is served on Fridays (Art Night in Hanapepe), but call ahead to check. The dining room turns Cinderella-like into a white and black café, with soft lighting and music. Entreés can include vegan lasagne, fresh fish, pasta, eggplant parmesan, as well as salads, soups, and appetizers.

Hanapepe, 3830 Hanapepe Road. 11am - 3pm (M-Th). 11am - 2pm (Fridays). Dinner on Fridays 6pm -9pm (call). Credit cards. Map 8

Shrimp Station 808.338.1242

Shrimp Station may claim the best tasting coconut shrimp on the planet ($11), but the main attraction here is its pricing. The menu features shrimp in several preparations, some more successful than others, and we liked shrimp tacos ($12) best. Shrimp styles include cajun, Thai, and sweet chili garlic ($11- $12). Beer battered shrimp ($11) is like coconut shrimp without the sweet coconut. You can also choose a shrimp burger ($8) or a more traditional shrimp cocktail ($4.75), or go unconventional with a hot dog and french fries ($3.75).

Waimea, 9652 Kaumualii Highway. 11am - 5pm. Credit cards. *www. shrimpstation.com* Map 8

Toi's Thai Kitchen 808.335.3111

Kahili ginger

You can't get more underground than Toi's Thai Kitchen. Its original home was a carport semi-attached to a bar called 'Traveler's Den' in sleepy Kekaha, with a half dozen formica dinette sets, some with card table chairs. Now you'll find Toi's in a shopping center in almost-as-sleepy Ele'ele, or you'll try to find it, huddled under the arm of Big Save. Painted cinder block walls are decorated by white lace curtains and plants, while fresh anthuriums brighten up the dozen formica tables. What comes out of the kitchen is much more special. Toi's has developed a loyal clientele who have spread the word, attracting newcomers who can't believe their eyes when they arrive – and are smiling when they leave.

We came in for lunch one afternoon, hungry and sandy from the beach. We loved Toi's saimin, Thai style – fresh white flat noodles float in a gently spiced broth colorful with vegetables, several varieties of bean sprouts and because the fishermen had been lucky, fresh and delicious ono. Rich and flavorful tofu soup was also terrific. Crispy spring rolls are served with fresh lettuce, mint leaves, and a zesty peanut sauce. The hot yellow curry pleased Jeremy, our spice enthusiast. Everyone loved Thai fried rice, so colorful and tasty that it was devoured to the last grain. Those who prefer American food can try hot, crisp french fries, sandwiches, or burgers.

Dinners include green papaya salad, dessert, and brown, jasmine, or sticky rice. Try Pad Thai, the tender chicken and fresh Thai noodles sweetened with coconut milk and fresh basil. Fresh eggplant sautéed with tofu and huge fresh mushrooms offers a marvelous contrast, both pungent and spicy. Be sure to try Toi's Temptation, a sweet curry made with your choice of chicken, beef, pork, or fish simmered in coconut milk and flavored with lemon grass, lemon, and basil leaves, and served with either potatoes or pineapples.

Ele'ele Shopping Center, Rt 50. Lunch 10:30am - 2pm; Dinner 5:30pm - 9:30pm (M - Sat). Credit cards. Map 8

Grove Café (Waimea Brew Co). . . 808.338.9733

Waimea Brewing Company has a new name for the dining room, but still serves its modest menu for lunch and dinner in the living room and on the porch of a restored planation house in Waimea Plantation Cottages Resort. You can order sandwiches, burgers, salads, or pu pus. Best is the fresh fish sandwich ($11) – juicy, tasty, attractively served in a basket with fries and spicy peanut coleslaw. Or try your local fish in a salad. As for home brew, four beers are typically on tap, two ales, a porter, a stout, and a wheat. Service is slow, bordering on pokey (not to be confused with ahi poke). So speak up right away about your need to get out and about, or sit back, enjoy the breeze, and take advantage of the free wireless.

The comfortable old planation house has wonderful wide verandas. An adjacent museum and gift shop has wonderful, reasonably priced stitchery, including beautiful patchwork and island style pillows made by 'Gramsy.'

Just west of Waimea Town, 9400 Kaumuali'i Hwy. 11am - 9pm daily. Credit cards. Map 8

Wrangler's Steakhouse 808.328.1218

After many years, Wrangler's dining room still retains the outlines and flavor of its historic building, where you expect to see Butch Cassidy amble in and take a chair. Ceilings are open to rafters, fly fans keep the air moving, and saddles and tools from the Hawaiian cowboys, the paniolos, make the decor. Tables are arranged on two levels for quiet and privacy, with a veranda for open air dining. On the lower level, you can try calzones, a terrific turkey wrap, home baked pizza with crispy crust, and deli sandwiches.

With most lunches ($8 - $12), Wrangler's offers a salad bar, with fresh greens, tasty home made pasta salad, even home made chips and salsa. Sandwiches and plate lunches include a 'plantation worker special' with beef teriyaki and tempura served in a traditional three tiered 'kau kau' pot. 'Wrangler Burger' is a juicy half-pounder on a sesame seed roll, with bacon, mushrooms and cheese, served with crispy, piping hot steak fries. Fresh ono sandwich is also first rate.

Service is friendly, prices reasonable, and Wrangler's gift shop features lovely items from local artists, including Hawaiian quilts, dolls, and stuffed animals. Deborah Tuzon of Waimea weaves placemats and jewelry of lauhala; Caz creates wonderful sunflower barrettes and headbands of colorful woven plaid paniolo cloth, and you can try Dennis Okihara's local grown 'Black Mountain' coffee. On your way to Koke'e or to Polihale, you'd be hard pressed to find a better spot.

Downtown Waimea, on Rt 50. 808.328.1218. Lunch 11am - 4 pm (M-F); Dinner 4pm - 8:30pm (M-Sat). Closed Sundays. Credit cards. Map 8

Index

A

B

C

Kauai Underground Guide
'Campaign for Kids'

The profit from each book sold benefits these outstanding non-profit agencies helping Kauai's children. Our donated dollars help individual children whose needs could not be met within the regular budget. Every dollar goes a long way, and there are no administrative costs.

- **The YWCA Family Violence Shelter** needs money for books, toys, clothes, writing materials and art supplies and child car seats. "We have almost no money in our regular budget for the special needs of individual children." 3904 Elua St, Lihue HI 96766 808.245.6362.

- **Friends of the Children's Justice Center** helps young victims of abuse and neglect. 4473 Pahee St, Suite M. Lihue HI 96766 808.245.6214.

- **Hale 'Opio** helps children referred by the Family Court. After-school learning programs include literacy, computer skills, photography, and special tutoring. 2959 Umi St, Lihue HI 96766. 808.245.2873.

- **Child and Family Service, Kauai** aims to strengthen families and foster the healthy development of children; it is Hawaii's oldest and largest private non-profit. 2970 Kele Street, Suite 203, Lihue, HI 96766 808 808.245.5914

Tax-deductible contributions can be sent directly to these fine agencies.

Order signed copies of the *Kauai Underground Guide 19th editon* by *mail* or *online* at www.explorekauai.com. Our exclusive CD of beautiful Hawaiian music by Keali'i Reichel is packaged FREE inside each book ($15.95). Free shipping.

Mahalo!
Lenore & Mirah

Papaloa Press

362 Selby Lane
Atherton CA 94027
papaloa@pacbell.net

Keep Up-to-Date on Kauai! For the latest updates, visit our web site
www.explorekauai.com